# PARCC ELA/Literacy Assessments

## Grades 6-8

**Dennis M. Fare, M.Ed.**
Assistant Superintendent
Mahwah Public Schools
Mahwah, New Jersey

**Research & Education Association**
Visit our website: www.rea.com

**Research & Education Association**
61 Ethel Road West
Piscataway, New Jersey 08854
E-mail: info@rea.com

## PARCC ELA/LITERACY ASSESSMENTS, GRADES 6–8

**Published 2015**

Printed in the United States of America

Library of Congress Control Number 2013936856

ISBN-13: 978-0-7386-1168-6
ISBN-10: 0-7386-1168-9

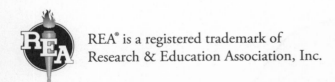

REA® is a registered trademark of
Research & Education Association, Inc.

## Dear Student,

*Let's be clear…*

The Common Core tests you'll soon be taking are unlike any tests you've faced.

But don't worry, we've got you covered.

If you haven't heard it already, you will begin hearing the name "PARCC" a lot. This is because the state where you attend school is part of a group of states that organized themselves as the Partnership for Assessment of Readiness for College and Careers, or PARCC.

These new tests mean it's "*Good-bye, bubble sheet,*" and "*Hello, computerized testing,*" and more important than the new format is what the PARCC assessments will want from you. They will test your ability to think, not just memorize stuff. You'll need to build essays, not simply answer multiple-choice questions that ask you to recall what seem like disconnected facts.

Just like a researcher or perhaps a lawyer, you will be required to use logic to present a clear, compelling case. You will need to make judgments using real-world sources, including printed text, audio, and video. You will need to decide what information should be believed, and why.

These tests — and the Common Core State Standards on which they are based — require careful critical thinking and solid writing skills.

Thankfully, much of what you need to help you understand and score well on the PARCC tests is right in this book.

Let's get started!

## Dear Teacher,

You and your students are part of a historic shift in American education.

The adoption of the Common Core State Standards marks the first time in the history of the nation that most of our states have opted to set the bar for K–12 education by ambitiously collaborating on setting and meeting internationally-benchmarked standards.

What does this mean to you?

Well, for one thing, tougher tests.

You likely live in a state that chose to become a member of one of two Common Core assessment consortia. This book was developed to address the English language arts/literacy assessments for the PARCC* consortium, whose members span 19 states, the District of Columbia and the U.S. Virgin Islands. Altogether, PARCC states educate about 22 million public K–12 students.

You've probably seen your share of screaming headlines about the Common Core, but now the big headline for you is that next-generation assessments are coming—and soon. So it's time to get ready.

There are plenty of books on the market that cover the theory behind the Common Core, as well as the curriculum that brings it into your classroom. This is not one of them. Instead, this is the first *practical* guide to Common Core *assessment*. It's a bracing tour of what makes the new assessments tick, brimming with test tips and carefully crafted standards-aligned practice—a workout, really—that reveals what your students most need to know to succeed on the new PARCC assessments for grades 6–8.

Your tour guide is author Dennis Fare, a veteran language arts supervisor and teacher in one of the nation's top school districts.

This is not test prep as you've come to know it because, truth be told, there's never been a battery of tests quite like the PARCC assessments.

Now, let's tackle the tests together.

---

* PARCC stands for Partnership for Assessment of Readiness for College and Careers.

# Contents

## Chapter 3: Narrative Writing Task

## Chapter 4: Literacy Analysis Task

## Chapter 5: The Research Simulation Task

## Chapter 6: The Research Simulation Task: English

## Chapter 7: The Research Simulation Task: History

## Chapter 8: The Research Simulation Task: Science

## Chapter 9: Research Simulation Task Practice Questions

## Chapter 10: Final Thoughts

## Acknowledgments

## Appendices

## About the Author

**Dennis M. Fare** holds a B.A. in English Writing and an M.Ed. in English Education. In 2014, Mr. Fare was named Assistant Superintendent of Mahwah (N.J.) Public Schools. Mr. Fare formerly served as the Supervisor of English Language Arts, Grades 6–12, for the Mahwah district, where he developed curriculum and supervised English Language Arts teachers. He taught English for many years at Hackensack (N.J.) High School and has also taught at the college level. Mr. Fare holds supervisor, principal, and superintendent certifications. He served as an AP reader for the AP English Language and Composition exam for the College Board and was also a rater for the SAT test. Mr. Fare's presentations to College Board conferences include: *AP Open Enrollment: From Theory to Practice; AP Online Curriculum*, and *AP Vertical Teaming: Working from the Ground Up.*

 ## Author's Acknowledgments

I would like to thank the following people for their invaluable input and support throughout this project: Dr. C. Lauren Schoen, Superintendent at Mahwah Public Schools; Christine Zimmermann, Director of Curriculum at Mahwah Public Schools; Brian Miller, Principal of Ramapo Ridge Middle School; Suzanne Straub, Assistant Principal of Ramapo Ridge Middle School; John P. Pascale, Principal of Mahwah High School; Linda Bohny, Assistant Principal of Mahwah High School; and Dominick Gliatta, Miriam Lezanski, Roger Pelletier, Danielle Poleway, Patricia Reinhart, and Kristen Trabona, all instructional supervisors at Mahwah Public Schools.

Further, I would like to acknowledge my parents, Dennis (Sr.) and Lois Fare. I would also like to thank Caseen Gaines for his help during the proposal phase of this project.

## About REA

Founded in 1959, Research & Education Association is dedicated to publishing the finest and most effective educational materials—including study guides and test preps—for students in middle school, high school, college, graduate school, and beyond.

Today, REA's wide-ranging catalog is a leading resource for teachers, students, and professionals. Visit *www.rea.com* to see a complete listing of all our titles.

## REA Acknowledgments

**Publisher:** Pam Weston

**Vice President, Editorial:** Larry B. Kling

**Senior Editor, PARCC Series:** Alice Leonard

**Managing Editor, Frontlist:** Diane Goldschmidt

**Copywriter:** Kelli Wilkins

**Cover Design:** Christine Saul

**Page Design:** Claudia Petrilli

**Copyeditor:** Anne McGowan

**Proofreader:** Ellen Gong

**Typesetter:** Kathy Caratozzolo

**Permissions:** Katherine Benzer, S4 Carlisle

# The PARCC Assessments At-a-Glance

Because PARCC is a new assessment system that is in development, not everything about it has been finalized. Based on the most recent guidance from the PARCC consortium, the following information is available.

The PARCC assessments in English Language Arts/Literacy (the content basis of this book) and Mathematics are designed to measure the degree to which students have learned the critical knowledge, skills and abilities essential for college and career success. While this guidebook focuses on grades 6-8, PARCC assessments will be administered in grades 3–11 beginning in the 2014–2015 school year. The assessments for each grade will be based on the Common Core State Standards for that grade level.

## Structure of the Tests

To effectively implement the PARCC design, assessments in both ELA/Literacy and Mathematics will be administered in two parts, a **performance-based assessment (PBA)**, administered after approximately 75% of the school year, and an **end-of-year assessment (EOY)**, administered after approximately 90% of the school year.

Each grade level of the ELA/Literacy PBA will include three tasks: a narrative task, a literary analysis task, and a research simulation task. For each task, examinees will be asked to read one or more texts, answer several short vocabulary and comprehension questions, and write an essay that requires examinees to gather evidence from the text(s). Each grade level of the ELA/Literacy EOY will consist of 4–5 texts, both literary and informational (including social science/historical, scientific, and technical texts in grades 6–11). Short-answer vocabulary and comprehension questions will also be associated with each text.

## Administration of the Tests

PBA and EOY assessments will be administered in a total of nine sessions. The PBA for each grade level will be administered in five sessions, three for ELA/Literacy and two for mathematics. The EOY for each grade level will be administered in four sessions, two for ELA/Literacy and two for mathematics. Individual examinees will be involved in testing sessions xii | PARCC ELA Literacy Grades 6–8

for both the PBA and EOY over a period of five to nine days. Refer to the following tables for a graphic representation of test components and times by grade(s).

## Performance-Based Component

|  | ELA/Literacy | | | Math | | |
|---|---|---|---|---|---|---|
|  | Literary Analysis | Research | Narrative | Session 1 | Session 2 | Total |
| Grades 6–8 | 80 min | 85 min | 50 min | 50 min | 50 min | 315 min |

## End-of-Year Component

|  | ELA/Literacy | | Math | | | |
|---|---|---|---|---|---|---|
|  | Session 1 | Session 2 | Session 1 | Session 2 | Total | Summative Total |
| Grades 6–8 | 70 min | 70 min | 55 min | 55 min | 250 min | 9 hours, 25 minutes |

## Test Results

Results of the ELA/Literacy assessments will be reported in three categories: (1) ELA/Literacy; (2) reading and comprehending a range of sufficiently complex texts independently (reading) and (3) writing effectively when using and/or analyzing sources (writing). ELA/Literacy results will be based on a composite of the examinees' reading and writing scores. Students will receive both a scaled score and performance-level scores for ELA/Literacy, and scaled scores for the reading and writing categories. Performance-level scores will be reported according to five levels.

In order to be deemed "CCR" (or "College and Career Ready"), students must earn a "4" or a "5" at the end of eleventh grade.

---

Readers should be aware that some materials used in this book—including contemporary articles and broadcast transcripts—are sourced from the United Kingdom and thus use British spellings and punctuation. We have included this content because it's considered fair game by developers of the PARCC assessments.

## CHAPTER 1

# Introduction

 ## The Common Core State Standards Initiative

This book gives what you most need to know about the PARCC assessments for English language arts/literacy.

In doing so, it proceeds from these five basic principles:

1. We believe in the PARCC assessments.

2. We believe in the Common Core Standards, which inform how the PARCC tests are being developed.

3. We believe the PARCC test battery assesses the very skills today's students most need to succeed in college and the workplace.

4. We believe in affording today's students the best possible shot at success in college and their chosen career.

5. We believe the PARCC assessments need the no-nonsense, practical perspective of the schoolhouse—and that's exactly what you'll find in this study guide.

The foundation for the PARCC tests lies in the Common Core State Standards. Adopted by the vast majority of U.S. states, the Common Core achieves for the first time in American history a near-common curriculum for the nation as a whole.

In essence, the PARCC is designed to assess whether or not students are making progress toward achieving the benchmarks set forth in the Common Core.

Thus, our book is closely aligned with the PARCC, and, by extension, the Common Core. For instance, most of the readings you will find in our book are taken from the reading suggestions from the Common Core (please see Appendix B of the Common Core: *http://www.corestandards.org/ELA-Literacy*). By using these reading suggestions and the curricular guidelines set forth in the Common Core English language arts document, we are giving you an advantage in taking the PARCC exam. Why, you might ask? The answer is simple: The more familiar you are with the literary and nonfiction texts of the Common Core, the better prepared you will be to take the PARCC assessment.

Therefore, we are supremely confident that the reading exercises and the activities within this book will help you on the PARCC exam.

While there are certainly a lot of standards, keep in mind that two standards will always be in play, regardless if the task is reading or writing. They are:

- Reading Standard One (1): Use of Evidence
- Reading Standard Ten (10): Complex Texts

 # Reading the Standards

Throughout this test prep guide, we have aligned each task to the Common Core standards. This is a natural alignment, as the test and Common Core standards are interlinked. The following chart will help guide you in understanding how to read the standards appropriately.

| Standard Strand | Title |
|---|---|
| RL | Reading Literature |
| RI | Reading Information |
| L | Language |
| W | Writing |
| SL | Speaking/Listening |
| RH | Reading History/Social Studies |
| RST | Reading Science/Technology |

# Overview of the PARCC

*PARCC* stands for *Partnership for the Assessment of Readiness for College and Careers*. We know—it's a long title! Throughout this guidebook, though, we will be referring to the test by its widely known acronym: PARCC.

The nature of the test makes it unlike any test you have ever taken. Three things make this so:

- The test is given on computer.

- The test is actually a series of tests given throughout the school year.

- What's on the test will require you to think in new and stimulating ways—both because of the content itself and the way it's presented.

So, how will this test be administered? First, you need to know that it's not actually just one test but a battery of tests. Thus, it will not be taken just on a single day of the school year, but rather several times throughout the year. Check out the timeline below, taken from the PARCC website:

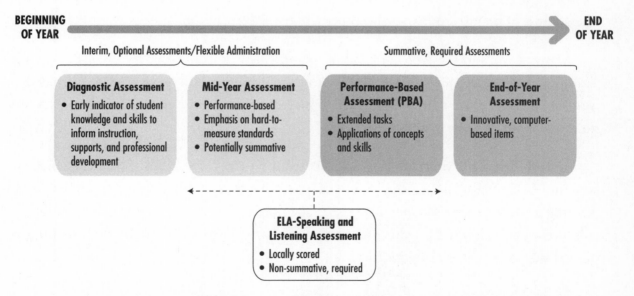

As shown above, you will be required to take the "Performance-Based Assessment" and the "End-of-Year Assessment." The "Diagnostic Assessment" and the "Mid-Year Assessment" are optional depending upon the state in which you live. The Performance-Based Assessments

(PBAs) consist of reading activities and three writing activities based upon these reading: (a) a narrative essay, (b) a literary analysis essay, and (c) a research-simulation task. This book will address the reading skills you will need as well as the writing skills for these three types of writing assessments.

Because this test will be taken on computer, your results will be returned to you much faster than what happens with pencil-and-paper exams. It is also very important to look at these practice questions in the context of keyboarding your responses. If you do not yet feel comfortable with keyboarding, it is time to practice these skills on your own!

Now that you are familiar with the structure of the PARCC, let's look over each of its question types together.

 ## Introduction to Interactive Reading

In every other test prep book you've ever read, or any English language arts classroom you've ever attended, you've most likely worked on strategies to engage with a printed text. While these strategies should not be forgotten, it is important to begin thinking of them in the context of brainstorming and working with a text via computer.

Many of you surf the Web daily. At this point, you're probably used to casually skimming, scanning, and reading texts online. If this isn't part of your daily, or even weekly, routine, then you should start. Since the PARCC is administered entirely as a computerized exam, it is time to think about this test in a different way.

The reading skills you will learn will help you on the "Performance-Based Assessment" and the "End-of-Year Assessment." Specifically, in Chapter 2 of this guidebook, you will begin looking at how to appropriately read, and take notes, from a screen. You will learn how to take what you've learned in your English language arts classes, and modify those techniques for the purposes of preparing for this test.

You've likely encountered reading comprehension sections in many tests, including any state test or even the SAT. Generally, you would read the passage or selection, and then answer a series of multiple-choice questions and/or open-ended questions. The PARCC, however, will assess reading in a more interactive manner. Often, you will answer questions as you read, as opposed to answering those questions after you've read.

Not only will you have to read a short reading selection, but you will also have to answer questions as you do so. You will need to electronically highlight text in relation to questions. You will need address how the reading selection raises specific points to support their viewpoint or argument. As you read, you will need to interactively investigate. While this sounds complicated, it is actually quite doable. The key is to be prepared, which is where this guidebook comes in!

As you read through the question types during the interactive reading chapter, be sure to review our "Thought Process" (a feature utilized throughout this book) as we navigate through the questions. This should serve as a model for you as you complete the interactive reading questions on your own.

Throughout your reading of this chapter, pay careful attention to the ways in which close-reading is modeled. If you are not aware of the language of authors in relation to their purposes, the questions will be more difficult to answer accurately. Think about how writers craft their viewpoints and project a desired effect upon the reader. You'll find that many of the question types in this particular chapter look closely at how you, as the reader/test-taker, can recognize how writers put together their viewpoints or arguments. This is what close and active reading successfully will clarify to you as you begin to have a greater understanding.

Also, according to PARCC requirements, the following word counts apply to all reading selections:

| Grade level | Word Count |
|---|---|
| Grades 6–8 | 400-1,000 words |

The PARCC requirements also have a complexity rating for each text, which follows this protocol:

| Grade level | PARCC "Complexity" Determination |
|---|---|
| Grades 6–8 | 905-1185 |

The balance of texts on the Performance-Based Assessments and End-of-Year Assessments will shift by grade band.

| Grade level | Types of texts |
|---|---|
| Grades 6–8 | • Approximately forty (40) percent literary texts<br>• Approximately sixty (60) percent informational text |

## Criteria for Selection of Authentic Texts

One goal of the PARCC is that students will be exposed to texts that are content-rich and challenging. These will be actual, authentic texts, not texts merely created for the test itself. Throughout this test prep guide, we have utilized texts specifically suggested from the Common Core.

## Criteria for Selection of Paired or Multiple Texts

As you work through the various tasks, you will notice that you will encounter questions that involve paired or multiple texts. These texts purposefully expose students to the domains of English language arts, science, history/social studies, technical subjects, and the arts. Through multiple texts, students will be able to analyze larger themes while also addressing informational validity and reliability.

# Introduction to Chosen Texts

Since the common core standards call for students to work with a variety of complex texts, this range will also be mirrored in the PARCC assessment.

## Examples of Literary Text Types:

- Poetry
- Drama
- Fiction
- Multimedia (in the form of film, radio, etc.)

## Examples of Informational Text Types:

- Literary non-fiction
- History/social science texts
- Science/technical texts
- Multimedia (texts that have both words and audio/video)

## More specific informational text examples:

- Advertisements
- Agendas
- Autobiographies
- Biographies
- Company profiles
- Contracts
- Correspondence
- Essays
- Feature articles
- Government documents
- Histories
- Interviews
- Journal articles
- Legal documents
- Magazine articles
- Memoirs
- News articles
- Opinion/editorial pieces
- Political cartoons
- Product Specifications
- Product/Service descriptions
- Recipes
- Reports
- Reviews
- Science investigations
- Speeches
- Textbooks
- Tourism guides
- Training manuals
- User guides/manuals

Please note that we have utilized this range of texts throughout our examples.

# Introduction to the PARCC's Performance-Based Tasks

- Narrative Writing Task (Performance-Based Assessment; 50 minutes)
- Literacy Analysis Task (Performance-Based Assessment; 80 minutes)
- Research Simulation Task (Performance-Based Assessment; 85 minutes)

Each of the three main writing tasks of the Performance-Based Assessment will assess very different skills. In order to work through these skills, it is crucial that you first become familiar with the setup of these types of questions. Don't worry, though, as we have mapped out each of the steps for tackling each of these question types!

Before we begin to discuss the three writing tasks, let us be clear on one very important point: Reading and writing on PARCC's Performance-Based Assessments are inter-connected and cannot, nor should they be, separated from each other. For instance, on the "Literary Analysis" task, you will write an analytic essay **based upon your reading** of the literary texts presented on the task. This fact completely distinguishes the PARCC from a test like the SAT. **In essence, on the PARCC, how well you write will depend upon how well you read.** We emphasize this point now and in most every chapter of this book.

Be sure to utilize the graphic organizers provided throughout this guidebook. They will help you in organizing your thoughts, and will help prepare your thinking. Remember that when you are sitting through this test, that the brainstorming and pre-writing stage is particularly essential to your success. By the time you sit down for this exam, you should be able to mentally visualize these easy-to-follow graphic organizers to manage your thinking with ease.

You may become nervous and anxious about thinking "on your feet." The setup of this guidebook will give you the confidence and skills needed to have the structure of the essays already pre-planned, and will give you the necessary foresight to predict what the PARCC test will ask you.

If you think you're a weak reader and writer, which many students do, you need to start seeing these tasks as doable, regardless of your training in your former English language arts classes. Even if you consider yourself a naturally strong reader and writer, each of the three main tasks of the "Performance-Based Assessment" may still seem difficult. But be patient. Look closely at the steps that we have clearly defined for you. If you can follow these steps, which we know you can do, then you can map out a well-thought response.

We have already mentioned that these performance-based tasks will be new exercises for you. With that said, do not let the title of this assessment, "English Language Arts," fool you. Not everything that you write will be based solely on what you've learned in your English class this year. These writing tasks are meant to be cross-curricular, which means that various subjects will be integrated into these writing tasks.

With each of these three reading and writing tasks, you will need to use the writing process in conjunction with your own content knowledge. This may require you to access your knowledge of different subject areas, including that of social studies, science, art, along with the reading and writing skills from your English language arts classes.

## Introduction to the Narrative Writing Task
(Performance-Based Assessment)

Now that you have been introduced to the structure of the test, and the purpose and philosophy behind the PARCC assessment, it is important to begin introducing you to each of the reading and writing tasks individually.

The narrative writing task has a 50-minute testing time and will require you to organize your thoughts in a way that is both easy to follow and interesting to read. When students think of a narrative, they instantly think of a story. This is understandable, especially because of the nature of narration. As we have discussed in the introduction of all of the writing tasks, you must not forget about all other subjects as you tackle this component of the test. Writing a story is just one of the various possibilities that might need to be completed.

Most simply, this task may require you, as the test-taker, to complete a story. The PARCC will provide you with an introduction, consisting usually of a few sentences, and you will need to take elements from that introduction and remain faithful to those details while completing a story independently. There is a delicate balance that needs to be mastered—through utilizing the details presented—and using them in a meaningful way throughout the presentation of your own narrative.

In this task, we will look at brainstorming strategies and graphic organizers that will help to organize and manage your thoughts creatively.

Along with this organization piece of this writing task, we will also look closely at the usage of language to create a desired effect upon the reader. We will focus our efforts on using language in a purposeful manner. We will review the steps associated with making the connections you need to work through this part of the test.

As discussed earlier, not only will you need to accomplish a creative short story rich in figurative language, the possibility still remains that this task may require you, as the test-taker, to complete either the organized description of a scientific process or historical account.

By integrating separate content areas, you will not only need to know how to organize your thoughts, but you will also have to use your content knowledge to complete the task. We will go through each of these possibilities, helping you to structure and prepare such a response, while also displaying your control of language throughout any writing situation.

## Introduction to the Literary Analysis Task
(Performance-Based Assessment)

The literary analysis task has an 80-minute time limit and will be difficult to organize at first, but with some practice, you'll find that writing this essay can be an interesting experience. Once you are comfortable with the format of this question, the other pieces will fall into place. You will need to use the helpful strategies from the interactive reading chapter to help with mastering the literary analysis task.

The goal here is to look at *two* different types of literary texts. These writings could consist of any of the following genres: poems, story excerpts, play excerpts, famous speech passages, or nonfiction article excerpts. These reading selections can be from a variety of content area backgrounds, but most likely, these reading selections will be, generally, brief. No matter what the situation, you will gain a great deal of practice looking at a wide assortment of different reading excerpts.

After you have read each of the two reading passages, you will need to compare and contrast them. This task will require you to look deeply at the content of the reading selections along with their use of language. When looking at this writing task, we will look closely at the purposeful usage of rhetorical and literary devices. Not only will we master the definitions of widely used devices, we will also take a look at how each device is most prevalently utilized for specific desired effects. Having this prerequisite knowledge will help you in mastering this writing task. We have created a quick reference guide for you to use in doing this.

As we have already mentioned, the content of these selections will vary. Selections will not only be English-based, but rather, may be related to social studies, science, or any of your technical subjects. It is your duty to make connections between these two texts, and to look at how they are both similar and different from each other.

This may be the most difficult writing task for you to organize easily but we will review an outline that will make the process that much more seamless in arranging your ideas. This will take a lot of practice, especially when you, as the test-taker, will have to compare and contrast the usage of language.

After you have looked at both content and language closely, you will have to connect the two together in your essay. You will be introduced to a framework to put these items together in a way that simplifies the drafting process.

## Introduction to the Research Simulation Task
(Performance-Based Assessment)

Initially, the Research Simulation Task, with an 85-minute time limit, seems tough, as it is supposed to mimic the skills that you often utilize to draft a traditional "research paper." Dreaded for years by students of all ages, the research paper requires a certain set of processes so you can be confident in putting all of its pieces together.

In the research simulation task, you will be given a variety of different sources related to a certain topic. This particular reading and writing experience is similar to a persuasive or argumentative essay, except you will be using information from the sources given to support claims in a written essay.

The subject of this task could pertain to any particular topic, from a contemporary social issue, to an issue related to any of the content areas. Like the other two writing tasks this essay will ask you to be familiar with a wide array of information in order to adequately respond to the writing prompt.

In this chapter, we will look closely at how to analyze a source. The sources are not all traditional texts, but rather may be considered "non-print" texts, where you will be able to extract information from a photograph, chart, graph, survey, painting, or advertisement in order to bolster or support the main thesis of your essay.

Not only will you learn how to organize your thoughts, as will be the case with structuring all other essays, but you will review how to look at a source to choose relevant information as support. You will be required to take this information and weave it together; we will discuss how the sources should "have a conversation" with one another. This will contribute to the flow of your essay, and will serve as a reasonable alternative to what many of you have known as the "research paper" that you have worked on, perhaps, in your English classes.

So, as you can tell, there is a great deal of detail that will go into framing your research simulation task. Not only do you have to be able to analyze each type of source in great detail, but you will also have to string the sources' information together in order to create a solid argument or viewpoint, while also keeping the power of language in mind throughout this experience.

We have found that many students, when having little to no experience with writing the research simulation task, will avoid many visual sources to support their written points because they are not comfortable with how to analyze these types of sources. Also, students often do not know how to make convincing connections between sources that might initially seem unrelated to one another. In the upcoming chapters, we will address these areas of concern.

## Introduction to the Speaking/Listening Task

Based on released information, we see the Speaking/Listening assessment as being much like a research simulation task, where students will utilize multiple sources to support their claims and perspectives through oral presentation. Keep this in mind as you work through the various RST chapters throughout this guidebook.

We do know that you will be required to complete this Speaking/Listening Assessment inside the classroom, but this will not be included in your summative scores. This component will be locally scored, which means that the scoring will be done by your classroom teacher.

 ## Special Education/Accommodations

Keep in mind that, according to the *PARCC Accommodations Manual*, even students who are not classified may still be eligible for test accommodations. This will be determined by the school building's principal or the principal's designee, as per data collected by the student's teacher(s) or administrator(s). Once it is determined that a student may need accommodations for the PARCC, a Personal Needs Profile (or "PNP") will need to be completed.

As you read through each of these chapters, be mindful of the accommodations that will be available to SWDs (students with disabilities). Through *the PARCC Accommodations Manual*, embedded electronic supports will be available to all students to use, including font magnification, highlighting tools, bolding, and underlining. The PARCC assessment will also include a computer-delivered system that provides features that are made available at the discretion of school-based educators, including background/font color and answer masking. Further accommodations exist to increase access while maintaining a valid and reliable student score, including Braille form, extended time, small group testing, and word-to-word native language dictionary. Paper-and-pencil tests will be available for students who need the specific support of this test format.

As teachers instruct you with respect to PARCC-related skills, differentiating instruction (by focusing on targeted instruction through different modes of learning) will help all the different students/learners in your classrooms to access these different assessment types. Computer-based keyboarding experiences should be occurring regularly, and the accommodations above should also be made available to you when needed so that the practice-testing environment mirrors that of the PARCC assessment as closely as possible.

# Performance Level Descriptors (PLDs)

After you complete the PARCC assessment, you will be provided with your performance-level descriptor, or "PLD." This will indicate your level of college and career readiness, according to the standards of the PARCC. A student's PLD is based on his or her performance as it relates to level of text complexity, range of accuracy, and usage of quality of evidence.

When reading the charts below, consider the following criteria—text complexity, range of accuracy, and quality of evidence.

## Text Complexity

PARCC uses two components for determining text complexity for all passages, including quantitative text complexity measures and qualitative judgments from rubrics.

## Accuracy

"Accurate"—The student is able to accurately state both the general ideas expressed in the text(s) and the key and supporting details. The response is complete and the student demonstrates *full* understanding.

"Mostly accurate"—The student is able to accurately state most of the general ideas expressed in the text(s) and the key and supporting details, but the response is incomplete or contains minor inaccuracies. The student demonstrates *extensive* understanding.

"Generally accurate"—The student is able to accurately state the gist of the text(s) but fails to accurately state the key and supporting details in the text or to connect such details to the overarching meaning of the text(s). The student demonstrates *basic* understanding.

"Minimally accurate"—The student is unable to accurately state the gist of the text(s) but is able to minimally state some of the key or supporting details with accuracy. The students do not connect the specific details of the text to the overarching meaning(s) of the text. The student demonstrates *minimal* understanding.

"Inaccurate"—The student is unable to accurately state either the gist of the text or the key and supporting details evident in the text.

## Quality of Evidence

"Explicit evidence"—The student shows how the explicit words and phrases (details) from the text support statements made about the meaning of the text.

"Inferential evidence"—The student shows how inferences drawn from the text support statements made about the meaning of the text.

The levels follow the criteria below:

## Grade 6

### PARCC English Language Arts/Literacy Performance Level Descriptors

| Level | Level of Text Complexity | Range of Accuracy | Quality of Evidence |
|---|---|---|---|
| 5 | Very complex | Accurate | Explicit/inferential |
|   | Moderately complex | Accurate | Explicit/inferential |
|   | Readily accessible | Accurate | Explicit/inferential |
| 4 | Very complex | Mostly accurate | Explicit/inferential |
|   | Moderately complex | Generally accurate | Explicit/inferential |
|   | Readily accessible | Accurate | Explicit/inferential |
| 3 | Very complex | Generally accurate | Explicit/inferential |
|   | Moderately complex | Generally accurate | Explicit/inferential |
|   | Readily accessible | Mostly accurate | Explicit/inferential |
| 2 | Very complex | Inaccurate | Explicit |
|   | Moderately complex | Minimally accurate | Explicit |
|   | Readily accessible | Generally accurate | Explicit/inferential |

## Grade 7

### PARCC English Language Arts/Literacy Performance Level Descriptors

| Level | Level of Text Complexity | Range of Accuracy | Quality of Evidence |
|---|---|---|---|
| 5 | Very complex | Accurate | Explicit/inferential |
| | Moderately complex | Accurate | Explicit/inferential |
| | Readily accessible | Accurate | Explicit/inferential |
| 4 | Very complex | Mostly accurate | Explicit/inferential |
| | Moderately complex | Accurate | Explicit/inferential |
| | Readily accessible | Accurate | Explicit/inferential |
| 3 | Very complex | Generally accurate | Explicit/inferential |
| | Moderately complex | Mostly accurate | Explicit/inferential |
| | Readily accessible | Accurate | Explicit/inferential |
| 2 | Very complex | Inaccurate | Explicit |
| | Moderately complex | Minimally accurate | Explicit/inferential |
| | Readily accessible | Mostly accurate | Explicit/inferential |

## Grade 8

### PARCC English Language Arts/Literacy Performance Level Descriptors

| Level | Level of Text Complexity | Range of Accuracy | Quality of Evidence |
|---|---|---|---|
| 5 | Very complex | Accurate | Explicit/inferential |
| | Moderately complex | Accurate | Explicit/inferential |
| | Readily accessible | Accurate | Explicit/inferential |
| 4 | Very complex | Mostly accurate | Explicit/inferential |
| | Moderately complex | Accurate | Explicit/inferential |
| | Readily accessible | Accurate | Explicit/inferential |
| 3 | Very complex | Generally accurate | Explicit/inferential |
| | Moderately complex | Mostly accurate | Explicit/inferential |
| | Readily accessible | Accurate | Explicit/inferential |
| 2 | Very complex | Inaccurate | Explicit |
| | Moderately complex | Minimally accurate | Explicit/inferential |
| | Readily accessible | Mostly accurate | Explicit/inferential |

In order to be deemed "college and career ready" for their grade level, students' progress on the PARCC ELA/literacy assessment will be determined by their performance-level descriptor. PLDs are further explained below:

| Level | Policy-Level Performance-Level Descriptor |
|-------|-------------------------------------------|
| 5 | Students performing at this level demonstrate a **distinguished command** of the knowledge, skills, and practices embodied by the Common Core State Standards assessed at their grade level. |
| 4 | Students performing at this level demonstrate a **strong command** of the knowledge, skills, and practices embodied by the Common Core State Standards assessed at their grade level. |
| 3 | Students performing at this level demonstrate a **moderate command** of the knowledge, skills, and practices embodied by the Common Core State Standards assessed at their grade level. |
| 2 | Students performing at this level demonstrate a **partial command** of the knowledge, skills, and practices embodied by the Common Core State Standards assessed at their grade level. |
| 1 | Students performing at this level demonstrate a **minimal command** of the knowledge, skills, and practices embodied by the Common Core State Standards assessed at their grade level. |

# End-of-Year (EOY) Assessment

The End-of-Year Assessment will consist of two 70-minute sessions in which you infuse all skills relevant to your work through the Performance-Based Assessments. You will need to read and write in relation to narrative, literary analysis, and research simulation tasks, just as you have practiced throughout the chapters of this guidebook.

The literacy skills found in each of these chapters, including the analysis of text and the working with text, will be helpful when ultimately completing the End-of-Year Assessment. As we will discuss further, reading and writing skills work hand-in-hand, which is a similar relationship between the skills needed for the Performance-Based Assessments and the End-of-Year Assessment.

Essentially, the reading and writing exercises that you complete throughout the Performance-Based Assessments will be ideal preparation for the End-of-Year Assessment.

# Looking at the Acronyms

The PARCC labels a lot of its components by acronyms, which is nothing new in the world of education. We wanted to put all of the acronyms in one place to help in clarification and explanation, as we understand that this will be a new language for all of us.

| Acronym | Actual Title | Explanation |
|---|---|---|
| PARCC | Partnership for Assessment of Readiness for College and Career | The name of this particular assessment's consortium. |
| ELA | English Language Arts | This refers to the literacy skills used throughout these PARCC assessments. |
| CCR | College and Career Readiness | In order for students to be deemed as "college- and career-ready," they will have demonstrated the academic knowledge, skills and practices necessary to enter directly into and succeed in entry-level, credit-bearing courses in college English Composition, Literature, and technical courses requiring college-level reading and writing. |
| CCSS | Common Core State Standards | These standards are aligned with the PARCC assessment. |
| OWG | Operational Working Group | The groups of professionals formed to work forward and to revise assessments. |
| PLD | Performance-Level Descriptor | A student's level determined by their performance on each assessment. |
| PBA | Performance-Based Assessment | This label is attributed to the three assessments you will take throughout the school year before the End-of-Year assessment. These include the narrative PBA, the literary analysis PBA, and the research simulation PBA. |

*(continued)*

| Acronym | Actual Title | Explanation |
|---------|--------------|-------------|
| MYA | Mid-Year Assessment | This assessment is taken in the middle of the school year. |
| EOY | End-of-Year Assessment | This assessment is taken at the end of the school year. |
| PCR | Prose-Constructed Response | The larger writing task that you will complete with each performance-based assessment. |
| EBSR | Evidence-Based Selected Response | When a second question on the PARCC is dependent on a student's answer to the first question. |
| TECR | Technology-Enhanced Constructed Response | A task that requires the student to use technology to capture student comprehension, including the following tasks: drag and drop, cut and paste, shade text, move items to show relationships. |
| WHST | Writing History, Science, and Technical Subjects | The interdisciplinary writing standard. |
| RST | Reading Science and Technical Subjects | The interdisciplinary reading standard. |
| RST | Research Simulation Task | The synthesis performance-based assessment that asks students to use information from a variety of sources to support their opinion. |
| PNP | Personal Needs Profile | An accommodation plan for a non-classified student or classified student |

## CHAPTER 2

# Interactive Literacy

## Introduction
(Performance-Based and End-of-Year Assessments)

Some people say that technology—especially the way that teens use it today, with its interactive features and touch screens—has changed the world. Certainly it has with the PARCC Assessment. Students and teachers who use this prep book are undoubtedly familiar with the "old way" of taking an exam. Take, for instance, the New Jersey ASK or the New York State ELA exam, as they've existed over the past several years. On those tests, students would read a passage, mark it up with a pencil if they were so inclined, and answer the multiple-choice items that followed. The PARCC, however, is quite different. This exam requires you to interact with texts in ways that were not possible even a few years ago.

This chapter is aligned with the following Common Core standards:

| Range | CCSS Alignment |
| --- | --- |
| RL.1-8; | RL.1: Cite strong and textual evidence. |
| | RL.2: Determine two or more themes. |
| | RL.3: Analyze the impact of the author's choices. |
| | RL.4: Determine the meaning of words and phrases. |
| | RL.5: Analyze how an author's choices contribute to its overall structure. |
| | RL.6: Analyze a case in which grasping a point of view requires distinguishing what is directly stated in a text. |
| | RL.7: Analyze multiple interpretations of a work. |
| RL.9-10 | RL.9: Demonstrate knowledge of foundational works of American literature, including how two or more texts from the same period treat similar themes. |
| | RL.10: Read and comprehend complex texts. |

*(continued)*

| RI.1-7; | RI.1: Cite strong and thorough textual evidence to support analysis. |
| | RI.2: Determine two or more central ideas of a text. |
| | RI.3: Analyze a complex set of ideas or sequence of events. |
| | RI.4: Determine the meaning of words and phrases. |
| | RI.5: Analyze and evaluate the effectiveness of the structure an author uses. |
| | RI.6: Determine an author's point of view or purpose in a text. |
| | RI.7: Integrate and evaluate multiple sources of information. |
| RI.9-10 | RI.9: Analyze U.S. documents of historical and literary significance. |
| | RI.10: Read and comprehend complex texts. |
| L.1-6 | L.1-2: Demonstrate command of the conventions of standard English grammar and usage. |
| | L.3: Apply knowledge of language to understand how language functions in different contexts. |
| | L.4: Determine or clarify the meaning of unknown and multiple-meaning words and phrases. |
| | L.5: Demonstrate understanding of figurative language, word relationships, and nuances in word meanings. |
| | L.6: Acquire and use accurately general academic and domain-specific words and phrases. |

To begin, let's clarify exactly what we mean by the term *interactive literacy* so that we can be prepared for the types of activities you will encounter on the PARCC. First, *interactive literacy* describes the specific reading and writing skills that are tested by the PARCC. These literacy skills include, but are not limited to four areas we'll explore in greater depth later on: inferring, interpreting, analyzing, and critiquing. Second, the term *interactive literacy* implies that the test-taker of the PARCC will use a computer interface to click on and manipulate the text as part of the reading process. So, in various ways, you will apply your literacy skills manner using a computer-based interactive approach.

Here's one more thing you should know about the PARCC assessment: The exam's reading passages will include as many nonfiction selections as fiction—meaning, the reading material you will come into contact with will differ from the traditional novels and short stories you might associate with your English language arts class. For this book, we will provide excerpts straight from the Common Core State Standards (CCSS) group. You should ask your teacher about the Common Core, particularly the suggested reading list.

To begin our preparation, let's see how we will use these literacy behaviors with a short excerpt from the Preamble and the First Amendment to the United States Constitution:

### Preamble

We, the People of the United States, in Order to form a more perfect Union, establish Justice, insure domestic Tranquility, provide for the common defense, promote the general Welfare, and secure the Blessings of Liberty to ourselves and our Posterity, do ordain and establish this Constitution of the United States of America.

### Amendment I

Congress shall make no law respecting the establishment of religion, or prohibiting the free exercise thereof; or abridging the freedom of speech, or of the press; or the right of people peaceably to assemble, and to petition the Government for a redress of grievances.

Even though you most likely have come in contact with these examples in your history class, let's approach the Preamble and the First Amendment from a literacy perspective. These two very short examples of text are very rich in vocabulary and profoundly deep in meaning. Let's look at the question below in order to illustrate one way in which the PARCC will require you to interact with the text on the computer screen:

Below are three claims that one could make based upon the Preamble and the First Amendment.

| | |
|---|---|
| **CLAIMS** | Choice 1: The founders of the Constitution guaranteed that slaves would be free. |
| | Choice 2: The founders of the Constitution were deeply concerned with citizens' rights to express their opinions. |
| | Choice 3: The founders of the Constitution were worried that the President or Congress would be too powerful. |

## PART A

Highlight the claim that is supported by the most relevant and sufficient evidence within the article.

## PART B

Click on two details within the text that best provide evidence to support the claim selected in Part A.

As you can see, with PART A and PART B, the PARCC requires that you find answers to the questions posed by going back, reading through portions of the text, and using the mouse to highlight parts of the passage that pertain to the answer that you previously identified as correct in the Claims box.

What did you choose for the correct answer in PART A? This item was quite tricky. Here's why. Choice 1, "The founder's of the Constitution guaranteed that slaves would be free," is part of our Constitution, but the banishment of slavery occurs in Amendment 13, not the Preamble or Amendment 1. Yes, the Preamble addresses issues of life and dignity, but in no way are slaves or slavery mentioned at all. Choice A, therefore, is not correct.

Let's now consider Choice 2: "The founders of the Constitution were deeply concerned with its citizens' rights to express their opinions." Once again, Choice 2 is very appealing as an answer. The Preamble talks about "the Blessings of Liberty" and the First Amendment discusses the famous terms "freedom of speech." These two reasons, therefore, lead us to believe that Choice 2 is a very strong candidate for being correct. However, before we commit to Choice 2, let's look at the third choice.

Choice 3 considers a very important topic of the Constitution: the separation of powers among the three branches of government. While Choice 3 does talk about making the United States a "more perfect union" and limiting Congress's power ("Congress shall make no law . . ."), the Preamble and the First Amendment do not directly talk about the three branches of government. Therefore, we can eliminate Choice 3. Choice 2 is clearly our answer!

Now, you might think that this test item wasn't too difficult, and we would agree; however, Part B requires that you select text in the Preamble *and* the First Amendment in order to support your answer. The PARCC is not only concerned with the correct answer; it is also concerned with your ability to *justify* your answer.

Here's what you should ask yourself, "Exactly HOW were the founders concerned with citizens' right to express their opinions?" "What text supports the citizens' right to express their opinions?" You guessed it! You can identify the selections, "abridging the freedom of speech" and "or the right of people peaceably to assemble" as prime examples. Great job! You have successfully completed parts A and B.

To summarize: *The PARCC is a new type of exam.* Using the latest in computer technology, the test will assess your ability to read, infer, interpret, analyze, and critique difficult text. The next section of our book will review the specific literacy skills you will need to perform successfully on the exam.

# Key Literacy Skills: Vocabulary and Context

One of the aims of the PARCC is to assess your ability not only to know vocabulary but to understand how context is used to create the meaning of a specific vocabulary term. A good way to tackle this part of the test is to think of it as solving a puzzle. Each word is a piece of the larger puzzle, or context. And all of them have to fit together to let you solve the puzzle.

So, two skills are being assessed:

1. To infer the meaning of a word based upon context, and
2. To identify the specific textual evidence used in the passage that gave rise to the meaning of the term.

Whew! Do not worry! It is really not as difficult as it may first seem.

Let's look at the previously quoted Preamble to the Constitution and the First Amendment from a vocabulary point of view. The text is reprinted below:

### Preamble

We, the People of the United States, in Order to form a more perfect Union, establish Justice, **insure** domestic Tranquility, provide for the common defense, promote the general Welfare, and secure the Blessings of Liberty to ourselves and our Posterity, do ordain and establish this Constitution of the United States of America.

### Amendment I

Congress shall make no law respecting the establishment of religion, or prohibiting the free exercise thereof; or abridging the freedom of speech, or of the press; or the right of people peaceably to assemble, and to petition the Government for a redress of grievances.

Below is the way PARCC will present the vocabulary question:

## PART A

What does the word *insure* mean in the text, "The Preamble to the Constitution"?

| | |
|---|---|
| a. to gather | b. to establish |
| c. to build | d. to guarantee |

## PART B

Which words from the lines of the text best help the reader understand the meaning of *insure?*

| | |
|---|---|
| a. this constitution of the United States of America | b. We, the people of the United States |
| c. in order to form . . . establish . . . provide for . . . promote | d. a more perfect union |

**TEST TAKING STRATEGY:** For Part A, the most effective and easiest way to go about answering the questions is to:

1. Read the sentence in the passage while inserting each letter for *insure*. For example, insert "a. to gather" for *insure*: "We, the People of the United States, in Order to form a more perfect Union, establish Justice, **to gather** domestic Tranquility." It is clear that "a. to gather" does not work, which leads us to step

2. Use the Process of Elimination to mentally "cross out" answers that do not work.

The only correct answer, therefore, that works for Part A, is "c. in order to form . . . establish . . . provide for . . . promote." OK. Now that we got the correct answer, you need to be aware of something very important when answering vocabulary items. Experienced teachers have seen that many students answer vocabulary items on standardized tests *without* looking back into the text and considering the context. That is a CRITICAL error. Here's the reason why:

Take, for example, a very popular term such as "Google." In the sentence, "I used Google to research the Constitution," the term *Google** refers to the Internet search engine. Everyone knows that! However, in the sentence, "I googled my name on the Internet," gives a different meaning to the term—in this case, "googled" is the act searching for data on the Internet. How about this sentence, "The English teacher informed his students that he would not allow "googling" as an accepted from of research." Here, the term *googling* refers to the research method of using the Internet search engine, Google. The point we are trying to make is simple: Without a *context*, you cannot identify the way in which the PARCC wants you to define a term. You might think you know what *Google* means, but that meaning can and will change depending on *how* it is used. With the PARCC, we are concerned with the *how*. The *how* gives rise to the *what*—the meaning of a word.

Now, let's move on to Part B to consider the literacy skills necessary to get that answer correct.

The first thing you will need to notice about Part B is that the correctness of its answer depends entirely on getting the correct answer to Part A. Fair or not, that's the way the test is designed, all the more reason to get you to consider the context when deciding on vocabulary choices.

---

*Google is a trademark of Google Inc.

So, for Part B, we just have to think backwards. Here's the process; ask yourself this question: When I decided that "to guarantee" was the correct answer for Part A, what specifically in the text caused me to get that answer? Once we ask this question, all that we have to do is complete the process of elimination again. Did "a. this constitution of the United States of America" lead us "to guarantee?" Did "b. We, the people of the United States?" lead us "to guarantee?" This process should be completed until we have eliminated all the answer choices that do not make sense. In this case, answer "c. in order to form . . . establish . . . provide for . . . promote" is the correct answer.

To summarize, we have discussed and illustrated the two-step process to answering vocabulary items on the PARCC correctly. 1.) Use the context in the passage to identify the correct answer choice, and 2.) Identify the specific terms in the context that directed us to that answer.

Below, we will provide more excerpts Chapter 1, "A City Ready to Burn," of Jim Murphy's *The Great Fire*.

Chicago in 1871 was a city ready to burn. The city boasted having 59,500 buildings, many of them—such as the Courthouse and the Tribune Building—large and ornately decorated. The trouble was that about two-thirds of all these structures were made entirely of wood. Many of the remaining buildings (even the ones proclaimed to be "fireproof") looked solid, but were actually **jerrybuilt** affairs; the stone or brick exteriors hid wooden frames and floors, all topped with highly flammable tar or shingle roofs. It was also a common practice to disguise wood as another kind of building material. The fancy exterior decorations on just about every building were carved from wood, then painted to look like stone or marble. Most churches had steeples that **appeared** to be solid from the street, but a closer inspection would reveal a wooden framework covered with cleverly painted copper or tin.

The situation was worst in the middle-class and poorer districts. Lot sizes were small, and owners usually filled them up with cottages, barns, sheds, and outhouses—all made of fast-burning wood, naturally. Because both Patrick and Catherine O'Leary worked, they were able to put a large addition on their cottage despite a lot size of just 25 by 100 feet. **Interspersed** in these residential areas were a variety of businesses—paint factories, lumberyards, distilleries, gasworks, mills, furniture manufacturers, warehouses, and coal distributors.

Wealthier districts were by no means free of fire hazards. Stately stone and brick homes had wood interiors, and stood side by side with smaller wood-frame houses. Wooden stables and other storage buildings were common, and trees lined the streets and filled the yards.

## Vocabulary Practice 1

### PART A

What does the word *jerrybuilt* mean in the text, "A City Ready to Burn"?

| a. built to code | b. poorly constructed |
|---|---|
| c. built to last | d. constructed of iron |

### PART B

Which words from the lines of the text best helps the reader understand the meaning of *jerrybuilt?*

| a. the stone or brick exteriors | b. remaining buildings |
|---|---|
| c. looked solid | d. common practice |

### Answers:

Part A: "b. poorly constructed"; Rationale: Using the process of elimination, "poorly constructed" substitutes best for *jerrybuilt*.

Part B: "c. looked solid"; Rationale: The phrase "looked solid" implies that the *jerrybuilt* structures had the appearance of being well-constructed.

## Vocabulary Practice 2

### PART A

What does the word *appeared* mean in the text, "A City Ready to Burn"?

| a. seemed | b. revealed |
|-----------|-------------|
| c. leaned | d. determined |

### PART B

Which words from the lines of the text best helps the reader understand the meaning of *appeared?*

| a. most churches had | b. a wooden framework |
|----------------------|------------------------|
| c. copper or tin | d. a closer inspection would reveal |

### Answers:

Part A: "a. seemed"; Rationale: Using the process of elimination, *seemed* is the only term that logically fits.

Part B: "d. a closer inspection would reveal"; Rationale: The phrase "a closer inspection would reveal" suggests that the building had an "appearance" of being solidly built.

## Vocabulary Practice 3

### PART A

What does the word *interspersed* mean in the text, "A City Ready to Burn"?

| a. engulfed | b. scattered |
|-------------|--------------|
| c. detailed | d. rebuilt |

## PART B

Which words from the lines of the text best help the reader understand the meaning of *interspersed?*

| a. businesses | b. coal distributers |
|---|---|
| c. were a variety | d. residential areas |

### Answers:

Part A: "b. scattered"; Rationale: Using the process of elimination, *scattered* is the only term that logically fits.

Part B: "c. were a variety"; Rationale: The phrase "were a variety" implies that the types of buildings described in the passage were mixed with the residential housing.

# Key Literacy Skills: Reading Comprehension and Comparative Thinking

Unlike other standardized tests that treat reading and writing as separate activities, the PARCC views the two (reading and writing) as one literacy event. For example, those familiar with the New Jersey ASK and the New York ELA know that those tests have a "a reading section" and then an essay-writing section. It's as if the tasks of reading and writing weren't related to each other! This is where the PARCC, in our opinion, is a far superior and FAIRER assessment of reading and writing skills.

As you will see through the course of this section, reading and writing are treated as interconnected activities; hence, we need to have a new outlook on how the PARCC, as a standardized test, treats the two as one.

The PARCC assessment tests literacy skills through three domains. These include:

a.  The Literary Analysis Section,

b.  The Narrative Writing Task, and

c.  The Research Simulation Task.

In this part of our book, we will cover and practice the literacy skills you will need to be successful on all three parts. In later chapters, we will take you through a detailed explanation of each section. For now, our intent is to prepare you for the general literacy skills required to tackle the PARCC successfully.

## The Literary Analysis Section: Literacy, Language Choices, and Comparative Thinking

In the Literary Analysis section of the PARCC, you will be faced with two thematically connected texts that you traditionally would associate with your language arts class. Works of "high literary value," from such greats as Frost and Twain, will be presented to you. For purposes of our preparation for the PARCC, we will consider Robert Frost's poem "The Road Not Taken," and an excerpt from Chapter 9 of Laurence Yep's novel *Dragonwings*, entitled "The Dragon Wakes." These two works will be treated under the theme of *choices*.

To begin, you will read Frost's poem "The Road Not Taken." While you read, you should focus very acutely on the language choices contained within the text. For instance, you should ask yourself questions like these while you read: "What figurative language did the author use and why? "What word choices within the text are repeated and why?" "What imagery and other literary devices did I notice and what is the connection of these literary devices to the text?"

The major point here that you should take away: **PAY ATTENTION TO THE LANGUAGE CHOICES WHILE YOU READ!** The makers of the PARCC care very much that you are able to bridge the connection between the author's language choices and the connection of those choices to the meaning of the text. OK, so here we go.

In order to practice the type of critical reading where language choices become the means to interpretation, we will give you the excerpt side-by-side with the thinking process. On the left is the text; on the right are examples of what you should be thinking about **WHILE** you read. **PAY ATTENTION TO THE LANGUAGE CHOICES.**

| "The Road Not Taken" | Thought Processes |
|---|---|
| Two roads diverged in a yellow wood,<br>And sorry I could not travel both<br>And be one traveler, long I stood<br>And looked down one as far as I could<br>To where it bent in the undergrowth;<br><br>Then took the other, as just as fair,<br>And having perhaps the better claim,<br>Because it was grassy and wanted wear;<br>Though as for that the passing there<br>Had worn them really about the same,<br><br>And both that morning equally lay<br>In leaves no step had trodden black.<br>Oh, I kept the first for another day!<br>Yet knowing how way leads on to way,<br>I doubted if I should ever come back.<br><br>I shall be telling this with a sigh<br>Somewhere ages and ages hence:<br>Two roads diverged in a wood, and I—<br>I took the one less traveled by,<br>And that has made all the difference. | • the speaker of the poem is faced with two paths<br><br>• there might be significance that the woods are "yellow"; maybe it's autumn<br><br>• speaker looks down one road as far as his eyes could see<br><br>• the speaker now considers the second road<br><br>• this road is "perhaps" more appealing "better claim"; it wanted "wear" or to be traveled down<br><br>• the speaker is faced with both paths<br><br>• the speaker keeps the first for "another day" and heads down the second path<br><br>• the speaker doesn't think he/she will ever come back to take the first path<br><br>• the speaker is now in the future<br><br>• the speaker took the one "less traveled by," meaning the more difficult path<br><br>• this difficult path "made all the difference"; or changed the speaker's life |

Our reading of the sample above, and the notations on the right side of the box, lead to an overwhelming theme. Can you infer what it is? Yes, you are correct! The answer here is any term or word similar to "choices." While the notes in the box above might seem lengthy and unnecessarily drawn out, we are showing you, in a slow-motion manner, the thought processes necessary for you to excel on the Literary Analysis section of the test. We promise that the notes in the right column will be very useful during the essay portion of the literary analysis.

**Next, let's look at some test questions that you will encounter when taking the Literary Analysis section:**

## PART A

Which of the following sentences best expresses a theme about "choice" present in the poem, "The Road Not Taken?"

  a. There are many chances in life that give the possibility of making wise choices.

  b. Easier choices are more desirable than difficult ones.

  c. Taking the unique choice in life can lead to the most benefit.

  d. Less difficult choices are easier to make.

  e. Life's choices depend upon how you feel about the situation.

So, how do we go about answering a question like this? The answer is straightforward and simple: If you take the time to read the passage, as shown above, taking note of the key words and phrases in the text, the answer is obvious: "c. Taking the unique choice in life can lead to the most benefit." Through a process of elimination, you should have realized that none of the other choices even come close. Frost even ends his poem with the lines, "I took the one less traveled by, / And that has made all the difference." Our answer, therefore, is a no-brainer.

Ah, but let's be clear: We are not suggesting that you outline and summarize the texts that you find on the PARCC assessment in the manner that we have. The more important point is for you to see the types of things you should "think while you read." The chart is a way for us to show you, in a slowed-down situation, what you will have to do in order to answer the PARCC's questions correctly. When taking the actual test, you will not have the luxury of indefinite time. Therefore, you will have to practice this type of close reading time and time again with your teachers.

**OK, now on to Part B of this literary analysis section. Please review the question below:**

## PART B

Select three pieces of evidence from Robert Frost's "The Road Not Taken" that support your answer in Part A.

a. Though as for that the passing there

b. I shall be telling this with a sigh/Somewhere ages and ages hence:

c. Two roads diverged in a wood, and I— /I took the one less traveled by,

d. And looked down one as far as I could/ To where it bent in the undergrowth;

e. And be one traveler, long I stood /And looked down one as far as I could

f. Yet knowing how way leads on to way,/ I doubted if I should ever come back.

g. And that has made all the difference.

Well, you might be thinking to yourself at this moment: "If I get the answer on Part A incorrect, then I will also get Part B incorrect, too." Unfair as it may seem to be, the answer is, "yes." This is all the more reason that you should heed our advice that when reading the passage, you must deliberately focus on the language choices in the text and think about the connection of these choices to the meaning of the work. To illustrate this point, let's look at the answer choices to Part B.

If you remember from our analysis of the excerpt from "The Road Not Taken" above, you will recall that the language choices in the passage led us to infer correctly that the major theme of the poem dealt with the positive outcomes that can result from making difficult choices, that there is benefit from being unique. Knowing this about the poem, our answer choices in Part B become very clearly obvious. Take a look above at the choices that do not fit with our theme positive outcomes can result from being unique. What's left will be the correct answer choices. Did you get it? Yes! You are correct. The only logical choices are c., f., and g..

To summarize, up to this point we have shown you how to interact with a difficult literary text through a focus on language choice and how to use this analysis of language choices to answer the multiple-choice questions correctly. Whew! That was a lot but we are not yet done!

Remember, on the Literary Analysis section, the PARCC will give you two texts in order to engage in some comparative thinking.

Let's, first, look at the second excerpt. It is an excerpt from Chapter 9 of Laurence Yep's novel, *Dragonwings*, entitled "The Dragon Wakes." As with the Frost excerpt, we will show you the type of thinking you need to be doing in order to be successful on the PARCC assessment. The left column shows the "The Dragon Wakes"; the right our focus on language choices and its connection to meaning.

| "The Dragon Wakes" | Our Critical Reading |
|---|---|
| By the time the winter rains came to the city, we were not becoming rich, but we were doing well. Each day we put a little money away in our cold tin can. Father never said anything, but I knew he was thinking about the day when we might be able to afford to bring Mother over. You see, it was not simply a matter of paying her passage over on the boat. Father would probably have to go over after her and escort her across. There had to be money for bribes—tea money, Uncle called it—at both ends of the ocean. Now that we no longer belonged to the Company, we somehow had to acquire a thousand dollars worth of property, a faraway figure when you can only save nickels and dimes. | • the family is doing better financially; they are actually starting to save in the "tin" can<br><br>• Family is saving for Mother<br>• Money is involved in bringing mother over; but the family must also "bribe" people in China and America<br>• the speaker and his father have left "the company"; perhaps the company is a business |
| And yet the hope that we could start our own little fix-it shop and qualify as merchants steadily grew with the collection of coins in the tin can. I was happy most of the time, even when it became the time for the New Year by the Tang people's reckoning. […] | • the family still has hope<br>• "Tin can" is repeated again; it is a symbol, a motif |
| We took the old picture of the Stove King and smeared some honey on it before we burned it in the stove. Later that evening we would hang up a new picture of the Stove King that we had bought in the Tang people's town. That was a sign the Stove King had returned to his place above our stove. After we had finished burning the old picture, we sat down to a lunch of meat pastries and dumplings. | • Stove King might be a reference to a Chinese deity?<br>• "Honey" is a reference to "sweetness"; to the goodness in life<br>• The burning and replacing of the "Stove King" is a sign of renewal<br>• The meat pastries and dumplings are symbolic of the goodness in the family's life |

So, what have we learned about "The Dragon Wakes" through completion of our analysis of the language choices:

- Through a steady effort, overtime, things get better: as shown through the fact that the family is able to slowly save money.

- Life's choices can sometimes be difficult: as shown through the fact that the Mother is living separately from the family in China.

- In the midst of difficulty there are still blessings and rewards: as shown through the honey image and the allusion to the "Stove King."

- Faith can be a blessing, as shown through the image of the Stove King and the meat pastries and dumplings.

At this point, you should be starting to see the literary and thematic connection between "The Road Not Taken" and the excerpt from "The Dragon Wakes." What those connections are will be dealt with below.

As discussed earlier, the PARCC writes its tests from the viewpoint that reading and writing are intimately connected activities. We agree wholeheartedly with this testing method and believe it plays to the advantage of you, the test-taker. Here's how: If you can adequately and competently read the texts from the literary analysis section, in a manner that we have demonstrated above, then the written portion of the exam shouldn't be that difficult at all. In the coming paragraphs, we will show you just how you can use the reading selections to your advantage when tackling the writing activities.

## Comparative Thinking

The skill of comparative thinking—or, stated more simply, comparison and contrast—represents a very high level of competent literacy activity. To be able to compare and contrast two texts that are of high literary value is quite an accomplishment. The good news here is that writing a successful comparison contrast essay is something ALL students are capable of doing if given the right tools and the right know-how.

To begin showing you the tools and knowledge necessary, let's tackle a typical literary analysis essay question that you will encounter on the PARCC using our excerpts from "The Road Not Taken" and "The Dragon Wakes" as the bases of analysis. On the actual PARCC, the test-creators have labeled this question a "Prose Constructed Response." Here's the test question:

## Prose Constructed Response Essay Question

Using what you have learned from reading the "The Road Not Taken" by Robert Frost, and the excerpt from the chapter, "The Dragon Wakes" by Laurence Yep, write an essay that provides an analysis of how *choice* is treated in the two texts.

As a starting point, you may want to consider what is emphasized, absent, or different in the two texts, but feel free to develop your own focus for analysis.

Develop your essay by providing textual evidence from both texts. Be sure to follow the conventions of Standard English.

As any good English teacher will tell you, the strongest guarantee to a successful essay is the pre-writing step. The PARCC is no different. Below, we will show you how to use a very simple graphic organizer with which to write a successful comparative thinking essay. This organizer will allow you (a) to record quotations that show the diction, tone, and intended effect of each literary selection, and (b) to record your thinking about these quotations. Both items (a & b) are absolutely essential for your success in the written portion of the literary analysis essay. As a quick review, let's define diction, tone, and intended effect:

- **Diction:** The words an author chooses in a text. Diction is a very deliberate and conscious choice by the author.

- **Tone:** The attitude of a text. Tone is the type of "emotion" of the text. Think of tone as when your parents are about to yell at you. You know that the tone of their voices will be negative. Also, think of tone when your parents are about to praise you. You know that the tone of their voices will be positive.

- **Intended Effect:** This is the purpose of the passage. Why did the author write this text? What meaning are we to get from it? What is the text meant to teach us?

In the organizer below, our thoughts appear in italics under the quotation. Lastly, the bottom row of the graphic organizer is reserved for our judgments about the theme of choice in each work.

## Top Hat Graphic Organizer for Prose Constructed Response

| Robert Frost's "The Road Not Taken" | Laurence Yep's "The Dragon Wakes" |
|---|---|
| **Key Phrases: diction, tone, intended effective** | |
| Two roads diverged in a yellow wood, | we were not becoming rich, but we were doing well. Each day we put a little money away in our cold tin can. |
| *The narrator has two choices* | |
| And sorry I could not travel both | *the family is slowly saving; theme of sacrifice* |
| *Both choices are appealing* | Father never said anything, but I knew he was thinking about the day when we might be able to afford to bring Mother over. |
| Then took the other, as just as fair, | |
| And having perhaps the better claim, | |
| *This path seems more appealing* | *The family, like in "The Road Not Taken," is on a difficult, yet rewording path* |
| And both that morning equally lay | |
| *There are two choices available to the narrator. S/he can go one way or the other* | Now that we no longer belonged to the Company, we somehow had to acquire a thousand dollars worth of property, a faraway figure when you can only save nickels and dimes. |
| Yet knowing how way leads on to way, | |
| I doubted if I should ever come back. | |
| *The narrator knows that once a decision has been made, there will be no "going back"* | *The family doesn't have the safety of "the company"* |
| Two roads diverged in a wood, and I— | And yet the hope that we could start our own little fix-it shop and qualify as merchants steadily grew with the collection of coins in the tin can. |
| I took the one less traveled by, | |
| And that has made all the difference. | |
| *The narrator chose the "unique path," the one that is "less traveled by"; the harder path made all the difference for him/her* | *The family depends upon hope, hard work, and steady devotion* |
| | We took the old picture of the Stove King and smeared some honey on it before we burned it in the stove. |

(continued)

*Honey is a symbol of sweetness and goodness*

That was a sign the Stove King had returned to his place above our stove.

*The family has faith in "renewal" and that the Stove King will bless them*

## How exactly is choice treated in both works?

In "The Road Not Taken" and "The Dragon Wakes," the concept of making difficult choices is an action that leads to promise, hope, and renewal; in addition, both works are laden with imagery that sends a message about making difficult choices. For instance, in "The Road Not Taken," Frost uses the symbolism of the "two roads and paths" as choices an individual can make. In other words, there are two ways to go: on the one hand, there is the easier path, and then there is the "one less traveled by," whose words connote the idea that the narrator has taken the difficult path. This choice, in turn, at the end of the narrator's life, has "made all the difference." Frost's poem teaches us that, in life, the difficult path, the one less traveled by, will be more rewarding than the easier one.

This idea of hard choices leading to reward is also echoed in "The Dragon Wakes," but through different imagery. In that short story, the family has sacrificed coming to America to pursue a better life. This decision, moreover, was made at the difficult choice of leaving Mother back in China. Despite this negativity, the family, through discipline and steadfastness is saving its money to bring Mother to America. Finally, even in the midst of this difficult time, the family finds renewal, strength, and faith in their actions—as seen through the references to the Stove King.

Overall, both works—"The Road Not Taken" and "The Dragon Wakes"—teach about the importance of making difficult decisions but that these difficult decisions can and will result in a satisfying reward.

Now that we have successfully broken down and analyzed the two texts, and now that we even have come to a conclusion about the role of choice in each, let's take a closer look at the essay question itself: Write an essay that provides an analysis of how choice is treated in the two texts.

With the top-hat graphic organizer this task now seems much easier and more manageable. The last box of the organizer contains the beginnings of a solid thesis statement for the essay. We just need to play with the words a little bit. Here's one example of a thesis statement that satisfies the essay question: *In Robert Frost's poem, "The Road Not Taken," and Laurence Yep's chapter, "The Dragon Awakes," making and accepting responsibility for difficult choices ultimately results in personal satisfaction and familial happiness.*

As you can see, a substantial amount of work was completed to get to this point: a.) the initial active reading and analyses of the works, b.) the completion of the top-hat graphic organizer, and c.) our development of a solid thesis statement.

The PARCC assessment is not meant to be an easy test. The good news is that if you follow the steps outlined in this text, you will be equiped with a series of tools and strategies to experience a high-degree of success. Our next item of business is to provide you with practice, using new texts, to be successful on the Literary Analysis section of the PARCC assessment.

# Literary Analysis: Independent Practice

The two works that will serve as the basis of this sample literary analysis are Nikki Giovanni's poem, "A Poem for My Librarian, Mrs. Long," and Walt Whitman's "O Captain! My Captain." We have placed "A Poem for My Librarian, Mrs. Long" in a two-column chart so you can begin your literary analysis, as we have modeled above. After you complete the chart, you will be given two reading comprehension questions. Finally, you will encounter a Prose Constructed Response for the two literary works, which will be accompanied by the top-hate graphic organizer in which to work.

Remember: Focus on the author's language choices and the connection of these choices to the meaning of the work.

## Reading Selection #1

| "A Poem for My Librarian, Mrs. Long"<br>(You never know what troubled little girl needs a book.) | My Thought Processes |
| --- | --- |
| At a time when there was not tv before 3:00 P.M.<br>And on Sunday none until 5:00<br>We sat on the front porches watching<br>The jfg sign go on and off greeting<br>The neighbors, discussing the political<br>Situation congratulating the preacher<br>On his sermon | |

(continued)

| "A Poem for My Librarian, Mrs. Long" (You never know what troubled little girl needs a book.) | My Thought Processes |
|---|---|
| There was always the radio which brought us<br>Songs from wlac in nashville and what we would<br>    now call<br>Easy listening or smooth jazz but when I listened<br>Late at night with my portable (that I was so proud of)<br>Tucked under my pillow<br>I heard nat king cole and matt dennis, june christy<br>and ella fitzgerald<br>And sometimes sarah vaughan sing black coffee<br>Which I now drink<br>It was just called music<br><br>There was a bookstore uptown on gay street<br>Which I visited and inhaled that wonderful odor<br>Of new books<br>Even today I read hardcover as a preference paperback<br>    only<br>As a last resort<br><br>And up the hill on vine street<br>(The main black corridor) sat our carnegie library<br>Mrs. Long always glad to see you<br>The stereoscope always ready to show you faraway<br>Places to dream about<br><br>Mrs. Long asking what are you looking for today<br>When I wanted Leaves of Grass or alfred north<br>    whitehead<br>She would go to the big library uptown and I now know<br>Hat in hand to ask to borrow so that I might borrow<br><br>Probably they said something humiliating since<br>    southern<br>Whites like to humiliate southern blacks | |

(continued)

| "A Poem for My Librarian, Mrs. Long"<br>(You never know what troubled little girl needs a book.) | My Thought Processes |
|---|---|
| But she nonetheless brought the books<br>Back and I held them to my chest<br>Close to my heart<br>And happily skipped back to grandmother's house<br>Where I would sit on the front porch<br>In a gray glider and dream of a world<br>Far away<br><br>I love the world where I was<br>I was safe and warm and grandmother gave me neck<br>   kissed<br>When I was on my way to bed<br><br>But there was a world<br>Somewhere<br>Out there<br>And Mrs. Long opened that wardrobe<br>But no lions or witches scared me<br>I went through<br>Knowing there would be<br>Spring | |

## PART A

Which of the following best expresses the tone in "A Poem for My Librarian, Mrs. Long"?

    a. Truth and wisdom

    b. Fear and anxiety

    c. Wonder and thanks

    d. Race and understanding

## PART B

Select three pieces of evidence from Giovanni's "A Poem for My Librarian, Mrs. Long" that support the answer to Part A.

a.  "A Poem for My Librarian, Mrs. Long"

b.  Even today I read hardcover as a preference paperback only / As a last resort

c.  I love the world where I was / I was safe and warm and grandmother gave me neck kissed

d.  Probably they said something humiliating since southern / Whites like to humiliate southern blacks

e.  But there was a world / Somewhere / Out there / And Mrs. Long opened that wardrobe

f.  We sat on the front porches watching / The jfg sign go on and off greeting

## Reading Selection #2

| Walt Whitman's "Oh Captain! My Captain!" | **My Thought Processes** |
|---|---|
| O Captain! my Captain! our fearful trip is done;<br>The ship has weather'd every rack, the prize we sought is won;<br>The port is near, the bells I hear, the people all exulting,<br>While follow eyes the steady keel, the vessel grim and daring:<br>But O heart! heart! heart!<br>O the bleeding drops of red,<br>Where on the deck my Captain lies,<br>Fallen cold and dead. | |

| Walt Whitman's "Oh Captain! My Captain!" | My Thought Processes |
|---|---|
| O Captain! my Captain! rise up and hear the bells;<br>Rise up—for you the flag is flung—for you the<br>    bugle trills;<br>For you bouquets and ribbon'd wreaths—for you the<br>    shores a-crowding;<br>For you they call, the swaying mass, their eager faces<br>    turning;<br>Here Captain! dear father!<br>This arm beneath your head;<br>It is some dream that on the deck,<br>You've fallen cold and dead.<br><br>My Captain does not answer, his lips are pale and still;<br>My father does not feel my arm, he has no pulse nor will;<br>The ship is anchor'd safe and sound, its voyage closed<br>    and done;<br>From fearful trip, the victor ship, comes in with<br>    object won;<br><br>Exult, O shores, and ring, O bells!<br>But I, with mournful tread,<br>Walk the deck my Captain lies,<br>Fallen cold and dead. | |

## Prose Constructed Response: "A Poem for My Librarian, Mrs. Long" and "O Captain! My Captain!"

Use what you have learned from reading "A Poem for My Librarian, Mrs. Long" and "O Captain! My Captain!" to write an essay that provides an analysis of how the idea of a *hero* is depicted in the two poems.

As a starting point, you may want to consider what is emphasized, absent, or different in the two texts, but feel free to develop your own focus for analysis.

Develop your essay by providing textual evidence from both texts. Be sure to follow the conventions of Standard English.

## Top Hat Graphic Organizer for Prose Constructed Response

| "A Poem for My Librarian, Mrs. Long"" | "O Captain! My Captain!" |
|---|---|
| Key Phrases: diction, tone, intended effective | |
| | |

How exactly is the idea of a hero treated in both works?

Write your Prose Constructed-Response Essay in a notebook or on loose-leaf paper.

# The Narrative Section: Tested Literacy Skills

As we discussed and have shown in the previous section, the PARCC treats reading and writing as one literacy event. The Narrative Task portion of the exam is no different, and, in fact, many of the literacy skills transfer easily from the Literary Analysis section. These skills include your ability to a.) define vocabulary in context, b.) identify terms that give rise to the meaning of vocabulary, c.) infer personality and character traits from narrative text, and d.) analyze character's motivations and desires. Last, the Narrative Section culminates in some form of creative and/or speculative writing.

To begin, we have an excerpt from Chapter 2 of Mark Twain's novel, *The Adventures of Tom Sawyer*, to serve as the basis of the Narrative Section skills that we will practice. As before, we will place the text in a two-column chart to show you the literacy skills in action that you will need to be successful on the narrative section.

When reading the narrative excerpt, you should focus on the ways in which the author presents and develops the main character. You should also focus on the underlying desires and motives of that main character. In our excerpt from *The Adventures of Tom Sawyer*, we will model these reading skills for you. Later on in this chapter, there will be another text with which you can practice independently.

| *The Adventures of Tom Sawyer,* excerpt from Ch. 2 | Our Thought Processes |
|---|---|
| But Tom's energy did not last. He began to think of the fun he had planned for this day, and his sorrows multiplied. Soon the free boys would come tripping along on all sorts of delicious expeditions, and they would make a world of fun of him for having to work—the very thought of it burnt him like fire. He got out his worldly wealth and examined it—bits of toys, marbles, and trash; enough to buy an exchange of *work*, maybe, but not half enough to buy so much as half an hour of pure freedom. So he returned his straitened means to his pocket, and gave up the idea of trying to buy the boys. At this dark and hopeless moment an inspiration burst upon him! Nothing less than a great, magnificent inspiration. | • Tom feels as though he is punished. He will have to work while the "free boys" come by.<br><br>• Tom's possessions are only enough for "a half an hour of pure freedom." |

*(continued)*

| *The Adventures of Tom Sawyer,* excerpt from Ch. 2 | Our Thought Processes |
|---|---|
| He took up his brush and went tranquilly to work. Ben Rogers hove in sight presently — the very boy, of all boys, whose ridicule he had been dreading. Ben's gait was the hop-skip-and-jump — proof enough that his heart was light and his anticipations high. He was eating an apple, and giving a long, melodious whoop, at intervals, followed by a deep-toned ding-dong-dong, ding-dong-dong, for he was personating a steamboat. As he drew near, he slackened speed, took the middle of the street, leaned far over to starboard and rounded to ponderously and with laborious pomp and circumstance — for he was personating the Big Missouri, and considered himself to be drawing nine feet of water. He was boat and captain and engine-bells combined, so he had to imagine himself standing on his own hurricane-deck giving the orders and executing them:<br><br>"Stop her, sir! Ting-a-ling-ling!" The headway ran almost out, and he drew up slowly toward the sidewalk.<br><br>"Ship up to back! Ting-a-ling-ling!" His arms straightened and stiffened down his sides.<br><br>"Set her back on the stabboard! Ting-a-ling-ling! Chow! ch-chow-wow! Chow!" His right hand, mean-time, describing stately circles — for it was representing a forty-foot wheel.<br><br>"Let her go back on the labboard! Ting-a-ling-ling! Chow-ch-chow-chow!" The left hand began to describe circles.<br><br>"Stop the stabboard! Ting-a-ling-ling! Stop the labboard! Come ahead on the stabboard! Stop her! Let your outside turn over slow! Ting-a-ling-ling! Chow-ow-ow! Get out that head-line! *lively* now! Come — out with your spring-line — what're you about there! Take a turn round that stump with the bight of it! Stand by that stage, now — let her go! Done with the engines, sir! Ting-a-ling-ling! SH'T! SH'T! SH'T!" (trying the gauge-cocks).<br><br>Tom went on whitewashing — paid no attention to the steamboat. Ben stared a moment and then said: "*Hi-Yi! You're* up a stump, ain't you!"<br><br>[…]<br><br>"Hello, old chap, you got to work, hey?" | • Tom dreads Ben Rogers will make fun of him.<br><br><br>• Twain represents boyhood freedom through Ben's pretending to be a steamboat.<br><br><br><br><br><br><br><br><br><br><br><br>• Tom is pretending he does not care; it's part of his plan. |

| The Adventures of Tom Sawyer, excerpt from Ch. 2 | Our Thought Processes |
|---|---|
| Tom wheeled suddenly and said:<br><br>"Why, it's you, Ben! I warn't noticing."<br><br>"Say—I'm going in a-swimming, I am. Don't you wish you could? But of course you'd druther *work*—wouldn't you? Course you would!"<br><br>Tom contemplated the boy a bit, and said:<br><br>"What do you call work?"<br><br>"Why, ain't *that* work?"<br><br>Tom resumed his whitewashing, and answered carelessly:<br><br>"Well, maybe it is, and maybe it ain't. All I know, is, it suits Tom Sawyer."<br><br>"Oh come, now, you don't mean to let on that you *like* it?"<br><br>The brush continued to move.<br><br>"Like it? Well, I don't see why I oughtn't to like it. Does a boy get a chance to whitewash a fence every day?"<br><br>That put the thing in a new light. Ben stopped nibbling his apple. Tom swept his brush daintily back and forth—stepped back to note the effect—added a touch here and there—criticised the effect again—Ben watching every move and getting more and more interested, more and more absorbed. Presently he said:<br><br>"Say, Tom, let *me* whitewash a little."<br><br>Tom considered, was about to consent; but he altered his mind:<br><br>"No—no—I reckon it wouldn't hardly do, Ben. You see, Aunt Polly's awful particular about this fence—right here on the street, you know—but if it was the back fence I wouldn't mind and *she* wouldn't. Yes, she's awful particular about this fence; it's got to be done very careful; I reckon there ain't one boy in a thousand, maybe two thousand, that can do it the way it's got to be done." | • Twain utilizes irony through the concept of "work."<br><br>• Tom is "tricking" Ben.<br><br><br><br><br><br><br><br><br><br><br><br><br><br><br>• Tom's hoax worked. |

| *The Adventures of Tom Sawyer,*<br>excerpt from Ch. 2 | **Our Thought Processes** |
|---|---|
| "No—is that so? Oh come, now—lemme just try. Only just a little—I'd let *you*, if you was me, Tom."<br><br>"Ben, I'd like to, honest injun; but Aunt Polly—well, Jim wanted to do it, but she wouldn't let him; Sid wanted to do it, and she wouldn't let Sid. Now don't you see how I'm fixed? If you was to tackle this fence and anything was to happen to it—"<br><br>"Oh, shucks, I'll be just as careful. Now lemme try. Say—I'll give you the core of my apple."<br><br>"Well, here—No, Ben, now don't. I'm afeard—"<br><br>"I'll give you *all* of it!"<br><br>Tom gave up the brush with reluctance in his face, but alacrity in his heart.<br><br>[…]<br><br>There was no lack of material; boys happened along every little while; they came to jeer, but remained to whitewash. By the time Ben was fagged out, Tom had traded the next chance to Billy Fisher for a kite, in good repair; and when he played out, Johnny Miller bought in for a dead rat and a string to swing it with—and so on, and so on, hour after hour. And when the middle of the afternoon came, from being a poor poverty-stricken boy in the morning, Tom was literally rolling in wealth. He had besides the things before mentioned, twelve marbles, part of a jews-harp, a piece of blue bottle-glass to look through, a spool cannon, a key that wouldn't unlock anything, a fragment of chalk, a glass stopper of a decanter, a tin soldier, a couple of tadpoles, six fire-crackers, a kitten with only one eye, a brass door-knob, a dog-collar—but no dog—the handle of a knife, four pieces of orange-peel, and a dilapidated old window sash.<br><br>He had had a nice, good, idle time all the while—plenty of company—and the fence had three coats of whitewash on it! If he hadn't run out of whitewash he would have bankrupted every boy in the village.<br><br>[…] | • "Reluctance in face and alacrity in heart"—Twain's diction perfectly represents Tom's character in that he is one way on the outside and another on the inside.<br><br>• Metaphor = "Slaughter of Innocents" refers to Tom's desire to deceive more of the town boys.<br><br>• Twain's list of Tom's materialistic gains is symbolic of boys and boyhood. These items are what amuse Tom and his friends. |

| *The Adventures of Tom Sawyer,* excerpt from Ch. 2 | **Our Thought Processes** |
|---|---|
| If he had been a great and wise philosopher, like the writer of this book, he would now have comprehended that Work consists of whatever a body is *obliged* to do, and that Play consists of whatever a body is not obliged to do. And this would help him to understand why constructing artificial flowers or performing on a tread-mill is work, while rolling ten-pins or climbing Mont Blanc is only amusement. There are wealthy gentlemen in England who drive four-horse passenger-coaches twenty or thirty miles on a daily line, in the summer, because the privilege costs them considerable money; but if they were offered wages for the service, that would turn it into work and then they would resign. [...] | • Tom is portrayed as very deceptive and very smart. <br><br><br> • Tom's discovery that "in order to make a man or a boy covet a thing, it is only necessary to make the thing difficult to attain" is representation of Twain's wit as an author |

Now that we have read and paid close attention to the language choices within the narrative passage, particularly the ways in which Mark Twain develops Tom's character and motivations, let's look at the type of reading comprehension questions the PARCC will ask.

# Narrative Section: Sample Questions

## PART A

Based upon the excerpt from *The Adventures of Tom Sawyer*, what can you infer about Tom's intelligence and understanding of human nature?

| a. Tom is driven to paint the fence properly out of respect for his Aunt Sally. | b. Tom understands that painting the fence is a long and hard process. |
|---|---|
| c. Tom knows how to blur the line between work and play. | d. Tom believes that if he gets his friends to paint the fence then he won't have to work. |

## PART B

What excerpt from the passage best supports your answer from Part A?

| | |
|---|---|
| a. The brush continued to move. "Like it? Well, I don't see why I oughtn't to like it. Does a boy get a chance to whitewash a fence every day?" | b. There was no lack of material; boys happened along every little while; they came to jeer, but remained to whitewash. |
| c. "No — no — I reckon it wouldn't hardly do, Ben. You see, Aunt Polly's awful particular about this fence — right here on the street, you know — but if it was the back fence I wouldn't mind and *she* wouldn't. | d. He had had a nice, good, idle time all the while — plenty of company — and the fence had three coats of whitewash on it! |

Now that you are done choosing the correct answer for each of the items above, we want to make one point here explicitly clear to you: If you read the sample selection with a critical eye — focusing on character development and character motivations — then the questions the PARCC throws at you are not so hard after all.

The annotations we have shown you above were an excellent aid for us to answer these narrative questions. Let's look at Part A: Through a process of elimination, the only viable choices are letters "c" and "d." Letters "a" and "b" should have been discarded as not applicable to answering the question. So, what's the correct choice? You got it! "B" is correct. While letter "d" represents a truth in the text — that if Tom gets his friends to paint the fence, then he won't have to — it does not tell us about Tom's intelligence and motivation. Only choice "c" does that. Because Tom understands that if he makes the fence look like it's fun, then his friends will be motivated for the pleasure of painting, so much so that they are willing to pay him for the honor!

Now, let's look at another type of narrative question PARCC will throw at you:

## PART A

Choose one word that describes Tom's personality as shown through the excerpt from *The Adventures of Tom Sawyer*. There is more than one correct choice listed below:

    a.  crafty

    b.  harmful

    c.  friendly

    d.  cunning

    e.  aggressive

    f.  responsible

    g.  mischievous

    h.  timid

## PART B

Find a sentence in the passage with details that support your response to Part A. On a computer-based test the instructions might be: "Click on that sentence and drag and drop it into the box below." Here, write your choices in the box.

| |
|---|
| |

Find another sentence in the passage with details that support your response to Part A.

| |
|---|
| |

As you can see from the passage above, the PARCC is giving you a little more space, in the form of options, to complete this series of questions. Let's look carefully at our Part A and consider our commentary on *The Adventures of Tom Sawyer*. Through a process of elimination, we can mentally cross out these choices: "aggressive, responsible, timid." If you consider our comments in the two-column chart above, you will clearly see that Tom is none of these choices. While Tom might be "friendly" in an indirect way, it does not match his behaviors and intentions within the passage.

So, we are now left with "a. crafty," "d. cunning," and "g. mischievous." Choices "a" and "d" are very close in meaning, since both mean "sneaky, sly, and tricky." Either of these choices would be acceptable. In addition, "g. mischievous" is also a viable option; it means, according to Merriam-Webster, to be "irresponsibly playful," as in mischievous behavior.

There is ample evidence from the text that would support such an answer. Here are some sentences below that you could choose:

- "Well, maybe it is, and maybe it ain't. All I know, is, it suits Tom Sawyer."

- "Ben, I'd like to, honest injun; but Aunt Polly—well, Jim wanted to do it, but she wouldn't let him; Sid wanted to do it, and she wouldn't let Sid. Now don't you see how I'm fixed? If you was to tackle this fence and anything was to happen to it—"

- If he hadn't run out of whitewash he would have bankrupted every boy in the village.

Excellent work! Now, let's consider the last portion of the Narrative Task section of the PARCC: The creative/speculative writing.

## Prose Constructed Response from Narrative Writing Task

One of the major points of this book you should absolutely understand by now is that the PARCC considers reading and writing to be a literacy event. As we have explained before, we believe that this part of the exam plays to your advantage as a test-taker. Consider, for a moment, the notes about the selection of *The Adventures of Tom Sawyer* that we have shown you. We cannot emphasize enough that this type of reading—where you question the characteristics and motivations of characters—is essential to your success. Let us show you another reason why this is true. Let's look at a sample Narrative Selection writing task:

## Narrative Writing Task

In this excerpt from *The Adventures of Tom Sawyer*, the text ends with Tom thinking "awhile over the substantial change which had taken place in his worldly circumstances...."

Write an original story to continue where the passage ended. In your story, be sure to use what you have learned about Tom as you tell what happens to him next.

Since the focus of this chapter is to show you the literacy skills you will need to be successful in such a narrative writing task, let's take a moment to engage, as we did in the previous Literary Analysis Section, with some prewriting.

---

The task at hand here is basically requiring two things from you: 1.) You need to develop an extension to the fence painting scene, and 2.) You need to make sure that your original story is based upon the characteristics of Tom as derived from your reading of the excerpt. *Whew!* That seems like a very hard task, but it is not really at all. This is where our notes on the excerpt become very useful again. We have learned all that we need to know about Tom; we just have to create a story based upon these characteristics.

Consider this very simple graphic organizer. It is set up to reveal Tom Sayer's defining characteristics. On the left side, we will identify Tom's defining personality traits. On the right, we will provide evidence from the text.

| Textual Evidence | Tom's Characteristics |
|---|---|
| Tom contemplated the boy a bit, and said: "What do you call work?" "Why, ain't *that* work?" Tom resumed his whitewashing, and answered carelessly: "Well, maybe it is, and maybe it ain't. All I know, is, it suits Tom Sawyer." | Tom is very witty. He knows human nature. He is very tricky and knows exactly how to fool Ben Rogers. |

*(continued)*

| Textual Evidence | Tom's Characteristics |
|---|---|
| "Ben, I'd like to, honest injun; but Aunt Polly—well, Jim wanted to do it, but she wouldn't let him; Sid wanted to do it, and she wouldn't let Sid. Now don't you see how I'm fixed? If you was to tackle this fence and anything was to happen to it—" | Tom is being manipulative. This is a hoax. |
| Tom gave up the brush with reluctance in his face, but alacrity in his heart. | Tom appears one way on the outside, but feels another way on the inside. |
| He had had a nice, good, idle time all the while—plenty of company—and the fence had three coats of whitewash on it! If he hadn't run out of whitewash he would have bankrupted every boy in the village. | Tom definitely prefers not to work! |
| Tom said to himself that it was not such a hollow world, after all. He had discovered a great law of human action, without knowing it—namely, that in order to make a man or a boy covet a thing, it is only necessary to make the thing difficult to attain. | Tom's insight into human nature is quite impressive. |

As you can see, we have ample ammunition now with which to create our original story about Tom Sawyer that will extend the excerpt above. The lessons you should have learned here are simple: 1.) Be actively engaged when you first read the excerpt from the Narrative Selection; be sure to comment on the character's PERSONALITY AND MOTIVATIONS and 2.) Always prewrite. Prewriting is never a waste of time. On the contrary, it actually speeds up the writing process.

So, now that we intimately know Tom's personality and motivations, let's conduct a bit of narrative prewriting. If you remember, the narrative writing task stated: Write an original story to continue where the passage ended. In your story, be sure to use what you have learned about Tom as you tell what happens to him next.

Here is a sample chart:

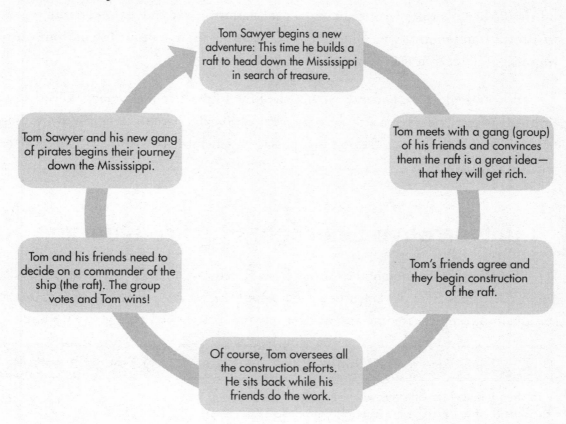

As you can clearly see through the graphic organizer above, we have created a step-by-step plan to write an original story about Tom's next adventure. The rationale of our tale comes directly from evidence within the text, and we are well on our way to achieving success on the Narrative Selection portion of the PARCC exam.

To summarize: The Narrative Selection will test your abilities in two primary areas: 1.) You will be required to *actively read* a sample narrative selection, paying attention to the focus character's personality development and motivations, and 2.) You will use the knowledge you gained from your *active reading* in order to write an original/creative story based upon the narrative selection.

We cannot emphasize to you enough that the single most critical aspect of this section of the PARCC is to test your ability to read narrative text and to understand a character's personality and motivation. All the PARCC's test-question items will stem from your ability to successfully read text in this way.

So, you might have guessed: Now is the time to practice the literacy skills that we have learned. You will be given a sample narrative selection and have to complete the reading questions and writing task based upon that passage. Remember the skills that you have learned, and GOOD LUCK!

## The Narrative Selection: Practice Question

Please read and annotate the excerpt from Rosemary Sutcliff's "The Golden Apple." This short tale comes from the larger book, *Black Ships Before Troy: The Story of the Iliad*. You will be asked to complete reading and writing activities based upon your active reading

| Excerpt from "The Golden Apple" | My Thought Processes |
|---|---|
| In the high and far-off days when men were heroes and walked with the gods, Peleus, king of the Myrmidons, took for his wife a sea nymph called Thetis, Thetis of the Silver Feet. Many guests came to their wedding feast, and among the mortal guests came all the gods of high Olympus. | |
| But as they sat feasting, one who had not been invited was suddenly in their midst: Eris, the goddess of discord, had been left out because wherever she went she took trouble with her; yet here she was, all the same, and in her blackest mood, to avenge the insult. | |
| All she did—it seemed a small thing—was to toss down on the table a golden apple. Then she breathed upon the guests once, and vanished. | |

*(continued)*

| Excerpt from "The Golden Apple" | My Thought Processes |
|---|---|
| The apple lay gleaming among the piled fruits and the brimming wine cups; and bending close to look at it, everyone could see the words "To the fairest" traced on its side. | |
| Then the three greatest of the goddesses each claimed that it was hers. Hera claimed it as wife to Zeus, the All-father, and queen of all the gods. Athene claimed that she had the better right, for the beauty of wisdom such as hers surpassed all else. Aphrodite only smiled, and asked who had a better claim to beauty's prize than the goddess of beauty herself. | |
| They fell to arguing among themselves; the argument became a quarrel, and the quarrel grew more and more bitter, and each called upon the assembled guests to judge between them. But the other guests refused, for they knew well enough that, whichever goddess they chose to receive the golden apple, they would make enemies of the other two. | |

## PART A

Based upon the excerpt from "The Golden Apple," what can you infer about Eris, the Goddess of Discord?

| | |
|---|---|
| a. That Eris, the Goddess of Discord, wants Aphrodite to eat the apple | b. That the Eris, Goddess of Discord, is jealous of Peleus, king of the Myrmidons |
| c. That Eris, the Goddess of Discord, is a bitter and resentful being | d. That Eris, the Goddess of Discord, wants Hera to eat the apple |

## PART B

What excerpt from the passage best supports your answer from Part A?

| | |
|---|---|
| a. Hera claimed it as wife to Zeus, the All-father, and queen of all the gods. | b. Eris, the goddess of discord, had been left out because wherever she went she took trouble with her; yet here she was, all the same, and in her blackest mood, to avenge the insult. |
| c. Aphrodite only smiled, and asked who had a better claim to beauty's prize than the goddess of beauty herself. | d. All she did—it seemed a small thing—was to toss down on the table a golden apple. Then she breathed upon the guests once, and vanished. |

## PART C

Choose one word that describes the Eris's personality as shown through the excerpt from "The Golden Apple." There is more than one correct choice listed below:

    a.  peaceful

    b.  vengeful

    c.  respectful

    d.  morbid

    e.  dedicated

    f.  spiteful

    g.  efficient

    h.  flattering

## PART D

Find a sentence in the passage with details that support your response to Part C. Click on that sentence and drag and drop it into the box below. (Here, write the sentence in the box.)

<br>

Find another sentence in the passage with details that support your response to Part C. Click on that sentence and drag and drop it into the box below. (Ditto.)

<br>

### Narrative Writing Task

In this excerpt from "The Golden Apple," the narrative ends with the three goddesses, Aphrodite, Athena, and Hera, at odds over who will get the apple.

Think about the characteristics of each of the three goddesses as presented in "The Golden Apple." Wrote an original story, starting where the excerpt ends.

Be sure to include details in your narrative that are consistent with the details of "The Golden Apple."

Please complete the graphic organizer to help you get started on your narrative. We have added a third column about Eris in order to keep your new tale consistent with that is written in our excerpt from "The Golden Apple."

| Eris's, the Goddess of Discord, Characteristics | The Three Goddess's Characteristics | Textual Evidence |
|---|---|---|
| | | |

**Please complete the graphic organizer to help you write your original narrative:**

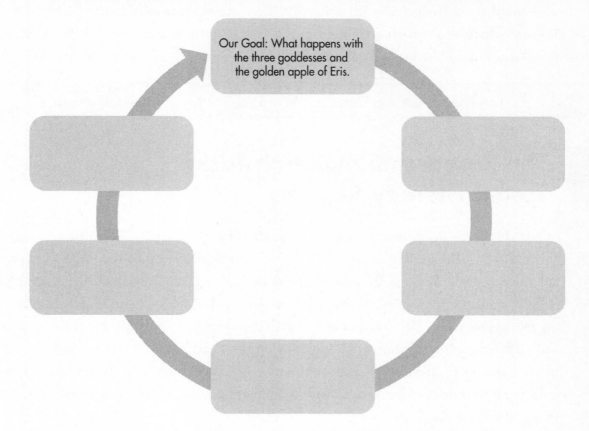

Our Goal: What happens with the three goddesses and the golden apple of Eris.

## ANSWERS:

Part A: b. That the Eris, Goddess of Discord, is jealous of Peleus, king of the Myrmidons. This is the only answer fully supported by the text. In no place in the text does Eris reveal her preference for which Goddess eats the apple.

Part B: b. Eris, the goddess of discord, had been left out because wherever she went she took trouble with her; yet here she was, all the same, and in her blackest mood, to avenge the insult.

Part C: The best answers are "b. vengeful" and "f. spiteful." These answer choices are supported by the fact that Eris wants to get revenge on King Peleus for not being invited to the wedding.

Part D: The following sentence from the excerpt, "The Golden Apple," best supports the idea that Eris is "vengeful" and "spiteful": "Eris, the goddess of discord, had been left out because wherever she went she took trouble with her; yet here she was, all the same, and in her blackest mood, to avenge the insult."

> Write your Narrative Response in a notebook or on loose-leaf paper.

 # The Research Simulation Task: Tested Literacy Skills

At this point in chapter 2, you might be thinking to yourself, "What more could be on the PARCC?" The answer clearly is, "A LOT." The next section of the PARCC is probably the most complicated and difficult of them all, and will require some of the same literacy skills—such as inferring, analyzing, and critiquing—but with one more difficult skill added on top: synthesizing. This section of Chapter 2 will explain in detail that the hard-acquired skill of synthesizing is, what it will look like on the PARCC, and how you will use that skill to read and write effectively. Lastly, it is with some excitement that in this chapter, we will go beyond traditional print text, as with the literary analysis and narrative tasks, and venture into graphic literacy. Here we go!

First things first: Let's start with, "What on earth is a research simulation task?" and "How can I do well on it?" As stated previously, the "Research Simulation Task" (aka RST) is a literacy event in which you will:

    a. support a position on a relevant issue

       by

    b. combining together two out of three sources.

What about the research you ask? By the term *research*, the PARCC does not mean you will "Google" the topic and find sources on your own. Actually, PARCC has done the research for you. You just have to be able to use the three sources given to write a solid, analytic essay.

This sounds difficult but it isn't if you practice the literacy skills outlined in this chapter. Are you ready? Let's look at an example of the RST section of the PARCC and break down, step-by-step, what you will need to do in order to shine! The RST is broken down into three sections. The first two literacy activities are reading and writing exercises that serve as the "warm-up" for the grand finale RST analytic essay.

The theme of our sample RST will be a contemporary issue, particularly about school uniforms. Let's look closely at the first step:

## Warm-up Task #1: Prose Constructed Response from Research Simulation Task (Summary)

As stated previously, the RST contains a minimum of 3 separate sources that pertain to a particular topic. Our topic of interest here is the issue of school uniforms in public schools.

The first source, an article published by the Associated Press that reports a major research study on the effectiveness of school uniforms. The entire text appears below. However, we must remember that when reading text, it is critical to interact with it WHILE YOU READ in a MEANINGFUL manner. When reading expository text such as the article that follows, these are some important questions to ask yourself while reading:

- What is the author's intent or motivation in writing the piece?

- Are the data (statistics) biased or unbiased?

- What do the data (statistics) reveal about the subject of the article?

- Is the author trying to prove a point? If so, what is that point?

- What other underlying messages do you notice in the text?

Now that we are equipped with our purpose for reading, we will place the text in a chart similar to the ones that you have already seen in this chapter. In the right column, are examples of the kinds of things you should be thinking when you read.

The article below discusses the integration of school uniforms in a large urban district.

| Local study says school uniforms may be a positive change! | Our Thought Processes |
|---|---|
| According to local data, a recent study reveals that since the requirement of school uniforms in our school districts, graduation, disciplinary, and attendance rates have all improved. | • Wow. Study reveals uniforms improve graduation, behavior, and attendance rates! |
| While this study has only been done on some, and not all, of our community's schools, it looks like this trend is positive academically on all levels. | • There weren't enough schools in the study to make the results 100%. |
| Six of the 20 schools in our district have instituted uniforms. Where do we go from here, though? Does this increase in graduation rate alone make such a change to be necessary? Local officials current discuss these questions today. | • Uniforms alone do not improve reading and math scores.<br><br>• Only 6 schools had uniforms. This number should be higher. |
| With an 11% increase in graduation rates in uniform-mandated schools, and a 4.6% decline in graduation rates in all other schools, the conversation and uniform debate has continued further. | • Wow! Graduation rates rose 11%.<br>• WOW! Non-uniform schools graduation rates fell 4.6%. |
| Four of the six of these uniform-mandated districts also stated that attendance has increased, and expulsion rates have fell. Is this enough data to push for a uniform-only policy? | • Attendance rates only increased in 4 of the 6 schools.<br><br>• Expulsion rate also fell. |
| One student, Adam LaMark, shared, "Uniforms have made things easier for me. My parents and I don't have to stress so much about what to wear every morning before going to school. It has helped our wallets also!" | • Uniforms are a good idea for troubled schools. |
| National surveys, especially recently, seem to declare that uniforms do not have a large impact positively on attendance, expulsion, and graduation rates as a whole. These surveys, though, are focused on student responses. All others involved in the educational process have not been nearly as surveyed as students. | • A national study seems to go against the study presented in this article. |

*(continued)*

| Local study says school uniforms may be a positive change! | Our Thought Processes |
|---|---|
| So, that leaves us thinking more about uniforms, especially how uniforms can both help and hinder the overall learning experience for our students. What about the impact on households, in general, however? These questions are still left up to debate in the continuing conversation amongst school districts and boards of education. | • Needed more schools for the study.<br>• The study did not factor parental involvement. |
| As we have spoken to various parents of these local districts, their opinions still vary. There is no absolute answer here. This, in itself, is frustrating for many who are actively entrenched in the uniform discussions. | • Some parents are against uniforms. |
| Some parents, and students alike, feel that uniforms take away student individuality. Overwhelmingly, many interviewed felt that individuality is what is most important for a teenager. And despite any uniform mandate, they did not totally change their students altogether. Peer pressure, and similar stresses and struggles remained present regardless. | • Some students are for it; some are against.<br>• Peer pressure, even with school uniforms, was still present. |

OK, so you might be asking yourself, "Why do I need to make so many annotations while I read?" "Why can't I just read the article?" From a literacy standpoint, the answer is simple: By annotating the text while you read you are more likely to retain information from the text that will help you with the questions on the PARCC that will follow. Let's show you how. Below is the first step of the three-step research simulation task:

## Prose Constructed Response from Research Simulation Task (Summary)

Student Directions

Based on the information in the text "Study says school uniforms might help attendance, graduation rates," write an essay that summarizes and explains the results of the research study.

Remember to use textual evidence to support your ideas.

After reading the above essay task, I am sure that you can see with certainty that the type of reading we are encouraging in this book—the type where you question the author's motives and the data within the text—will help you ace this relatively simple essay. What the PARCC is trying to do with this writing activity is to question and challenge your ability to summarize difficult, expository text. In the sample passage shown above, the difficulty lies in the understanding and balancing of all the data and statistics present. By annotating the text as you go along, the summary essay should be a piece of cake!

**Next, let's go to the second step in the RST section of the PARCC:**

### Warm-up Exercise #2: Making Claims

The second portion of the RST will ask you to consider another piece of text based upon the same theme as text #1, in this case school uniforms. What's exciting and dynamic about the PARCC assessment is that for them, the term *text* means just more than writing. Sometimes on the PARCC they will challenge you with all types of non-traditional text: graphs, charts, videos, artwork, etc. . . . . The basic principle, however, of interacting with the text stays the same.

As you view the graph below, you will want to ask yourself some of the following questions: "What is the purpose of the graph? What does it portray?" "Is the graph from a trusted source? What is the overall message or theme of the graph?" "What can you infer from the graph?"

OK. So, let's take a shot at this. Below you will find a graphic organizer that you should use while viewing the graph, "Do school uniforms make students more or less competitive about clothing?"

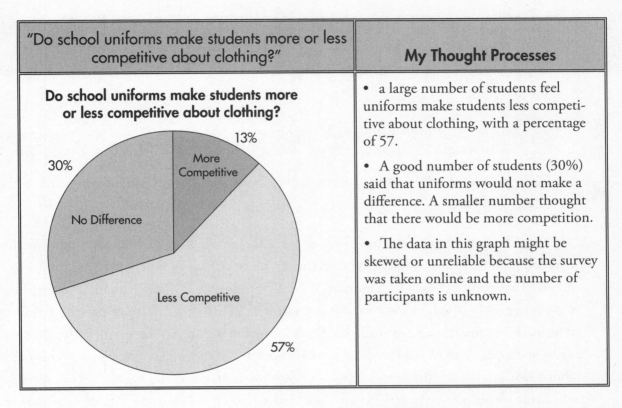

| "Do school uniforms make students more or less competitive about clothing?" | My Thought Processes |
|---|---|
| **Do school uniforms make students more or less competitive about clothing?**<br><br>13%<br>More Competitive<br><br>30%<br>No Difference<br><br>Less Competitive<br><br>57% | • a large number of students feel uniforms make students less competitive about clothing, with a percentage of 57.<br><br>• A good number of students (30%) said that uniforms would not make a difference. A smaller number thought that there would be more competition.<br><br>• The data in this graph might be skewed or unreliable because the survey was taken online and the number of participants is unknown. |

The chart above is based on an online survey given in March 2010 for a teenage magazine. All participants/voters were to be students in 6–8 grade.

Now that we have successfully dealt with the graph, let's see what the PARCC has in store for you. The next activity in the RST should be very familiar to you because we've practiced it already in this chapter:

Below are three claims that one could make based upon the graph, "Do school uniforms make students more or less competitive about clothing?"

| | |
|---|---|
| **CLAIMS** | Claim A: There is evidence that school uniforms increase reading and math scores. |
| | Claim B: Requiring school uniforms is an issue for middle school students. |
| | Claim C: More middle school students feel that uniforms would not make a difference in competitiveness about clothing. |

## PART A

Highlight the claim that is supported by the most relevant and sufficient evidence within the graph.

## PART B

Click on two details within the graph that best provide evidence to support the claim selected in Part A.

Now it's time to consider our three choices and whether or not the data supports these choices. Choice A is a no-brainer; it discusses an issue that is nowhere to be found in the graph. That choice is easy to eliminate. Claim B, however, is quite relevant and we need to look closer at the graph to see if we can support it. Claim B reads, "Requiring school uniforms is an issue for middle school students." Let's go to the numbers. The graph states that about 57% of middle school students say school uniforms would make students less competitive about clothing. Next, the graph states that 30% of students at the middle school say school uniforms would not matter. This suggests that Claim B, "Requiring school uniforms is an issue for middle school students," is our choice.

However, before we jump to conclusions, let's look at Claim C: "More middle school students feel uniforms would not make a difference in competitiveness about clothing." This claim is not true, as the size of the graph representing that view is much smaller. There you have it! Our answer is Claim B.

Great. Now, let's consider Part B on the PARCC, "Click on two details within the graph that best provide evidence to support the claim selected in Part A." Because of all the hard inferential work we did for Part A, this activity is pretty much a breeze. All we would have to do is click on the lightest part and the dark gray parts of the graph. About 57% of students at the middle school feel that uniforms would make students less competitive; and 13% feel uniforms make students more competitive. Therefore, Claim B—requiring school uniforms is an issue—is supported by the light gray and dark gray data. These data support the notion that school uniforms is more of a relevant issue for middle school students, because 70% of the students felt they make a difference.

At this point in our exploration of the RST, we moved from an activity that asked you to summarize data-rich text and an activity in which you analyzed a graph. These two activities will now culminate in the final section of the RST: "The Prose Constructed Response from Research Simulation Task (Analytical Essay)."

## RST Task Three: The Prose Constructed Response from Research Simulation Task (Analytical Essay)

Here's what the question looks like:

You have reviewed three sources regarding school uniforms. These three pieces provide information to begin drafting your own argument.

- **Source A:** Local study says school uniforms may be a positive change!

- **Source B:** Do school uniforms make students more or less competitive about clothing?

- **Source C:** Does school discipline over uniform infractions go too far?

Should students be required to wear uniforms in public school? Write an informative piece that addresses the question and supports your position with evidence from at least two of the three sources. Be sure to acknowledge competing views. Give examples from past and current events or issues to illustrate and clarify your position. You may refer to the sources by their titles (Source A, Source B, Source C).

That question prompt is pretty intense, but it is not impossible to tackle. Let's take it one step at a time. First, let's start with the issue of Source C, the video, because we have not yet interacted with that item. Just like ALL of the other texts covered in this chapter, we will employ the same literacy skills to deconstruct the video. In our chart below, we left space for us to record our thoughts. Some questions you might wish to consider while watching the video are: "What is the purpose or intent of the video (i.e. to inform or persuade)?" "Is the video based upon a scientific study or is it based upon anecdotal evidence?" "What types of data are used to back up claims?" "Does the video have a bias to it?" "What does the video want us to learn?"

Great, now that we are set with questions to help us, let's look carefully at the video and take notes while we view.

- As you will quickly realize, the PARCC is a "multimedia" text in which you find traditional text (essays and fiction), pictures and art, and, finally, video or audio. We are aware that access to the Internet might be a problem for some of you. Therefore, each time a video appears in our book, we will provide a brief, succinct summary so that you can use this information as you write.

### "Does School Discipline Over Uniform Infractions Go Too Far?"

This news report documents issues around school districts that have implemented a dress code for their students. Some larger cities around the country—such as Philadelphia and Chicago—have instituted school dress code policies. Proponents of the dress code argue that school uniforms reduce violence and promote a sense of equity in the buildings—meaning, since all students have the same dress, there is less emphasis on who wears what and why. Opponents argue that implementing a dress code takes away individuality and expressions of creativity. Lastly, in the video, the difference between dress code and school uniform is made. A dress code being a set of guidelines that students must follow and a uniform being clothes students are required to wear. When asked in the video, most students were in favor of a dress code but not a school uniform.

> **"Does School Discipline over Uniform Infractions Go Too Far?"** *www.freespeech.org*
>
> ## My Thought Processes
>
> - Student interviews show that such uniform policies, and their infractions, may have impact on particularities of color.
> - As a result of these infractions, students and parents may feel inconvenienced.
> - Many students may be missing school class time.
> - Consistency of rules is an issue.
> - Students may feel harassed by school administration.

Now that we have analyzed the video, let's consider again the RST question: *Should students be required to wear uniforms in public school?* It is important to consider that we are only required to use two of the three sources. That should be a piece of cake. OK, so let's eliminate one of our choices. Source A will prove to be useful because the data presented in the article actually came from a scientific study. The data, therefore, is trustworthy. It contains a high-level of validity in the sense that we can trust the data. Source B, on the other hand, while useful because it gives students' perspectives, is a bit unreliable because of the voting that was done over the Internet. That leaves us with Source C. The strength of Source C is that the videographer took the time to interview real students and to give perspectives from those most affected by the dress code: the students.

The next issue, and it is a critical step, is to decide where we stand on the issue. We would like to note that at this point in our writing you should put aside your personal feelings on the matter of school uniforms and stick with what you feel the texts could support in a possible answer. For instance, while you might think that not having school uniforms is a pretty cool idea, the data sources might be more beneficial to argue the other side. In this case, the data seem to better support the notion that public schools should require uniforms. Therefore, we will take a stand on that viewpoint.

As you probably know by now, the most significant step in answering the literacy questions posed on the PARCC is the groundwork, or the reading annotations and the prewriting activities. For the RST, prewriting is absolutely 100% critical. Let's look at the chart below to show how you could effectively prewrite for the RST activity.

| | |
|---|---|
| **Thesis: Students in public school should be required to wear school uniforms.** | |
| **Source A**<br>Local study says school uniforms may be a positive change! | **Source C**<br>"Does School Discipline over Uniform Infractions Go Too Far?" |
| • Wow. Study reveals uniforms improve graduation, behavior, and attendance rates!<br><br>• There weren't enough schools in the study to make the results 100%.<br><br>• Uniforms alone do not improve reading and math scores.<br><br>• Only 6 schools had uniforms. This number should be higher.<br><br>• Wow! Graduation rates rose 11%.<br><br>• WOW! Non-uniform schools graduation rates fell 4.6%.<br><br>• Attendance rates only increased in 4 of the 6 schools.<br><br>• Expulsion rate also fell.<br><br>• Uniforms are a good idea for troubled schools.<br><br>• A national study seems to go against the study presented in this article.<br><br>• Needed more schools for the study.<br><br>• The study did not factor in parental involvement.<br><br>• Some parents are against uniforms.<br><br>• Some students are for it; some are against.<br><br>• Peer pressure, even with school uniforms, was still present. | • Student interviews show that such uniform policies, and their infractions, may have impact on particularities of color.<br><br>• As a result of these infractions, students and parents may feel inconvenienced.<br><br>• Many students may be missing school class time.<br><br>• Consistency of rules is an issue.<br><br>• Students may feel harassed by school administration. |

**Common Themes Between the Two Sources:**

• Safety, focus on learning, Reduction in peer pressure

Now that we have completed our prewriting for the RST, we need to consider some special components within the essay itself that will be critical for you in the composition of your essay.

## Synthesis of Sources: Get Them Talking Together!

The RST is not your typical literary analysis or narrative writing task. It requires, as we have discussed, that you synthesize the two sources you are required to use. So, exactly how do you synthesize your sources? What on earth does that mean? In terms of literacy, to synthesize is to take two or more sources and treat them as if they were one. So, in our case here, we have to treat the research article and the video as if they were one. How do we do that? Once again, the answer is simpler than you think: 1.) Organize your essay according to thematic topics, and 2.) Get your sources talking to each other.

Now, let's consider the prewriting work we completed above. We provided ourselves with some good ammunition in terms of textual support, but, more importantly, we identified common themes between the two sources in the last row of our chart. Therefore, we have the themes by which we will write our essay. The next step is to get the sources talking with each other. Check out the outline below:

I. Introduction

    a. Introductory technique

    b. Thesis statement

II. Body

    a. Theme 1: Safety

        i. Sources A & C (talking together)

    b. Theme 2: Focus on Learning

        i. Sources A & C (talking together)

    c. Theme 3: Refute First Amendment

        i. Sources A & C (talking together)

III. Conclusion

    a. Introductory technique revisited

    b. Thesis Statement restated

    c. So what question

So, here we have the skeleton of our RST paper. Let's talk about the introduction first.

As with all good writing, the start of a paper must in some way grab the reader's attention. This can be accomplished in myriad ways such as: a quotation, a startling statement, an anecdote, etc. Our personal favorite is the rhetorical question. You will see it in action below. In addition to the rhetorical, we must remember to end our introductory paragraph with a solid thesis statement.

Here's our sample introductory paragraph for the RST.

> What is it that makes America great? Is it our commitment to hard work and social mobility? Yes. Is it our willingness to defend our liberty and freedoms? Yes. Is it our innovation and scientific advancements? Yes. The common denominator to all these ideals is our educational system. In fact, without education, the democratic experiment of America cannot be. We owe it to ourselves, therefore, to make our schools the best they can be. Part of improving our schools would be to require students to wear school uniforms. The simple requirement of school uniforms will make our educational system, and therefore, America, stronger.

While probably not the best introduction, it does illustrate exactly how you can catch your reader's attention with a series of rhetorical questions and also provide to the reader a solid thesis statement. Let's look at the body paragraph next. Remember, we decided to organize our paper by themes. In our sample below, we will also illustrate the skill of having your sources talk with each other.

> Ask any principal or teacher what is most necessary to receive a quality education, and you will hear one resounding answer: safety. It is a simple fact that learning cannot occur without a sense of safety and security in a school building.

Take, for example, Source C, the audio clip entitled, "Does School Discipline over Uniform Infractions Go Too Far?" various students discuss their experiences in dealing with often frivolous, or unnecessary, uniform infractions. These students, though, need to understand the importance of implementing rules that will make this mandate more long lasting. Such infraction policies will do just that. In Source A, however, we see solid local data that discusses how, despite such a nuisance as these infractions, the concept of uniforms is both important to student performance and overall school culture. The implication of these statistics is simple: How could graduation rates rise and dropout rates fall without safer schools? Based on this article in Source A, we can thank the simple change of school uniforms for these positive outcomes.

Next, requiring school uniforms would go a long way in keeping students focused on the most important aspect of their schooling: their learning. In today's modern world, there are quite enough distractions teens face: cell phones, media, dating, and yes, clothing! Take, for example, the students who were featured in Source A. It is a simple fact that a more orderly environment is a place where more learning takes place. Moreover, nothing can be more distracting from learning than school violence. The student interviews in Source C, while discussing the headache of such uniform infractions, the larger ideas that argue that school uniforms "reduce school violence by making students equal" and " and that school uniforms also eliminate "peer pressure" may still remain present. Therefore, both sources may both content that uniforms can indeed an atmosphere in school more conducive to learning.

Finally, when discussing school uniforms, the First Amendment always becomes an issue. Both Sources, A and C, present the argument that requiring school uniforms limits students' freedom of speech. Superficially, this might seem like a plausible idea. However, an individual's right to freedom of speech must be balanced against the greater good of the school building. Even with school uniforms, students can still express themselves through things like their hair, shoes, and even nail polish. Providing safe and rigorous schools, therefore, trumps an individual's right to wear, say, a Chicago Bulls t-shirt or baggy pants.

Now that we have given you a sample body, let's look at the important parts of the essay that you will have to write when you take the RST for real. The first point to notice is that these body paragraphs are organized by theme: safety and learning. By choosing these two ideas, we were able in our essay to allow the two sources to talk with each other. For instance, the first source provided anecdotal evidence about safety, while the second source produced statistics and facts about safety. Hence, our sources were "talking with each other" in a way that presented a structured and logical response to the RST prompt. The important thing to remember here is simple: Pick a theme for each of your body paragraphs and make sure that both sources discuss the same theme. Ask yourself, "What does source A say about the theme? "How dos source B complement or refute source A?" Doing so will ensure that the sources talk with each other.

Now, let's consider our sample conclusion:

> What more precious resource does America have other than its children? The short answer to that question is nothing. However, without a solid education, America's most precious commodity does not have a bright future. It is absolutely imperative, therefore, that we provide our children with the best education possible. After all, our democracy depends upon it. Through the simple act of requiring our children to wear uniforms to school, we are going a long way in ensuring a bright future for them, and for our country.

True to the outline we presented above, this sample conclusion fulfills all of the requirements. First, we repeated our use of the rhetorical question as we did in our introduction. Next, we restated our thesis, and finally, we answered that "So What?" question. That "So What" question being, "Why is this essay and my position on the topic important?"

OK, now that we have broken down the RST into its parts and have shown you an example of a RST essay in action, it is time for you to prepare yourself for the PARCC and practice on your own. Before we go to your practice RST, however, we need to discuss with you an issue surrounding multimedia.

## A Word about Validity

An article is not just an article. A video is not just a video. There are characters; there are messages; there are purposes. We often take text and, in this case, non-print text for granted, in the sense that we "believe" what they are reading or what they are viewing is a valid, or trustworthy, source of information.

Students need to be cognizant of the fact, however, that all texts are not created equal. Take, for example, the use of the multimedia video on the PARCC assessment. As a test-taker, you need to make yourself acutely aware that the information you are reading is credible, and, if it is not, you should make this observation known in the essays that you write for the research simulation task.

Who is providing this information? What is the background of the author/creator of this information? When is this information from? These sorts of questions should be asked when dealing with all types of information, whether that information is part of a traditional text or otherwise. Images, multimedia videos, and standard articles and passages can all be slanted with some sort of bias. Do not let this distract your argument, however. Concentrate on being conscious of such bias in the delivery of information, and using this information in the most valid way that you can. Couple this given information with your own know-how and real-life experiences.

These practices will inevitably make your argument stronger and that much more persuasive in nature.

## Sample RST Essay Practice

For your sample RST essay, we will give you the three texts first and then the actual RST question. Be sure to follow the steps in the practice as they will help you succeed when you actually take the exam. The topic of this RST is President Abraham Lincoln.

## Source A

| Abraham Lincoln's great laws of truth, integrity: A long career ruled by honesty<br>*www.greatamericanhistory.net/honesty.htm* | **My Thought Process** |
|---|---|
| Mary Todd Lincoln once wrote to a friend that "Mr. Lincoln . . . is almost monomaniac on the subject of honesty."<br><br>The future president was first called "Honest Abe" when he was working as a young store clerk in New Salem, Ill. According to one story, whenever he realized he had shortchanged a customer by a few pennies, he would close the shop and deliver the correct change-regardless of how far he had to walk.<br><br>People recognized his integrity and were soon asking him to act as judge or mediator in various contests, fights, and arguments. According to Robert Rutledge of New Salem, "Lincoln's judgment was final in all that region of country. People relied implicitly upon his honesty, integrity, and impartiality."<br><br>As a member of the Illinois legislature and later in his law practice, he took advantage of his reputation for honesty and fairness to help broaden his constituency. His good name helped win him four consecutive terms in the legislature.<br><br>Lincoln soon moved to Springfield, Ill., and began his law practice, a profession at which he admitted there was a "popular belief that lawyers are necessarily dishonest." His advice to potential lawyers was: "Resolve to be honest at all events; and if in your judgment you cannot be an honest lawyer, resolve to be honest without being a lawyer. Choose some other occupation, rather than one in the choosing of which you do, in advance, consent to be a knave." | |

*(continued)*

| Abraham Lincoln's great laws of truth, integrity: A long career ruled by honesty www.greatamericanhistory.net/honesty.htm | My Thought Process |
|---|---|
| According to Judge David Davis, in whose court Lincoln practiced for many years, "The framework for [Lincoln's] mental and moral being was honesty, and a wrong cause was poorly defended by him." Another judge who had worked with Lincoln agreed, saying "Such was the transparent candor and integrity of his nature that he could not well or strongly argue a side or a cause he thought wrong." | |
| Lincoln was ethical not only in his legal dealings with clients, but with his personal relationships. | |
| Always comfortable telling jokes and stories around the men of Springfield, he usually was awkward and self-conscious around women. In Lincoln's early political years, he wrote "I want in all cases to do right, and most particularly so in all cases with women." This was a principle to which he remained true all of his life. Today, historians tell us there is not a single credible story of Lincoln's being unfaithful to his wife. | |
| The Reverend Albert Hale of Springfield's First Presbyterian Church said, "Abraham Lincoln has been here all the time, consulting and consulted by all classes, all parties, and on all subjects of political interest, with men of every degree of corruption, and yet I have never heard even an enemy accuse him of intentional dishonesty or corruption." | |
| An example of an "enemy's" respect came in 1858, during Lincoln's Senate race against the powerful incumbent, Stephen A. Douglas. The senator, having competed with Lincoln in the legislature and many Illinois courtrooms, knew his opponent well. | |

(continued)

| Abraham Lincoln's great laws of truth, integrity: A long career ruled by honesty<br>*www.greatamericanhistory.net/honesty.htm* | My Thought Process |
|---|---|
| Responding to the news that Lincoln was to be his adversary, Douglas said: "I shall have my hands full. He is the strong man of his party—full of wit, facts, dates-and the best stump speaker, with his droll ways and dry jokes, in the West. He is as honest as he is shrewd, and if I beat him my victory will be hardly won."<br><br>Lincoln lost his Senate bid to Douglas. Two years later, however, he found himself running against the same man for the presidency. When Douglas was told of Lincoln's victory, he unselfishly told his informants: "You have nominated a very able and very honest man."<br><br>By the time Lincoln was president, statements he had made previously, such as "I have never tried to conceal my opinions, nor tried to deceive anyone in reference to them," and "I am glad of all the support I can get anywhere, if I can get it without practicing any deception to obtain it" had become a source of strength for him as a leader.<br><br>Everyone, even his bitterest political opponents, knew exactly where they stood with Lincoln. Because he didn't have to waste time convincing his opponents of his sincerity, he was able to devote his energies to solving political issues and winning the war.<br><br>Lincoln as commander in chief was honest and straightforward with his generals, always telling them directly what he did and did not appreciate about them. An example of his candor is the following excerpt from a letter to Maj. Gen. Joseph Hooker in early 1863: | |

*(continued)*

| Abraham Lincoln's great laws of truth, integrity: A long career ruled by honesty *www.greatamericanhistory.net/honesty.htm* | **My Thought Process** |
|---|---|
| "I have placed you at the head of the Army of the Potomac. Of course I have done this upon what appear to me to be sufficient reasons, and yet I think it best for you to know that there are some things in regard to which I am not quite satisfied with you. I believe you to be a brave and a skillful soldier, which of course I like . . . I have heard, in such a way as to believe it, of your recently saying that both the army and the government needed a dictator. Of course it was not for this, but in spite of it, that I have given you the command. Only those generals who gain successes can set up dictators. What I now ask of you is military success, and I will risk the dictatorship."<br><br>Finally, in search for the reason Lincoln was so adamant about honesty, a quote by one of his closest friends, Leonard Swett, is revealing:<br><br>"He believed in the great laws of truth, the right discharge of duty, his accountability to God, the ultimate triumph of the right, and the overthrow of wrong." | |

## Source B

### Abraham Lincoln: Life and Death (video)

Born February 12, 1809, in Kentucky, Abraham Lincoln spent his youth on farms in rural America. Self-educated, he began to study law in 1835, only after he was elected to the Illinois State Legislator as a member of the Whig Party. In 1846, Lincoln secured a spot in the U.S. House of Representatives. After his two years in Congress, Lincoln became a successful lawyer. In 1854, Lincoln challenged the Kansas-Nebraska Act, which was essentially a pro-slavery bill. Soon after, the Whig Party dissolved and the Republican Party was born, of which Lincoln has great influence. Next in his political career, Lincoln ran for the U.S. Senate against Douglas, but ultimately lost the race. The debates during this race contained some of Lincoln's finest speeches, one of which contained his famous words, "A house divided against itself cannot stand." Despite this loss, in 1960, Lincoln was decisively elected President in 1860. Two years into the Civil War, Lincoln issued The Emancipation Proclamation, symbolically freeing slaves in the Southern, rebellious states. Lincoln was re-elected by a landslide in 1864. On April 14, 1865, Lincoln was assassinated by John Wilkes Booth. In his death, Lincoln became one of the best presidents in the history of America.

| Abraham Lincoln: Life and Death<br>*www.watchmojo.com/video/id/9180/* |
| --- |
| My Thought Process |

## Source C

| The Youth of Indiana Becomes the President of the United States<br>*www.nps.gov/nr/twhp/wwwlps/ lessons/126libo/126facts4.htm* | My Thought Processes |
| --- | --- |
| The boy who grew up on the Indiana frontier eventually became the leader of the nation and did so at a critical point in its history. After moving to Illinois, Abraham Lincoln worked at several different jobs before he became a lawyer. His success as a lawyer led him to Springfield, the capital of Illinois, where his long interest in politics became a serious part of his life. In 1834, he was elected to the Illinois House of Representatives where he served three terms. In 1846, he was elected to the United States House of Representatives and in 1858 he ran for Senator from Illinois. Although he lost that election, he gained national prominence, partially through debates with Stephen A. Douglas on the issue of slavery. Two years later, in 1860, he was elected President of the United States, just as the crisis over slavery and secession peaked. Many of the qualities and characteristics that would help him to lead the country through the Civil War were born and nurtured during his formative years between the ages of 7 and 21.<br><br>**Quotes from Abraham Lincoln:**<br><br>**"In this country, one can scarcely be so poor, but that, if he will, he can acquire sufficient education to get through the world respectably."**<br><br>**" . . . I am never easy . . . when I am handling a thought, till I have bounded it north and bounded it south, and bounded it east, and bounded it west."**<br><br>Abraham Lincoln's intelligence was invaluable in making the many difficult decisions that came with being President during a time of crisis. He worked hard all his life to educate himself, in spite of many obstacles and challenges, and while President he continued to learn. As a boy he listened to his father and friends talk about the issues of the day, and then worked the idea in his | |

*(continued)*

| The Youth of Indiana Becomes the President of the United States *www.nps.gov/nr/twhp/wwwlps/ lessons/126libo/126facts4.htm* | My Thought Processes |
|---|---|
| mind until he understood it. His stepmother, Sarah Bush Johnston Lincoln, later recalled that he would repeat things over and over until it was fixed in his mind. As President, he listened carefully to his generals and advisors and read books on military strategy in a continual effort to learn and understand.<br><br>**"Labor is the great source from which nearly all, if not all, human comforts and necessities are drawn."**<br><br>**"Labor is the true standard of value."**<br><br>Growing up on the Indiana frontier, Abraham Lincoln learned at an early age that hard work was necessary for survival. He spent long days working with his father to clear the land, plant, and tend the crops. He hired himself out to work for neighboring farmers as a means of bringing additional money in for the family. When he decided to become a lawyer, he read and studied diligently and advised others to do the same. Certainly as President, he knew that it was going to take a lot of hard work to save the Union. He put in long hours attending to the countless details of running the country, including spending the entire night, sometimes, at the telegraph office, waiting for the latest news from his generals. He believed in the virtue of hard work not only for himself but for others. In response to a woman seeking work for her sons in 1865, he forwarded her request to one of his generals with a note stating, "The lady bearer of this says she has two sons who want to work. Wanting to work is so rare a want that it should be encouraged." | |

*(continued)*

| The Youth of Indiana Becomes the President of the United States www.nps.gov/nr/twhp/wwwlps/ lessons/126libo/126facts4.htm | My Thought Processes |
|---|---|
| . . . resolve to be honest at all events; and if in your own judgment you cannot be an honest lawyer, resolve to be honest without being a lawyer." Honesty and integrity were character traits that Abraham learned early in life, possibly from observing his father. Thomas Lincoln was described by those who knew him as "a sturdy, honest . . . man." A young and impressionable boy was certainly impressed by the regard with which neighbors and friends held Thomas, and determined to emulate his behavior. Abraham exhibited his own sense of honesty on a number of occasions, enough so to earn him the nickname of "Honest Abe." As a teen, he had borrowed a book about George Washington from a neighbor and while it was in his possession, the book was damaged. Not having any money to pay for the damage, Abraham honestly told his neighbor what happened and offered to work off the value of the book. For three days he worked in the man's fields as payment for the damaged book. Such a strong sense of integrity later became a hallmark of his presidency. | |

(continued)

| The Youth of Indiana Becomes the President of the United States<br>*www.nps.gov/nr/twhp/wwwlps/ lessons/126libo/126facts4.htm* | My Thought Processes |
|---|---|
| "With malice toward none; with charity for all; with firmness in the right, as God gives us to see the right, let us strive on to finish the work we are in; to bind up the nation's wounds; to care for him who shall have borne the battle, and for his widow, and his orphan…"<br><br>Abraham Lincoln has long been revered for his compassion as so eloquently stated in his Second Inaugural Address. There were also instances of him granting clemency to deserters and of writing heartfelt letters of condolence to bereaved families. Perhaps because he had experienced loss himself at a young age, he was able to empathize with those in pain. But his acts of kindness were not limited to just people. At the age of eight he killed a wild turkey and was so distraught that he resolved never to hunt animals again. A childhood friend remembered that one day at school Abraham "… came forward … to read an essay on the wickedness of being cruel to helpless animals." Whatever its origins were, the compassion that led him to urge the binding of the nation's wounds, after the terrible devastation of the Civil War, helped ensure the country's survival of its trial by fire. | |

*(continued)*

| The Youth of Indiana Becomes the President of the United States www.nps.gov/nr/twhp/wwwlps/ lessons/126libo/126facts4.htm | My Thought Processes |
|---|---|
| "I recollect thinking then, boy even though I was, that there must have been something more than common that those men struggled for." <br><br> "I hold, that in contemplation of universal law, and of the Constitution, the Union of these States is perpetual." <br><br> Abraham Lincoln held very strong beliefs about the sanctity of preserving the Union. In his mind the Founding Fathers envisioned a form of government unlike any the world had ever known and they sacrificed everything to create it. The ideas of freedom, equality of opportunity, and representative government were the foundation upon which a new nation was built. As a young man in Indiana, he read biographies of George Washington and Benjamin Franklin and accounts of the revolutionary struggle they, and others, waged and endured. The impression they left on him was strong and lasting. So much so that when he found himself faced with secession, he did not hesitate, but resolved to preserve the Union. That decision, based on beliefs formed during his youth, significantly impacted the United States of the 1860s, and the United States of today, which still exists due to his resolve. | |

# Research Simulation Task: Practice Question

## Abraham Lincoln

You have read and reviewed three texts describing President Abraham Lincoln. All three include discuss the qualities that made him one of the greatest presidents in our country's history. These sources include:

- **Source A:** Abraham Lincoln's great laws of truth, integrity: A long career ruled by honesty, *www.greatamericanhistory.net/honesty.htm*

- **Source B:** Abraham Lincoln: Life and Death: *www.watchmojo.com/video/id/9180/*

- **Source C:** The Youth of Indiana Becomes the President of the United States, *www.nps.gov/nr/twhp/wwwlps/lessons/126libo/126facts4.htm*

Write an essay that analyzes the personality traits that made Abraham Lincoln a truly great president. You must support your thesis with evidence from at least two of the three sources.

| Source | Source |
|---|---|
|  |  |

What specific personality traits made Abraham Lincoln great?

Write your Essay in a notebook or on loose-leaf paper.

## CHAPTER 3

# Narrative Writing Task

##  Introduction
(Performance-Based Assessment)

As we discussed in the introduction to the narrative writing task, you must know that organization and style are absolutely needed to be successful with this exercise. Whether you have to write a short story narrative, write a rhetorical speech, finish a scientific process, or complete a historical account, your writing must follow a specific formula.

To begin, let's review some common literary and rhetorical devices. You will need to master these in order to prove that you have the command over language that the PARCC expects you to have.

We have separated the common rhetorical and literary devices into two categories: diction devices and syntactical devices. Diction devices use words, and syntactical devices address sentence structure in order to develop a writer's style. Your goal here is to use a combination of both.

Take the time to review the chart below, including the definitions and examples of some devices that we have highlighted. Research these further online or in your English classes!

These are some common rhetorical and literary devices:

### Diction devices:

| Rhetorical/literary device | Definition | Example |
|---|---|---|
| Apostrophe | An exclamatory passage in a speech or poem addressed to a person or object (typically one who/which is dead or absent). | "Twinkle, twinkle, little star. How I wonder what you are." |

(continued)

| Rhetorical/literary device | Definition | Example |
|---|---|---|
| Hyperbole | Exaggerated statements or claims not meant to be taken literally. | "I'm so hungry I could eat a horse!" |
| Imagery | Visually descriptive or figurative language, | "Her eyes glittered like a star-lit night against the ocean's surface." |
| Metaphor | A figure of speech in which a word or phrase is applied to an object or action to which it is not literally applicable. | "He remained *the light of my life*, being my best friend and the only person that I could trust." |
| Onomatopoeia | A word that is spelled the way that it sounds. | " *'Boom!'* The car hit the tree, and all became silent that day." |
| Paradox | A seemingly absurd or self-contradictory statement or proposition that when investigated or explained may prove to be well founded or true. | "At the end of the day, it turns out that *it is cruel to be kind*." |
| Personification | The attribution of a personal nature or human characteristics to something nonhuman. | "The leaves *danced* in the wind that day." |
| Simile | A figure of speech involving the comparison of one thing with another thing of a different kind, using the words "like," or "as." | "The postal worker moved from house to house, *as busy as a bee*." |
| Symbol | A thing that represents or stands for something else. | "*The American flag* waved proudly that day, representing the freedom that we have come so far to achieve." |

## Syntactical devices:

| Rhetorical/literary device | Definition | Example |
|---|---|---|
| Anadiplosis | Repetition of the final words of a sentence or line at the beginning of the next. | "Fear leads to *anger. Anger* is just something that we can hide away from." |
| Anaphora | The repetition of a word or phrase at the beginning of successive clauses. | "*Here comes* the wind. *Here comes* the fire. *Here come* the days we have been waiting for." |
| Antithesis | A contrast or opposition between two things. | "Colonial Africa and the Western World portrayed a distinct difference in culture." |
| Asyndeton | Omission of the conjunctions that ordinarily join coordinate words or clauses (as in "I came, I saw, I conquered"). | "I went to the *store, park, library, school, church.*" |
| Epanalepsis | Repetition after intervening words. | "*The thought* of the stars that night brought back so many memories that it was, in the first, worth *the thought*." |
| Epistrophe | The repetition of a word at the end of successive clauses or sentences. | "I want *the best.* I deserve *the best.* I think what is most important is to have *the best.*" |
| Polysyndeton | Using several conjunctions in close succession, especially where some might be omitted (as in "he ran and jumped and laughed for joy"). | "I went to the *store, and park, and library, and school, and church.*" |
| Rhetorical Question | A statement that is formulated as a question but that is not supposed to be answered. | "What do I do from here?" "How do I cope?" |

There are plenty of devices out there, but we wanted to give you those that we found to be the easiest to use with regard to the writing of a narrative. In order to see results with this section of the PARCC, you will need to purposefully use language. You cannot use language in such a way unless you know specific devices. So, you can memorize the devices, or rather, you can learn them through practice. We suggest that you use them as you practice, especially with the sample prompts that we have constructed for you. This will help for these stylistic strategies to become routine for you.

Beyond the control and command over language, you should also be able to organize your thoughts in a logical manner. You will have to refer to the PARCC rubric (on the next page) as we continue through the three writing prompts.

Keep in mind that your response should be readable, but it should also be appropriate to the writing topic. As you know, you do not write a short story in your English language arts class the way that you would write a lab report in your biology class.

So, where do we begin? We have come up with a step-by-step guide to help you manage and outline your steps in responding to the question:

| What is the question asking of you? | | |
| --- | --- | --- |
| **To write a story?** | **To complete a historical account?** | **To complete a scientific procedure?** |
| • What are the elements of the short story?<br><br>• Who is the original main character?<br><br>• What are the character traits of that character?<br><br>• How can you be true to that character throughout the rest of the story? | • What parts of the historical account have already been revealed?<br><br>• How do I continue through the historical account?<br><br>• How does this historical account conclude?<br><br>• How can I use literary devices to engage the reader? | • What parts of the scientific procedure have already been revealed?<br><br>• How do I continue through the entire scientific process?<br><br>• How does this scientific process conclude? |

# Evaluating the Narrative Writing Task

You might ask yourself, exactly how is the PARCC going to grade my narrative writing task. The good news is that we have very clear and precise guidance in this area. Below, we have two items:

1. A writing/scoring checklist that you can use to revise and edit your work, and

2. The rubric the PARCC will use to evaluate your work.

As you write your narrative responses, utilize the scoring checklist and scoring rubrics (found at the back of the book), to assist you in constructing an excellent essay. *If you use these tools after each practice essay, you will start to internalize what the PARCC expects of you.* That will definitely help you.

# English Language Arts Narrative Writing Task

As you continue to review the literary devices, along with the thought process that goes along with this task and its rubric, keep in mind the following structure for your narrative. Be sure to remember where the narrative left off. Continue it from there, and be true to the structure of the short story. We will review this diagram as we look at some sample responses.

This type of organizer, called "Freytag's Pyramid," should help assist you in your brainstorming and pre-writing. Put an identifiable notation next to the part of the short story where you should begin, based on your completed reading of the selection given. Then, make sure to hit all remaining parts of the short story as you move through the narrative writing task.

# Freytag's Pyramid

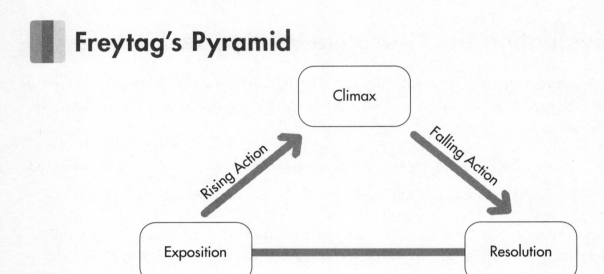

We have put this pyramid into an easy-to-use graphic organizer in the back of the book. Thinking about this task in a chronological way will help you organize your ideas in a timely manner. Remember, we understand that this task is extremely doable for you, but to save time, we want you to organize your thoughts as quickly as possible.

Think about the point at which you are beginning your story—Is the story currently in the rising action? Has the conflict already occurred? Be true to the story that has already been started for you.

Review the graphic organizer as we begin looking at models.

*(continued)*

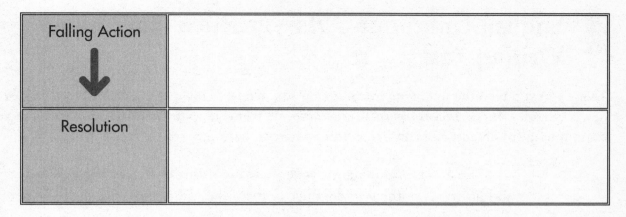

We are going to start by looking at an authentic text (in this case, a short story) and completing it, while also using some of the devices listed in the beginning of this section. Do not worry if you have never read this story before. This task is asking you to take what you have read so far and use the conventions present in this story to move it forward.

| CCSS Alignment | | |
|---|---|---|
| | RL.1 | Cite strong and textual evidence. |
| | RL.2 | Determine two or more themes. |
| | RL.3 | Analyze the impact of the author's choices. |
| | RL.5 | Analyze how an author's choices contribute to its overall structure. |
| | L.3 | Apply knowledge of language to understand how language functions in different contexts. |
| | L.5 | Demonstrate understanding of figurative language, word relationships, and nuances in word meanings. |
| | W.3 | Write narratives to develop real or imagined experiences. |
| | W.5 | Develop and strengthen writing as needed by planning, revising, editing, and rewriting. |
| | W.6 | Use technology to produce, publish, and update individual writing products. |

[ELA TASK GENERATION MODEL FOR NARRATIVE TYPE: 1PBA]

# English Language Arts—Practice Narrative Writing Task

Today you will read the following introduction to the tale, "Down the Rabbit's Hole," a part of Lewis Carroll's *Alice's Adventures in Wonderland*. As you read, pay close attention to characterization, usage of details, and conflict as you prepare to write a narrative story:

ALICE was beginning to get very tired of sitting by her sister on the bank, and of having nothing to do: once or twice she had peeped into the book her sister was reading, but it had no pictures or conversations in it, "and what is the use of a book," thought Alice, "without pictures or conversations?"

So she was considering in her own mind (as well as she could, for the hot day made her feel very sleepy and stupid) whether the pleasure of making a daisy-chain would be worth the trouble of getting up and picking the daisies, when suddenly a White Rabbit with pink eyes ran close by her.

There was nothing so *very* remarkable in that; nor did Alice think it so *very* much out of the way to hear the Rabbit say to itself, "Oh dear! Oh dear! I shall be too late!" (when she thought it over afterwards, it occurred to her that she ought to have wondered at this, but at the time it all seemed quite natural); but when the Rabbit actually *took a watch out of its waistcoat-pocket*, and looked at it, and then hurried on, Alice started to her feet, for it flashed across her mind that she had never before seen a rabbit with either a waistcoat-pocket, or a watch to take out of it, and burning with curiosity, she ran across the field after it, and was just in time to see it pop down a large rabbit-hole under the hedge.

In another moment down went Alice after it, never once considering how in the world she was to get out again.

The rabbit-hole went straight on like a tunnel for some way, and then dipped suddenly down, so suddenly that Alice had not a moment to think about stopping herself before she found herself falling down what seemed to be a very deep well.

Either the well was very deep, or she fell very slowly, for she had plenty of time as she went down to look about her, and to wonder what was going to happen next. First, she tried to look down and make out what she was coming to, but it was too dark to see anything; then she looked at the sides of the well and noticed that they were filled with cupboards and book-shelves: here and there she saw maps and pictures hung upon pegs. She took down a jar from one of the shelves as she passed; it was labeled "ORANGE MARMALADE," but to her disappointment it was empty; she did not like to drop the jar for fear of killing somebody underneath, so managed to put it into one of the cupboards as she fell past it.

Down, down, down. Would the fall *never* come to an end? "I wonder how many miles I've fallen by this time?" she said aloud. "I must be getting somewhere near the centre of the earth. Let me see: that would be four thousand miles down. I think—"

Down, down, down. There was nothing else to do, so Alice soon began talking again. "Dinah'll miss me very much to-night, I should think!" (Dinah was the cat.) "I hope they'll remember her saucer of milk at tea-time. Dinah, my dear, I wish you were down here with me! There are no mice in the air, I'm afraid, but you might catch a bat, and that's very like a mouse, you know. But do cats eat bats, I wonder?" And here Alice began to get rather sleepy, and went on saying to herself, in a dreamy sort of way, "Do cats eat bats? Do cats eat bats?" and sometimes, "Do bats eat cats?" for, you see, as she couldn't answer either question, it didn't much matter, which way she put it. She felt that she was dozing off, and had just begun to dream that she was walking hand in hand with Dinah, and saying to her very earnestly, "Now, Dinah, tell me the truth: did you ever eat a bat?" when suddenly, thump! thump! down she came upon a heap of sticks and dry leaves, and the fall was over.

## Practice Narrative Writing Task

In the above excerpt, the author develops an interesting situation where the narrator, Alice, is experiencing a rather shocking series of circumstances! Think about the narrator's current situation regarding her fall, her feelings, along with the details surrounding Alice at this moment in the story.

Write an original story to continue where the passage ends. In your story, be sure to use what you have learned about the character of Alice as you tell what happens next.

| Exposition ⬇ | |
|---|---|
| Rising Action ⬇ | |
| Climax ⬇ | |
| Falling Action ⬇ | |
| Resolution | |

Here is our model essay, designed to plausibly carry the Lewis Carroll story forward:

As Alice landed, she looked around. She hasn't been able to sleep in days, but continued to relentlessly think in rhymes that made almost no sense at all.

"Can a lime tell time?"

"Does a dream seem?"

Alice straightened her once-ironed dress, as she attempted to smooth out its wrinkles. She searched the limited space around her for the White Rabbit. Her head felt heavy, as she searched the room's walls, adorned by similar cabinetry that she remembered while falling through the rabbit-hole.

The first cabinet revealed a small pin, labeled with the message, "FOUND." Alice laughed to herself, as she pinned her new treasure to the collar of her dress. She felt anything but found, though; she felt lost; she felt sad; she felt confused.

Crunch. Crunch. Crunch. Alice could hear a rustle in an almost-hidden cabinet in the corner of this room. She opened the door to reveal the White Rabbit! Alice jumped, startled that the rabbit was not merely a figment of her imagination. The rabbit handed Alice a carrot. Alice held onto this carrot, as it acted as a key into a doorway.

"Don't catch a cold! The carrot connects the keyhole!" the White Rabbit screeched.

Alice, still thinking in rhymes, asked the rabbit for directions to get home.

"Follow the fool! Trail the trolley!" the White Rabbit riddled.

"Follow the fool! Trail the trolley!" the White Rabbit repeated.

Alice shook her head in confusion. She used the carrot as a key in an adjacent doorway. Once opened, she entered a world of utter beauty. Glistening, icy gems reflected beams of sunlight upon Alice's pale face. A winding waterway flowed into a central point of this picturesque scene. The flowers began to bloom as Alice passed their budding presence, and Alice could not resist but look around in wonderment.

Following the rabbit as he ranted to himself, Alice could see a small nook in the distance. She hurried as the White Rabbit increased his pace. She ran. She ran. She ran. The sun smiled down on them, shining brighter, as they drew closer to the nook.

Reaching the small area, Alice looked at its grassy wall. The White Rabbit hopped into the water, as he yelled, "Look there!" The rabbit was never to be seen again.

Looking at the mirror in front of her, Alice said to herself, "Home is within myself." She grabbed the small mirror from its roots, held it close to her, and closed her eyes. Home was the comfort within herself.

Alice realized that she would finally sleep well that night, as she lay on the grassy knoll beneath her, holding firm to the mirror within her sturdy grasp.

**Read through this model narrative writing response. We have filled out the graphic organizer, linking our story to its corresponding elements. Fill in any other details that you think may link appropriately.**

| | |
|---|---|
| **Exposition** ↓ | • Alice sees a rabbit, who seems to be checking his watch and is in a rush.<br>• Setting: It seems as if the characters are in a wooded forest. |
| **Rising Action** ↓ | • Alice follows the rabbit, who still seems to be in a rush. |
| **Climax** ↓ | • Alice takes a very long fall down the rabbit-hole.<br>• Alice is extremely confused at her predicament. |
| **Falling Action** ↓ | • Alice searches the room for the White Rabbit.<br>• Alice enters one of the cabinets, where she finds the White Rabbit. |
| **Resolution** | • The White Rabbit explains the rest of Alice's quest to come, as he disappears in the water. |

Now, take the time to identify some literary devices, and try to recognize how the usage of these devices affects the overall effect of the short story as a whole.

Here are some we found:

**Metaphor:** *Alice straightened her once-ironed dress*

**Foreshadowing:** *The first cabinet revealed a small pin, labeled with the message, "FOUND."*

**Anaphora:** *She felt anything but found . . .; she felt lost; she felt sad; she felt confused.*

**Onomatopoeia:** *Crunch. Crunch. Crunch.*

**Alliteration:** *"Don't catch a cold! The carrot connects the keyhole!"*

**Imagery:** *Glistening, icy gems reflected beams of sunlight upon Alice's pale face. A winding waterway flowed into a central point of this picturesque scene. The flowers* *began to bloom as Alice passed their budding presence, and Alice could not resist but look around in wonderment.*

**Repetition:** *She ran. She ran. She ran.*

**Personification:** *The sun smiled down on them, shining brighter, as they drew closer to the nook.*

Now that you have reviewed the model essay, along with the devices used throughout, take the time to jot down notes about the impact these devices have on the overall effect of the story. Use the note-taking chart below:

| Device | Impact on story |
|---|---|
| metaphor | |
| foreshadowing | |
| anaphora | |
| onomatopoeia | |
| alliteration | |
| imagery | |
| repetition | |
| details | |
| personification | |

The narrative writing task is one where you need to keep a few things in mind at all times:

- The elements of the short story.

- The need to stay true to the original story.

- The use of literary devices to contribute to the impact of the story.

# English Language Arts—Practice Narrative Writing Task #1

| CCSS Alignment | |
|---|---|
| RL.1 | Cite strong and textual evidence. |
| RL.2 | Determine two or more themes. |
| RL.3 | Analyze the impact of the author's choices. |
| RL.5 | Analyze how an author's choices contribute to its overall structure. |
| RL.10 | Read and comprehend complex texts. |
| L.3 | Apply knowledge of language to understand how language functions in different contexts. |
| L.5 | Demonstrate understanding of figurative language, word relationships, and nuances in word meanings. |
| W.3 | Write narratives to develop real or imagined experiences. |
| W.5 | Develop and strengthen writing as needed by planning, revising, editing, and rewriting. |
| W.6 | Use technology to produce, publish, and update individual writing products. |

[ELA TASK GENERATION MODEL FOR NARRATIVE TYPE: 1PBA]

Today you will read the following introduction to the novel, *Little Women*, by Louisa May Alcott. As you read, pay close attention to characterization, usage of details, and conflict as you prepare to write a narrative story:

"Christmas won't be Christmas without any presents," grumbled Jo, lying on the rug.

"It's so dreadful to be poor!" sighed Meg, looking down at her old dress.

"I don't think it's fair for some girls to have plenty of pretty things, and other girls nothing at all," added little Amy, with an injured sniff.

"We've got Father and Mother and each other," said Beth contentedly from her corner.

The four young faces on which the firelight shone brightened at the cheerful words, but darkened again as Jo said sadly, "We haven't got Father, and shall not have him for a long time." She didn't say "perhaps never," but each silently added it, thinking of Father far away, where the fighting was.

Nobody spoke for a minute; then Meg said in an altered tone, "You know the reason Mother proposed not having any presents this Christmas was because it is going to be a hard winter for everyone; and she thinks we ought not to spend money for pleasure, when our men are suffering so in the army. We can't do much, but we can make our little sacrifices, and ought to do it gladly. But I am afraid I don't." And Meg shook her head, as she thought regretfully of all the pretty things she wanted.

"But I don't think the little we should spend would do any good. We've each got a dollar, and the army wouldn't be much helped by our giving that. I agree not to expect anything from Mother or you, but I do want to buy *Undine and Sintram* for myself. I've wanted it *so* long," said Jo, who was a bookworm.

"I planned to spend mine in new music," said Beth, with a little sigh, which no one heard but the hearth brush and kettle holder.

"I shall get a nice box of Faber's drawing pencils. I really need them," said Amy decidedly.

"Mother didn't say anything about our money, and she won't wish us to give up everything. Let's each buy what we want, and have a little fun. I'm sure we work hard enough to earn it," cried Jo, examining the heels of her shoes in a gentlemanly manner.

"I know *I* do—teaching those tiresome children nearly all day, when I'm longing to enjoy myself at home," began Meg, in the complaining tone again.

"You don't have half such a hard time as I do," said Jo. "How would you like to be shut up for hours with a nervous, fussy old lady, who keeps you trotting, is never satisfied, and worries you till you're ready to fly out of the window or cry?"

"It's naughty to fret, but I do think washing dishes and keeping things tidy is the worst work in the world. It makes me cross, and my hands get so stiff, I can't practice well at all." And Beth looked at her rough hands with a sigh that any one could hear that time.

"I don't believe any of you suffer as I do," cried Amy, "for you don't have to go to school with impertinent girls, who plague you if you don't know your lessons, and laugh at your dresses, and label your father if he isn't rich, and insult you when your nose isn't nice."

## Practice Narrative Writing Task #1

*50 Minutes*

In the above passage, the author develops an interesting exchange among a group of sisters. Think about their relationships, as each is revealed through the author's usage of dialogue.

Write an original story to continue where the passage ended. In your story, be sure to use what you have learned about the sisters as you tell what happens next.

| Exposition | |
| --- | --- |
| Rising Action | |
| Climax | |
| Falling Action | |
| Resolution | |

Write your original story to show how you think the passage ended.
Put it on loose-leaf paper or in a notebook. Be sure to check the
scoring checklist and the scoring rubrics chart in the back of the book.

# English Language Arts—Practice Narrative Writing Task #2

| CCSS Alignment | |
| --- | --- |
| RL.1 | Cite strong and textual evidence. |
| RL.2 | Determine two or more themes. |
| RL.3 | Analyze the impact of the author's choices. |
| RL.5 | Analyze how an author's choices contribute to its overall structure. |
| RL.10 | Read and comprehend complex texts. |
| L.3 | Apply knowledge of language to understand how language functions in different contexts. |
| L.5 | Demonstrate understanding of figurative language, word relationships, and nuances in word meanings. |
| W.3 | Write narratives to develop real or imagined experiences. |
| W.5 | Develop and strengthen writing as needed by planning, revising, editing, and rewriting. |

[ELA TASK GENERATION MODEL FOR NARRATIVE TYPE: 1PBA]

**Today you will read the following introduction to the novel, *The Adventures of Tom Sawyer*, by Mark Twain. As you read, pay close attention to characterization, usage of details, and conflict as you prepare to write a narrative story:**

All nature was wide awake and stirring, now; long lances of sunlight pierced down through the dense foliage far and near, and a few butterflies came fluttering upon the scene.

Tom stirred up the other pirates and they all clattered away with a shout, and in a minute or two were stripped and chasing after and tumbling over each other in the shallow limpid water of the white sandbar. They felt no longing for the little village sleeping in the distance beyond the majestic waste of water. A vagrant current or a slight rise in the river had carried off their raft, but this only gratified them, since its going was something like burning the bridge between them and civilization.

They came back to camp wonderfully refreshed, glad-hearted, and ravenous; and they soon had the camp-fire blazing up again. Huck found a spring of clear cold water close by, and the boys made cups of broad oak or hickory leaves, and felt that water, sweetened with such a wildwood charm as that, would be a good enough substitute for coffee. While Joe was slicing bacon for breakfast, Tom and Huck asked him to hold on a minute; they stepped to a promising nook in the river-bank and threw in their lines; almost immediately they had reward. Joe had not had time to get impatient before they were back again with some handsome bass, a couple of sun-perch and a small catfish—provisions enough for quite a family. They fried the fish with the bacon, and were astonished; for no fish had ever seemed so delicious before. They did not know that the quicker a fresh-water fish is on the fire after he is caught the better he is; and they reflected little upon what a sauce open-air sleeping, open-air exercise, bathing, and a large ingredient of hunger make, too.

They lay around in the shade, after breakfast, while Huck had a smoke, and then went off through the woods on an exploring expedition. They tramped gayly along, over decaying logs, through tangled underbrush, among solemn monarchs of the forest, hung from their crowns to the ground with a drooping regalia of grape-vines. Now and then they came upon snug nooks carpeted with grass and jeweled with flowers.

They found plenty of things to be delighted with, but nothing to be astonished at. They discovered that the island was about three miles long and a quarter of a mile wide, and that the shore it lay closest to was only separated from it by a narrow channel hardly two hundred yards wide. They took a swim about every hour, so it was close upon the middle of the afternoon when they got back to camp. They were too hungry to stop to fish, but they fared sumptuously upon cold ham, and then threw themselves down in the shade to talk. But the talk soon began to drag, and then died. The stillness, the solemnity that brooded in the woods, and the sense of loneliness, began to tell upon the spirits of the boys. They fell to thinking. A sort of undefined longing crept upon them. This took dim shape, presently—it was budding homesickness. Even Finn the Red-Handed was dreaming of his doorsteps and empty hogsheads. But they were all ashamed of their weakness, and none was brave enough to speak his thought.

## Practice Narrative Writing Task #2

50 Minutes

In the above passage, the author developed a distinct setting for the rest of this story. Think about the relationships of these characters in this setting, the events leading to the characters' sense of shame and weakness, along with the details the author used to build the characters in this story.

Write an original story to continue where the passage ended. In your story, be sure to use what you have learned about the characters and setting as you tell what happens next.

| Exposition | |
|---|---|
| Rising Action | |
| Climax | |
| Falling Action | |

| Resolution | |
|---|---|
| | |

Write your original story on loose-leaf paper or in a notebook. Be sure to use the scoring checklist and the rubrics chart in the back of the book.

# English Language Arts—Practice Narrative Writing Task #3

| CCSS Alignment | |
|---|---|
| RL.1 | Cite strong and textual evidence. |
| RL.2 | Determine two or more themes. |
| RL.3 | Analyze the impact of the author's choices. |
| RL.5 | Analyze how an author's choices contribute to its overall structure. |
| RL.10 | Read and comprehend complex texts. |
| L.3 | Apply knowledge of language to understand how language functions in different contexts. |
| L.4 | Determine or clarify the meaning of unknown and multiple-meaning words and phrases. |
| L.5 | Demonstrate understanding of figurative language, word relationships, and nuances in word meanings. |
| W.3 | Write narratives to develop real or imagined experiences. |
| W.5 | Develop and strengthen writing as needed by planning, revising, editing, and rewriting. |
| W.6 | Use technology to produce, publish, and update individual writing products. |

[ELA TASK GENERATION MODEL FOR NARRATIVE TYPE: 1PBA]

Today you will read the following introduction to the novel, *A Wrinkle in Time*, by Madeleine L'Engle. As you read, pay close attention to characterization, usage of details, and conflict as you prepare to write a narrative story.

It was a dark and stormy night.

In her attic bedroom Margaret Murry, wrapped in an old patchwork quilt, sat on the foot of her bed and watched the trees tossing in the frenzied lashing of the wind. Behind the trees clouds scudded frantically across the sky. Every few moments the moon ripped through them, creating wraithlike shadows that raced along the ground.

The house shook.

Wrapped in her quilt, Meg shook.

She wasn't usually afraid of weather. —It's not just the weather, she thought. —It's the weather on top of everything else. On top of me. On top of Meg Murry doing everything wrong.

School. School was all wrong. She'd been dropped down to the lowest section in her grade. That morning one of her teachers had said crossly, "Really, Meg, I don't understand how a child with parents as brilliant as yours are supposed to be can be such a poor student. If you don't manage to do a little better you'll have to stay back next year."

During lunch she'd roughhoused a little to try to make herself feel better, and one of the girls said scornfully, "After all, Meg, we aren't grade-school kids anymore. Why do you always act like such a baby?"

And on the way home from school, as she walked up the road with her arms full of books, one of the boys had said something about her "dumb baby brother." At this she'd thrown the books on the side of the road and tackled him with every ounce of strength she had, and arrived home with her blouse torn and a big bruise under one eye.

Sandy and Dennys, her ten-year-old twin brothers, who got home from school an hour earlier than she did, were disgusted. "Let *us* do the fighting when it's necessary," they told her.

—A delinquent, that's what I am, she thought grimly.

—That's what they'll be saying next. Not Mother. But Them. Everybody Else. I wish Father—

But it was still not possible to think about her father without the danger of tears. Only her mother could talk about him in a natural way, saying, "When your father gets back—"

Gets back from where? And when? Surely her mother must know what people were saying, must be aware of the smugly vicious gossip. Surely it must hurt her as it did Meg. But if it did she gave no outward sign. Nothing ruffled the serenity of her expression.

—Why can't I hide it, too? Meg thought. Why do I always have to *show* everything?

The window rattled madly in the wind, and she pulled the quilt close about her. Curled up on one of her pillows, a gray fluff of kitten yawned, showing its pink tongue, tucked its head under again, and went back to sleep.

Everybody was asleep. Everybody except Meg. Even Charles Wallace, the "dumb baby brother," who had an uncanny way of knowing when she was awake and unhappy, and who would come, so many nights, tiptoeing up the attic stairs to her—even Charles Wallace was asleep.

How could they sleep? All day on the radio there had been hurricane warnings. How could they leave her up in the attic in the rickety brass bed, knowing that the roof might be blown right off the house and she tossed out into the wild night sky to land who knows where?

Her shivering grew uncontrollable.

## Practice Narrative Writing Task #3

50 Minutes

In the above excerpt, the author develops an interesting situation for Meg Murry. Think about how the rest of Meg's world remains asleep as she is wide-awake.

Write an original story to continue where the passage ended. In your story, be sure to use what you have learned about the character of Meg as you tell what happens next.

| Exposition | |
| --- | --- |
| Rising Action | |
| Climax | |
| Falling Action | |
| Resolution | |

Write your original story to continue where the passage ended on loose-leaf paper or in a notebook. Look at the scoring checklist and the scoring rubrics chart in the back of the book to see how you are improving.

 ## Narrative Writing Task: Historical Account— Introduction

Now that you have read through the narrative writing task basics, and worked through a few practice questions, it is time to review the steps in taking these same skills and applying them to a similar task, only related to social studies.

As we mentioned in the introduction, the following questions should be considered when working through this type of task:

- What parts of the historical account have already been revealed?
- How do I continue through the historical account?
- How does this historical account conclude?
- How can I use literary devices to engage the reader?

The PARCC will ask you to refer to your knowledge of history in order to complete a historical account. Keep in mind, though, that you must not forget the skills from the previous pages, while also referencing your knowledge of history with accuracy.

Think of this more as a "narrative description" rather than a narrative story. You are still using diction and syntactical devices, *but you will not be following the same exact structure of the short story.*

You should, however, work through this prompt chronologically, moving from beginning to end of this historical account, using vivid language to paint a picture in the reader's mind, just as you would with any narrative.

Today you will read the beginning of a historical account, related to the Boston Tea Party. As you read, pay close attention to historical details and conflict as you prepare to complete a historical account.

| CCSS Alignment | |
|---|---|
| RI.3 | Analyze a complex set of ideas or sequence of events and explain how specific individuals, ideas, or events interact and develop over the course of the text. |
| RI.10 | Read and comprehend literary nonfiction at the high end of the grade's text complexity. |
| WHST.1 | Introduce precise, knowledgeable claims, and create an organization that logically sequences the claims. |
| WHST.2 | Write informative texts, including the narration of historical events, scientific procedures, or technical processes. |
| L.3 | Apply knowledge of language to understand how language functions in different contexts. |
| L.4 | Determine or clarify the meaning of unknown and multiple-meaning words and phrases. |
| L.5 | Demonstrate understanding of figurative language, word relationships, and nuances in word meanings. |
| W.3 | Write narratives to develop real or imagined experiences. |
| W.5 | Develop and strengthen writing as needed by planning, revising, editing, and rewriting. |
| W.6 | Use technology to produce, publish, and update individual writing products. |

[ELA TASK GENERATION MODEL FOR NARRATIVE TYPE: 1PBA]

On the morning of December 16, 1773, over 5,000 colonists met at the Old South Meeting House to plan the protest of the Tea Act, passed by Parliament on May 10, 1773. Over 100 colonists disguised as Mohawk Indians then raided the three docked ships of the British East India Company. This movement, known as the Boston Tea Party, was organized by a patriotic group led by Samuel Adams, referred to as the "Sons of Liberty."

## Narrative Writing Task: Historical Account — Introduction

50 minutes

In the above passage, a historical account of the Boston Tea Party is introduced. Think about the sequence of events that led to the Boston Tea Party, and share these events in a well-written narrative description.

Complete this historical account, and discuss the series of events that led to the Boston Tea Party. In your narrative, be sure to use accurate details from what you have learned about these events as you explain what happened beforehand.

Look to see how we modeled our response using the graphic organizer on the next page to begin structuring our thoughts.

| Introduction of Historical Account |
| --- |
| • 1764: The Sugar Act—British imposed tax on sugar and molasses to raise revenue. |

| Sequence of Main Events | | |
| --- | --- | --- |
| **Event 1** | **Event 2** | **Event 3** |
| • The Currency Act <br> • 1765: Quartering Act <br> • The Stamp Act | • 1766: The Stamp Act is repealed <br> • 1767: Townsend Acts <br> • 1768: Massachusetts Circular Letter | • 1770: Boston Massacre <br> • 1773: Tea Act |

| Completion of Historical Account |
| --- |
| • 5,000 colonists met at the Old South Meeting House to plan the protest of the Tea Act. <br> • Over 100 colonists disguised as Mohawk Indians raided docked ships of the British East India Company. <br> • Tea was thrown overboard. |

After we have worked through our graphic organizer, and structured our thoughts, it is then time to write. As we do, we must remember that we do not write in social studies the same way that we write for English language arts. While we are using figurative language to help the reader envision the historical account, we are also basing our accounts on facts, not exaggerations. So, let's get started!

## Model essay:

Upon the control of Parliament, a series of acts led to revolts and rampage of its colonists against their governing body. Political unrest and financial uncertainty contributed to the events that would lead up to what we now consider the Boston Tea Party today.

Starting in 1764, the British began their financial power over United States colonists with the passing of the Sugar Act, which imposed a tax on all sugar and molasses sold. The Currency Act, and the Quartering Act, and the Stamp Act, and the Townshend Acts all contributed to the tension that grew between the colonists and the Parliament. As a result, the Parliament then quickly controlled colonial currency (The Currency Act), the housing of British soldiers in the American colonies (The Quartering Act), the taxing for all printed material to be stamped (The Stamp Act), and the duties placed on colonists in overseeing the imports of glass, lead, paints, paper, and tea (The Townshend Acts).

The colonists felt betrayed by the government. The colonists felt almost helpless. The colonists felt as if they had no other options. With the increase in taxes and imposing actions, colonists could not help but feel overpowered — as overpowered as the forces they had no control over. Taxes, levies, and the feeling of powerlessness made colonists feel alone and unsupported, in a way that reminded them of why they were fighting in the first place. Colonists drowned in their own dismay.

The Townshend Acts met a variety of upset from the colony of Massachusetts. Written by Samuel Adams, the Massachusetts Circular Letter argued that the Townshend Acts were unconstitutional because the colony of Massachusetts was not represented by Parliament. While this request was revoked, revolts by colonists ensued, especially since they had lost all faith in their government and had no other options than to react with violence. What else were they to do? Where were they to turn?

From the announcement of the selection of seven chosen Loyalists for the East India Company, the Boston Massacre, and the impacts of the Tea Act, further unrest existed in Massachusetts. The Tea Act was eventually protested, hurling pounds and pounds of tea overboard, splashing to the depths, never to surface again.

Now, take the time to identify some **literary devices** that you can notice, and try to recognize how the use of these literary devices impacts the overall effect of the historical account.

## Model essay:

Upon the control of Parliament, a series of acts led to revolts and rampage of its colonists against their governing body. Political unrest and financial uncertainty contributed to the events that would lead up to what we now consider the Boston Tea Party today.

Starting in 1764, the British began their financial power over United States colonists with the passing of the Sugar Act, which imposed a tax on all sugar and molasses sold. The Currency Act, and the Quartering Act, and the Stamp Act, and the Townshend Acts all contributed to the tension that grew between the colonists and the Parliament. As a result, the Parliament then quickly controlled colonial currency (The Currency Act), the housing of British soldiers in the American colonies (The Quartering Act), the taxing for all printed material to be stamped (The Stamp Act), and the duties placed on colonists in overseeing the imports of glass, lead, paints, paper, and tea (The Townshend Acts).

The colonists felt betrayed by the government. The colonists felt almost helpless. The colonists felt as if they had no other options. With the increase in taxes and imposing actions, colonists could not help but feel overpowered — as overpowered as the forces they had no control over. Taxes, levies, and the feeling of powerlessness made colonists feel alone and unsupported, in a way that reminded them of why they were fighting in the first place. Colonists drowned in their own dismay.

The Townshend Acts met a variety of upset from the crumbling colony of Massachusetts. Written by Samuel Adams, the Massachusetts Circular Letter argued that the Townshend Acts were unconstitutional because the colony of Massachusetts was not represented by Parliament. While this request was revoked, revolts by colonists ensued, especially since they had lost all faith in their government and had no other options than to react with violence. What else were they to do? Where were they to turn?

From the announcement of the selection of seven chosen Loyalists for the East India Company, the Boston Massacre, and the impacts of the Tea Act, further unrest existed in Massachusetts. The Tea Act was eventually protested, hurling pounds and pounds of tea overboard, splashing to the depths, never to surface again.

## We found:

**Alliteration:** revolts and rampage

**Polysyndeton:** *The Currency Act, and the Quartering Act, and the Stamp Act, and the Townshend Acts*

**Anaphora:** *The colonists felt betrayed by the government. The colonists felt almost helpless. The colonists felt as if they had no other options.*

**Simile:** *overpowered as the forces they had no control over*

**Personification:** *Colonists drowned in their own dismay.*

**Alliteration:** *crumbling colony*

**Rhetorical questions:** *What else were they to do? Where were they to turn?*

**Imagery:** *The Tea Act was eventually protested, hurling pounds and pounds of tea overboard, splashing to the depths, never to surface again.*

Now that you have reviewed the model essay, along with the devices used throughout, take the time to jot down notes about the impact these devices have on the overall effect of the story. Use the note-taking chart below:

| Device | Impact on story |
|---|---|
| alliteration | |
| polysyndeton | |
| anaphora | |

*(continued)*

| Device | Impact on story |
|---|---|
| simile | |
| personification | |
| rhetorical question | |
| imagery | |

## Historical Account—Practice Narrative Description Task #1

| CCSS Alignment | |
|---|---|
| RI.3 | Analyze a complex set of ideas or sequence of events and explain how specific individuals, ideas, or events interact and develop over the course of the text. |
| RI.10 | Read and comprehend literary nonfiction at the high end of the grade's text complexity. |
| WHST.1 | Introduce precise, knowledgeable claims, and create an organization that logically sequences the claims. |
| WHST.2 | Write informative texts, including the narration of historical events, scientific procedures, or technical processes. |
| L.3 | Apply knowledge of language to understand how language functions in different contexts. |
| L.4 | Determine or clarify the meaning of unknown and multiple-meaning words and phrases. |

*(continued)*

| CCSS Alignment | |
|---|---|
| L.5 | Demonstrate understanding of figurative language, word relationships, and nuances in word meanings. |
| W.3 | Write narratives to develop real or imagined experiences. |
| W.5 | Develop and strengthen writing as needed by planning, revising, editing, and rewriting. |
| W.6 | Use technology to produce, publish, and update individual writing products. |

[ELA TASK GENERATION MODEL FOR NARRATIVE TYPE: 1PBA]

**Today you will read the beginning of a historical account, related to the Age of Chaos. As you read, pay close attention to historical details and conflict as you prepare to complete a historical account.**

Around 235 A.D., often known as the Age of Chaos, many different military leaders took over power, while many rulers died from revolts, plagues, fires, and Christian persecutions. Upon control of Diocletian in 285 A.D., the Roman Empire was then split into two, ruled by four caesars.

## Historical Account — Practice Narrative Description Task #1

50 Minutes

In the above passage, a historical account of the Fall of the Roman Empire has been introduced. Think about the sequence of events that occurred after the Roman Empire was split into two parts and ruled by four caesars, and share these events in a well-written narrative description.

Complete this historical account, and discuss the Fall of the Roman Empire. In your narrative, be sure to use accurate details from what you have learned about these events as you explain what happens next.

| Introduction of Historical Account |
| --- |
| |

| Sequence of Main Events | | |
| --- | --- | --- |
| Event 1 | Event 2 | Event 3 |
| | | |

| Completion of Historical Account |
| --- |
| |

Now write your essay on loose-leaf paper or in a notebook. Be sure to use the checklists at the back of the book to see how you have done.

# Historical Account—Practice Narrative Description Task #2

| CCSS Alignment | |
|---|---|
| RI.3 | Analyze a complex set of ideas or sequence of events and explain how specific individuals, ideas, or events interact and develop over the course of the text. |
| RI.10 | Read and comprehend literary nonfiction at the high end of the grade's text complexity. |
| WHST.1 | Introduce precise, knowledgeable claims, and create an organization that logically sequences the claims. |
| WHST.2 | Write informative texts, including the narration of historical events, scientific procedures, or technical processes. |
| L.3 | Apply knowledge of language to understand how language functions in different contexts. |
| L.4 | Determine or clarify the meaning of unknown and multiple-meaning words and phrases. |
| L.5 | Demonstrate understanding of figurative language, word relationships, and nuances in word meanings. |
| W.3 | Write narratives to develop real or imagined experiences. |
| W.5 | Develop and strengthen writing as needed by planning, revising, editing, and rewriting. |
| W.6 | Use technology to produce, publish, and update individual writing products. |

[ELA TASK GENERATION MODEL FOR NARRATIVE TYPE: 1PBA]

**Read the beginning of a historical account, related to the Mongol Empire. As you read, pay close attention to historical details and conflict as you prepare to complete a historical account.**

Being one of the most fast-growing empires of the world, the Mongol Empire successfully united with Turkic tribes, and in 1206, Genghis Khan was named the Empire's universal ruler. Genghis Khan led the Mongol army across Asia, Europe, and the Middle East. They soon gained control over almost all the areas they passed through.

## Historical Account — Practice Narrative Description Task #2

50 minutes

In the above passage, a historical account of the rise of the Mongol Empire is introduced. Think about the sequence of events that occurred after Genghis Khan unified the Mongol Empire, and discuss these events in a well-written narrative description.

Complete this historical account, and discuss the Mongol Empire experience. In your narrative, be sure to use accurate details from what you have learned about these events as you explain what happens next.

| Introduction of Historical Account |
| --- |
| |

| Sequence of Main Events | | |
| --- | --- | --- |
| Event 1 | Event 2 | Event 3 |
| | | |

| Completion of Historical Account |
| --- |
| |

| Complete your historical account on loose-leaf paper or in a notebook. |
| --- |

# Historical Account—Practice Narrative Description Task #3

| CCSS Alignment | |
|---|---|
| RI.3 | Analyze a complex set of ideas or sequence of events and explain how specific individuals, ideas, or events interact and develop over the course of the text. |
| RI.10 | Read and comprehend literary nonfiction at the high end of the grade's text complexity. |
| WHST.1 | Introduce precise, knowledgeable claims, and create an organization that logically sequences the claims. |
| WHST.2 | Write informative texts, including the narration of historical events, scientific procedures, or technical processes. |
| L.3 | Apply knowledge of language to understand how language functions in different contexts. |
| L.4 | Determine or clarify the meaning of unknown and multiple-meaning words and phrases. |
| L.5 | Demonstrate understanding of figurative language, word relationships, and nuances in word meanings. |
| W.3 | Write narratives to develop real or imagined experiences. |
| W.5 | Develop and strengthen writing as needed by planning, revising, editing, and rewriting. |
| W.6 | Use technology to produce, publish, and update individual writing products. |

[ELA TASK GENERATION MODEL FOR NARRATIVE TYPE: 1PBA]

**Read the beginning of the historical account, related to the French and Indian War. As you read, pay close attention to historical details and conflict as you prepare to complete a historical account.**

In 1753, French troops from Canada marched south into the Ohio Valley. In response, Britain protests this invasion and claims Ohio as its own. A very young George Washington surrenders his army after being defeated by the French and the Indians at Fort Necessity. As a result, the British implement a plan to defeat the French.

## Historical Account — Practice Narrative Description Task #3

50 minutes

In the above passage, a historical account of the beginning of the French and Indian War is introduced. Think about the sequence of events that occurred after the British implement a plan to defeat the French and share these events in a well-written narrative description.

Complete this historical account, and discuss the French and Indian War experience. In your narrative, be sure to use accurate details from what you have learned about these events as you explain what happens next.

| Introduction of Historical Account |
| --- |
| |

| Sequence of Main Events | | |
| --- | --- | --- |
| Event 1 | Event 2 | Event 3 |

| Completion of Historical Account |
| --- |
| |

Write your completion of the article about the French and Indian War on loose-leaf paper or in a notebook. Be sure to check the scoring checklist and the scoring rubrics guides in the back of the book.

# Narrative Writing Task: Scientific Process— Introduction

You have already read through the narrative writing task basics, and worked through a series of practice questions for English language arts and history. It is time to review the steps in taking these same skills and applying them to a similar task, only now it's related to science.

As we have mentioned in the introduction, the following questions should be considered when working through this type of task:

- What parts of the scientific procedure have already been revealed?

- How do I continue through the entire scientific process?

- How does this scientific process conclude?

The PARCC will ask you to refer to your knowledge of scientific procedures in order to complete a scientific process. Keep in mind, though, that you must not forget the skills from the previous pages, while also accurately referencing your knowledge of science.

Think of this more as a "narrative description," rather than a narrative story (just as you did with your historical account). You are still using diction and syntactical devices, but you will not be following the same exact structure of the short story. *Your focus with the scientific process task is to focus on the use of details and organize these steps with precision.*

We also encourage science and English classes to work on traditional stories where scientific processes are involved, using characters and creative plot choices to move through each phase of the process in an interesting manner!

You should, however, work through this prompt chronologically, moving from beginning to end of this scientific process using vivid language to paint a picture in the reader's mind, just as you would with any narrative.

**Read the beginning of a scientific process, related to glacier formation. As you read, pay close attention to scientific details as you prepare to complete the scientific process.**

| CCSS Alignment | |
|---|---|
| RI.3 | Analyze a complex set of ideas or sequence of events and explain how specific individuals, ideas, or events interact and develop over the course of the text. |
| RI.10 | Read and comprehend literary nonfiction at the high end of the grade's text complexity. |
| WHST.1 | Introduce precise, knowledgeable claims, and create an organization that logically sequences the claims. |
| WHST.2 | Write informative texts, including the narration of historical events, scientific procedures, or technical processes. |
| L.3 | Apply knowledge of language to understand how language functions in different contexts. |
| L.4 | Determine or clarify the meaning of unknown and multiple-meaning words and phrases. |
| L.5 | Demonstrate understanding of figurative language, word relationships, and nuances in word meanings. |
| W.3 | Write narratives to develop real or imagined experiences. |
| W.5 | Develop and strengthen writing as needed by planning, revising, editing, and rewriting. |
| W.6 | Use technology to produce, publish, and update individual writing products. |

[ELA TASK GENERATION MODEL FOR NARRATIVE TYPE: 1PBA]

As snow remains in the same area year-round, this snow accumulation transforms into ice. Each year, more snowfall adds more layers of snow that bury the previous years' layers.

## Narrative Writing Task: Scientific Process

50 minutes

In the above passage, a scientific process of glacier formation has been introduced. Think about the sequence of events that occurred after the layers of snow are collected and share the following stages in a well-written, logically organized narrative description.

Complete this scientific process, and discuss the important stages that occur during the rest of glacier formation. In your narrative, be sure to use accurate facts from what you have learned about these stages as you explain what happens next.

---

Look to see how we modeled our response using the graphic organizer below to begin structuring our thoughts:

| Introduction to Scientific Process |
|---|
| • Snow remains in the same area year-round. |
| • This snow accumulates to transform into ice. |
| • Each year, new layers of snow bury old layers. |

| Sequence of Scientific Process | | |
|---|---|---|
| **First Steps** | **Second Steps** | **Third Steps** |
| • The layers force the snow to gradually grow larger in size.<br><br>• This makes the air pockets between the flakes of snow become smaller.<br><br>• Snow compacts and increases in density. | • After two winters, the snow turns into "firn," which refers to the state in between snow and glacier ice. | • Over time, larger ice crystals become so compressed that the snow turns to ice.<br><br>• After dozens, hundreds, or even thousands of years, the ice eventually gets compressed so much that the air is forced out.<br><br>• Glacial ice appears blue. |

| Completion of Scientific Process |
|---|
| • Since the glacier becomes so heavy, it starts to move. |
| • Glacial movement: spreading and basal slip. |

After we have worked through our graphic organizer, and structured our thoughts, it is now time to write. As we do, we must remember that we do not write in science the same way that we write for English language arts or social studies. While we are describing the process we are paying particular attention to what is important in science—the facts! So, let's get started!

When writing for science, it is important to focus our efforts on the logical, sequential steps of the scientific process, and not necessarily the literary devices used. You must move through the scientific process in an easy-to-follow manner.

## Model essay:

In an area, snow remains year-round, which will eventually transform into ice. Annually, new layers of snow bury old layers, and the formation of glaciers finally begins.

As the layers of snowfall accumulate, the snow grows larger in size gradually. This makes the air pockets between the flakes of snow become smaller. As a result, the snow compacts and increases in density. Often, after two winters of snowfall, snow turns into firn, which refers to the state in between snow and glacier ice.

Over time, larger ice crystals become so compressed that the snow turns into solid ice. After dozens, hundreds, or even thousands of years, the ice eventually gets compressed so much that the air is forced out, which causes the glacial ice to appear blue.

Due to the compression of snow into ice, and the long amount of time the compression process takes, the glacier becomes so heavy that it begins to move. Spreading movement occurs when the weight of the glacier becomes too burdensome that it begins to move on its own, spreading out. Basal slip movement occurs when the glacier forms on a slope. Once pressure causes a small piece of the base of the glacier to melt, this water formation creates enough friction for the glacier to subsequently move down the slope.

You will notice a difference in this response over our narratives regarding English language arts topics and historical accounts. The narrative description of the scientific process is straightforward and delineates and sequentially organizes the necessary steps that move this scientific process forward to completion.

Try out similar responses with our practice questions!

# Scientific Process—Practice Narrative Description Task #1

| CCSS Alignment | |
|---|---|
| RI.3 | Analyze a complex set of ideas or sequence of events and explain how specific individuals, ideas, or events interact and develop over the course of the text. |
| RI.10 | Read and comprehend literary nonfiction at the high end of the grade's text complexity. |
| WHST.1 | Introduce precise, knowledgeable claims, and create an organization that logically sequences the claims. |
| WHST.2 | Write informative texts, including the narration of historical events, scientific procedures, or technical processes. |
| L.3 | Apply knowledge of language to understand how language functions in different contexts. |
| L.4 | Determine or clarify the meaning of unknown and multiple-meaning words and phrases. |
| L.5 | Demonstrate understanding of figurative language, word relationships, and nuances in word meanings. |
| W.3 | Write narratives to develop real or imagined experiences. |
| W.5 | Develop and strengthen writing as needed by planning, revising, editing, and rewriting. |
| W.6 | Use technology to produce, publish, and update individual writing products. |

**Read the beginning of a scientific process, related to the phases of the moon. As you read, pay close attention to scientific details as you prepare to complete the scientific process.**

The new moon occurs when the Moon is in position between the Earth and the Sun. Since the Moon is interfering with the lighted Sun, therefore, the Moon's dark side is facing the Earth, which is the start of this process before beginning of a new crescent.

## Scientific Process — Practice Narrative Description Task #1

50 minutes

In the above passage, a scientific process of moon phases is introduced. Think about the sequence of events that occur after the new moon phase and share the following phases in a well-written, logically organized narrative description.

Complete this scientific process, and discuss the consecutive phases, using examples to illustrate your point. In your narrative, be sure to use accurate facts from what you have learned about these phases, noting the role of the phases that occur after the new crescent as you explain what happens next.

| Introduction of Scientific Process |
| --- |
| |

| Sequence of Scientific Process | | |
| --- | --- | --- |
| First Steps | Second Steps | Third Steps |

| Completion of Scientific Process |
| --- |
| |

Your assignment is to complete this scientific process, and discuss the consecutive phases, using examples to illustrate your point. Write your completion on loose-leaf paper or in a notebook, being sure to use the charts in the back of the book.

# Scientific Process—Practice Narrative Description Task #2

| CCSS Alignment | |
| --- | --- |
| RI.3 | Analyze a complex set of ideas or sequence of events and explain how specific individuals, ideas, or events interact and develop over the course of the text. |
| RI.10 | Read and comprehend literary nonfiction at the high end of the grade's text complexity. |
| WHST.1 | Introduce precise, knowledgeable claims, and create an organization that logically sequences the claims. |
| WHST.2 | Write informative texts, including the narration of historical events, scientific procedures, or technical processes. |
| L.3 | Apply knowledge of language to understand how language functions in different contexts. |
| L.4 | Determine or clarify the meaning of unknown and multiple-meaning words and phrases. |
| L.5 | Demonstrate understanding of figurative language, word relationships, and nuances in word meanings. |
| W.3 | Write narratives to develop real or imagined experiences. |
| W.5 | Develop and strengthen writing as needed by planning, revising, editing, and rewriting. |
| W.6 | Use technology to produce, publish, and update individual writing products. |

[ELA TASK GENERATION MODEL FOR NARRATIVE TYPE: 1PBA]

**Read the beginning of a scientific process, related to erosion and deposition. As you read, pay close attention to scientific details as you prepare to complete the scientific process.**

Erosion occurs when soil and rock are removed from the Earth's surface by processes that often involve wind and water, transporting and depositing these materials elsewhere. As rainfall increases, falling raindrops work to create small pockets in the soil, ejecting soil particles.

## Scientific Process — Practice Narrative Description Task #2

50 minutes

In the above passage, a scientific process of erosion and deposition is introduced. Think about the sequence of events that occur after the soil particles are initially ejected by falling raindrops and share the following stages in a well-written, logically organized narrative description.

Complete this scientific process, and discuss the consecutive stages, using examples to illustrate your point. In your narrative, be sure to use accurate facts from what you have learned about these stages as you explain what happens next. Be sure to also discuss the possible benefits and drawbacks to the erosion and deposition process.

| Introduction of Scientific Process | | |
| --- | --- | --- |
| | | |
| Sequence of Scientific Process | | |
| First Steps | Second Steps | Third Steps |
| | | |

(continued)

| Completion of Scientific Process |
| --- |
|  |

Complete the scientific process and discuss the consecutive stages, using examples to illustrate your point. When finished, consult the scoring checklist and the rubrics chart in the back of the book.

# Scientific Process—Practice Narrative Description Task #3

| CCSS Alignment | |
| --- | --- |
| RI.3 | Analyze a complex set of ideas or sequence of events and explain how specific individuals, ideas, or events interact and develop over the course of the text. |
| RI.10 | Read and comprehend literary nonfiction at the high end of the grade's text complexity. |
| WHST.1 | Introduce precise, knowledgeable claims, and create an organization that logically sequences the claims. |
| WHST.2 | Write informative texts, including the narration of historical events, scientific procedures, or technical processes. |
| L.3 | Apply knowledge of language to understand how language functions in different contexts. |
| L.4 | Determine or clarify the meaning of unknown and multiple-meaning words and phrases. |
| L.5 | Demonstrate understanding of figurative language, word relationships, and nuances in word meanings. |

*(continued)*

| CCSS Alignment | |
|---|---|
| W.3 | Write narratives to develop real or imagined experiences. |
| W.5 | Develop and strengthen writing as needed by planning, revising, editing, and rewriting. |
| W.6 | Use technology to produce, publish, and update individual writing products. |

[ELA TASK GENERATION MODEL FOR NARRATIVE TYPE: 1PBA]

**Read the beginning of a scientific process, related to the seven characteristics of life. As you read, pay close attention to scientific details as you prepare to complete the scientific process.**

Throughout the study of life science, seven characteristics of life exist. The first two:

1. Living things are composed of cells, and

2. Living things have different levels of organization.

## Scientific Process — Practice Narrative Description Task #3

50 minutes

In the above passage, the first two characteristics of life are introduced. Think about the sequence of characteristics that follow, and in a well-written, logically organized narrative description, apply all characteristics of life to a living thing.

Apply these characteristics as they relate to a living thing of your choice, using examples to illustrate your point in proving that all characteristics of life are successfully met. In your narrative, be sure to use accurate facts from what you have learned about these characteristics as you explain what happens next.

| Introduction of Scientific Process |
| --- |
| |

| Sequence of Scientific Process | | |
| --- | --- | --- |
| First Steps | Second Steps | Third Steps |
| | | |

| Completion of Scientific Process |
| --- |
| |

| Complete your assignment on loose-leaf paper or in a notebook. |
| --- |

## CHAPTER 4

# Literary Analysis Task

## Introduction
(Performance-Based Assessment)

As we have emphasized repeatedly throughout this book, the makers of the PARCC view reading and writing as connected activities. One feeds off the other. This principle holds true for the literary analysis section of the exam. The good news about this fact is that once you get the reading down, half the battle is won. The writing, then, just becomes an extension of the hard work you did with the reading.

In this chapter, therefore, we will show you exactly how you should interact with (or analyze) the texts in the PARCC literary analysis task so that you can write a terrific essay. Don't worry, we will provide you with ample practice to put these principles of analysis into action.

First, you should know that the literary analysis task requires that you read and interact with two texts of "high literary value." By "high literary value," we mean that the texts are found in most middle school language arts departments around the country and that these texts contain writing that is rich with theme, symbolism, and literary devices. Most of the authors and literary works used in this chapter can be found in the Common Core State Standards for English language arts. Be sure to ask your teacher for the Common Core's recommended reading list. The more works you read from the Common Core list, the better off you will be.

While we work on the literary analysis, though, when reading these texts, we will be keenly focused on the author's choice of words (i.e. the author's diction) and how these words give rise to a thematic message of the text. Our focus is to see how the author's deliberate choice of words creates a thematic message within the text. Sound difficult? Don't worry. Analysis of text gets easier the more that you do it. Here are some questions that you could ask yourself *while you read*:

- Are there any words or terms that are symbolic? For example, the American flag is a symbol of freedom. What symbolism do you notice in the text?

- Are any words or terms repeated? Often repeated words/terms have significance in terms of theme.

- Is any irony present (i.e. the writer means the opposite of what's being said)?

- What type of imagery is used? Why? Imagery is used when there are words in the text that deal with sight, smell, touch, and taste.

- What is the tone (attitude) of the passage? How do you know? For example, the tone of a "funeral" is quite different from the tone of a "wedding."

- Do you see any patterns in the language the author uses? For instance, poets often repeat structures of words. Think of your favorite music for examples.

- Does the author use a special dialect? If so, why? The best example of dialect that you know would most likely be Mark Twain's *The Adventures of Tom Sawyer*, which contains the Southern Missouri dialect.

- Are there any literary devices used? Examples include simile, metaphor, rhetorical questions, etc.

- What might be the theme or the message of the text? How do you know?

You do not have to memorize the above questions, although they are very helpful. The more important thing is to understand that authors carefully and deliberately choose specific words (diction) to create a theme, or a message. Your job is to find these terms in order to find the message.

Our first piece of literature is called "The World's Reward," from James A. Honey's *South-African Folk Tales*. This text places a heavy emphasis on African Americans' experiences during slavery, and it is a folktale. As you might know, folktales are stories loosely based in fact and contain events that might seem larger than life.

As in the previous chapters, we place the text in the left side of a two-column chart. On the right side of the column, we jot down our thoughts about the text as we read. Pay attention to the ideas on the right side of the chart as you read the left. We wrote down these thoughts to show you how to interact with a text. This process of interacting with (i.e. analyzing) the text is absolutely necessary for you to be able to complete the literary analysis essay. As you read "The World's Reward" and our thoughts, ask yourself, "Why was this comment written?" and "What does the comment have to do with the thematic message of Honey's piece?"

| "The World's Reward" (from James A. Honey's South-African Folk Tales) | Our Thought Processes |
|---|---|
| Once there was a man that had an old dog, so old that the man desired to put him aside. The dog had served him very faithfully when he was still young, but ingratitude is the world's reward, and the man now wanted to dispose of him. The old dumb creature, however, ferreted out the plan of his master, and so at once resolved to go away of his own accord. | • The relationship between the man and dog is similar to what we know today. The dog is loyal to his master. |
| After he had walked quite a way he met an old bull in the veldt. | • The dog learns of his master's plan to dispose of him, as he is now aged. |
| "Don't you want to go with me?" asked the dog. | |
| "Where?" was the reply. | |
| "To the land of the aged," said the dog, "where troubles don't disturb you and thanklessness does not deface the deeds of man." | |
| "Good," said the bull, "I am your companion." | |
| The two now walked on and found a ram. | |
| The dog laid the plan before him, and all moved off together, until they afterwards came successively upon a donkey, a cat, a cock, and a goose. | |
| These joined their company, and the seven set out on their journey. | |
| Late one night they came to a house and through the open door they saw a table spread with all kinds of nice food, of which some robbers were having their fill. It would help nothing to ask for admittance, and seeing that they were hungry, they must think of something else. | • Meeting other animals along the way, the dog leads the pack to a new place, where they cannot gain easy entrance. |
| Therefore the donkey climbed up on the bull, the ram on the donkey, the dog on the ram, the cat on the dog, the goose on the cat, and the cock on the goose, and with one accord they all let out terrible (threatening) noises (cryings). | |

(continued)

| "The World's Reward" (from James A. Honey's South-African Folk Tales) | Our Thought Processes |
| --- | --- |
| The bull began to bellow, the donkey to bray, the dog to bark, the ram to bleat, the cat to mew, the goose to giggle gaggle, and the cock to crow, all without cessation.<br><br>The people in the house were frightened perfectly limp; they glanced out through the front door, and there they stared on the strange sight. Some of them took to the ropes over the back lower door, some disappeared through the window, and in a few counts the house was empty.<br><br>Then the seven old animals climbed down from one another, stepped into the house, and satisfied themselves with the delicious food.<br><br>But when they had finished, there still remained a great deal of food, too much to take with them on their remaining journey, and so together they contrived a plan to hold their position until the next day after breakfast.<br><br>The dog said, "See here, I am accustomed to watch at the front door of my master's house," and thereupon flopped himself down to sleep; the bull said, "I go behind the door," and there he took his position; the ram said, "I will go up on to the loft"; the donkey, "I at the middle door"; the cat, "I in the fireplace"; the goose, "I in the back door"; and the cock said, "I am going to sleep on the bed." | • The animals successfully startled those in the house, and then subsequently entered. |
| The captain of the robbers after a while sent one of his men back to see if these creatures had yet left the house.<br><br>The man came very cautiously into the neighborhood, listened and listened, but he heard nothing; he peeped through the window, and saw in the grate just two coals still glimmering, and thereupon started to walk through the front door. | • After eating, the animals then took their places inside the house. The robbers returned! |

*(continued)*

| "The World's Reward" (from James A. Honey's South-African Folk Tales) | Our Thought Processes |
|---|---|
| There the old dog seized him by the leg. He jumped into the house, but the bull was ready, swept him up with his horns, and tossed him on to the loft. Here the ram received him and pushed him off the loft again. Reaching ground, he made for the middle door, but the donkey set up a terrible braying and at the same time gave him a kick that landed him in the fireplace, where the cat flew at him and scratched him nearly to pieces. He then jumped out through the back door, and here the goose got him by the trousers. When he was some distance away the cock crowed. He thereupon ran so that you could hear the stones rattle in the dark. | • After the robbers entered, the animals attacked as planned. |
| Purple and crimson and out of breath, he came back to his companions. | • The robber then returned to meet his fellow robbers, frightened. |
| "Frightful, frightful!" was all that they could get from him at first, but after a while he told them. | |
| "When I looked through the window I saw in the fireplace two bright coals shining, and when I wanted to go through the front door to go and look, I stepped into an iron trap. I jumped into the house, and there someone seized me with a fork and pitched me up on to the loft, there again some one was ready, and threw me down on all fours. I wanted to fly through the middle door, but there some one blew on a trumpet, and smote me with a sledge hammer so that I did not know where I landed; but coming to very quickly, I found I was in the fireplace, and there another flew at me and scratched the eyes almost out of my head. I thereupon fled out of the back door, and lastly I was attacked on the leg by the sixth with a pair of fire tongs, and when I was still running away, some one shouted out of the house, 'Stop him, stop h—i—m!'" | • The robber details his account of being attacked by the animals. |

(continued)

> ### Thematic Messages Found in Text
>
> The first item to remember with "The World's Reward" is that it is a folktale, and, as such, it is highly symbolic. The text is built around the notion of relationships, involving both humans and animals, and the idea of relying on one's master; these animals are slaves—once needed by their owners—whose ability to finally talk and take control becomes apparent once they search for freedom. In the story, the dog finds out about the plan of his own disposal by the master to whom he has remained loyal. Because of this knowledge, I believe, the dog, and his fellow animals (as slaves were often treated), finally find their voices and take action. As a result, they are, in essence, free.

Let's break down what just happened with our analysis of Honey's text.

1. As we read, we asked ourselves the importance of the words the author chose, and

2. We thought about how these words create meaning within the text, and lastly,

3. We identified major themes we found in Honey's text and recorded these themes at the bottom of our chart with a brief explanation.

These are the three steps you need to take each time you are presented with literature on the literary analysis section.

At this point, you might be saying, "Well, that's not that bad! How hard could the literary analysis be?" The answer: It's doubly hard! On the PARCC, when you finally write your literary analysis essay, you will have to compare a second text to the first. This skill, that of comparison, is the next topic of this chapter.

## The Second Text

In keeping in line with the theme of racism, we have another text for you, this time a poem entitled "Caged Bird," by the famous African American poet Maya Angelou. This second text presents some formidable challenges to us because it is a different genre than Honey's work. However, you can be assured that both works—that of Honey's and Angelou's—will be connected thematically. As is true throughout this book, we give you a chart in which Angelou's poem appears in the left column and our thought processes appear on the right. As with Honey's work, we can use the following questions to guide us in our analysis:

- Are there any words or terms that are symbolic in nature?

- Are any words or terms repeated?

- Is any irony present (i.e., the opposite of what's being said)?

- What type of imagery is used? Why?

- What is the tone (attitude) of the passage? How do you know?

- Do you see any patterns in the language the author uses?

- Does the author use a special dialect? If so, why?

- Are there any literary devices used? (i.e., simile, metaphor, rhetorical questions, etc.)

- What might be the theme or the message of the text? How do you know?

| Maya Angelou's "Caged Bird" | Our Thought Processes |
|---|---|
| A free bird leaps<br>on the back of the wind<br>and floats downstream<br>till the current ends<br>and dips his wing<br>in the orange sun rays<br>and dares to claim the sky.<br><br>But a bird that stalks<br>down his narrow cage<br>can seldom see through<br>his bars of rage<br>his wings are clipped and<br>his feet are tied<br>so he opens his throat to sing.<br><br>The caged bird sings<br>with a fearful trill<br>of things unknown<br>but longed for still<br>and his tune is heard<br>on the distant hill<br>for the caged bird<br>sings of freedom. | • Symbolism of the bird and flying: freedom<br><br>• beautiful imagery: "orange sun rays"<br>• "dares" implies something is dangerous about flying<br>• bird trapped inside cage<br>• "bars of rage" could be symbolic of what it is that is actually keeping the bird trapped<br><br>• The birds sings "fearfully" about the freedom it doesn't have.<br>• The bird doesn't have freedom. |

(continued)

| Maya Angelou's "Caged Bird" | Our Thought Processes |
|---|---|
| The free bird thinks of another breeze<br>and the trade winds soft through the sighing trees<br>and the fat worms waiting on a dawn bright lawn<br>and he names the sky his own<br>But a caged bird stands on the grave of dreams<br>his shadow shouts on a nightmare scream<br>his wings are clipped and his feet are tied<br>so he opens his throat to sing.<br><br>The caged bird sings<br>with a fearful trill<br>of things unknown<br>but longed for still<br>and his tune is heard<br>on the distant hill<br>for the caged bird<br>sings of freedom.<br><br>Maya Angelou, "Caged Bird" from *Shaker, Why Don't You Sing?* Copyright © 1983 by Maya Angelou. Used by permission of Random House, Inc. | • Angelou contrasts the caged bird with a "free bird."<br><br>• Imagery of nature; the free bird is one with nature<br><br>• He calls the sky his own.<br><br>• These two birds are in contrast to each other.<br><br>• Angelou repeats this section; doing so emphasizes the rage and anger of the caged bird. |

### Thematic Messages

As with the Honey text, Angelou's poem is rich with symbolism. In her poem, there are two "birds": the caged and the free. The caged bird is full of rage; the free bird is one with nature and full of freedom. Perhaps the birds Angelou writes about are people? Some people get trapped with rage, just like the first bird in her poem. Those birds "free from rage" experience the beauty of nature and harmony with the world. In her poem, external reality is represented of spiritual reality.

As you can see, Maya Angelou's poem and Honey's tall tale hold some significant similarities. For one thing, both works are about "finding freedom." Both works also have a deep spiritual tone to them. This knowledge will help us greatly in our literary analysis essay.

Having read both texts carefully and having completed our textual analyses, we are ready to turn our attention to the literary analysis writing prompt:

| CCSS Alignment | |
|---|---|
| RL.1 | Cite strong and textual evidence. |
| RL.2 | Determine two or more themes. |
| RL.3 | Analyze the impact of the author's choices. |
| RL.5 | Analyze how an author's choices contribute to text's overall structure. |
| RL.9 | Demonstrate knowledge of foundational works of American literature, including how two or more texts from the same period treat similar themes and topics. |
| L.1 | Demonstrate command of the conventions of standard English grammar and usage when writing. |
| L.3 | Apply knowledge of language to understand how language functions in different contexts. |
| L.5 | Demonstrate understanding of figurative language, word relationships, and nuances in word meanings. |
| W.3 | Write narratives to develop real or imagined experiences. |
| W.5 | Develop and strengthen writing as needed by planning, revising, editing, and rewriting. |
| W.6 | Use technology to produce, publish, and update individual writing products. |

[ELA TASK GENERATION MODEL: 7A.1PBA]

## Literary Analysis Writing Prompt

Student Directions

80 Minutes

Use what you have learned by reading James A. Honey's "The World's Reward" and Maya Angelou's "Caged Bird" to write an essay that analyzes how both texts treat the theme of freedom.

Develop your essay by providing textual evidence from both sources. Be sure to follow the conventions of Standard English.

At this point in our preparation, you should be 100% convinced that reading carefully—that is, paying attention to the author's word choices and understanding the connection of these choices to the meaning of the text—is a sure way to succeed on the written portion of the literary analysis. Our hard work has paid off and we are two steps ahead in the planning and writing of our essay.

So, let's now turn our attention to the actual planning of the literary analysis essay. Make no mistake about it, planning is also vitally necessary and NOT a step you can skip. **Even under timed conditions and even just some brief and basic prewriting will pay dividends.** Look at the graphic organizer below to see exactly how you could prewrite for an essay such as the one that we build in the pages that follow.

| Issue of Freedom | |
| --- | --- |
| "The World's Reward" | "Caged Bird" |
| **Physical and Spiritual Enslavement** | **Physical and Spiritual Enslavement** |
| "Once there was a man that had an old dog, so old that the man desired to put him aside. The dog had served him very faithfully when he was still young, but ingratitude is the world's reward, and the man now wanted to dispose of him."<br><br>"Late one night they came to a house and through the open door they saw a table spread with all kinds of nice food, of which some robbers were having their fill. It would help nothing to ask for admittance, and seeing that they were hungry, they must think of something else." | But a bird that stalks<br>down his narrow cage<br>can seldom see through<br>his bars of rage<br>his wings are clipped and<br>his feet are tied<br>so he opens his throat to sing.<br><br>The caged bird sings<br>with a fearful trill<br>of things unknown<br>but longed for still<br><br>But a caged bird stands on the grave of dreams<br>his shadow shouts on a nightmare scream<br>his wings are clipped and his feet are tied<br>so he opens his throat to sing. |

*(continued)*

| Physical and Spiritual Freedom | Physical and Spiritual Freedom |
|---|---|
| "The old dumb creature, however, ferreted out the plan of his master, and so at once resolved to go away of his own accord."<br><br>"The bull began to bellow, the donkey to bray, the dog to bark, the ram to bleat, the cat to mew, the goose to giggle gaggle, and the cock to crow, all without cessation."<br><br>"I thereupon fled out of the back door, and lastly I was attacked on the leg by the sixth with a pair of fire tongs, and when I was still running away, some one shouted out of the house, 'Stop him, stop h—i—m!' " | The free bird thinks of another breeze<br>and the trade winds soft through the sighing trees<br>and the fat worms waiting on a dawn bright lawn<br>and he names the sky his own |

**Thesis Statement:**

James A. Honey's "The World's Reward" and Maya Angelou's "Caged Bird" present this truth: spiritual freedom is possible even in the midst of physical enslavement.

We are quite sure that if you read and examined the table above, you would see the absolute value in prewriting. The two minor themes—physical enslavement and spiritual freedom—come directly from our analytic reading of the texts. In addition, not only do we have a solid thesis statement based upon evidence in the texts, we have supporting quotations to incorporate into our essay. As you continue to prepare for the literary analysis section of the PARCC, you should make the process of prewriting and analyzing text second nature for you.

# Writing the Literary Analysis Essay

One of the major ideas of this chapter is the following: A little bit of preparation (pre-writing) goes a long way. Even under a timed situation, a quick outline can ensure that your literary analysis essay has structure and organization. Check out our sample outline below:

I. Introduction

    a. Opening technique

    b. Thesis statement

II. Body

    a. Physical and spiritual enslavement

    b. Physical and spiritual freedom

III. Conclusion

    a. Rework the introductory technique

    b. Rework thesis

    c. Answer the "So What?" question

Each of the items in our outline above serves as guidance in the flow and organization of the essay. We will now take you through each step.

As with all essay writing, the literary analysis requires that you utilize a writing technique to grab the reader's attention. These techniques include, but are not limited to, a rhetorical question, an anecdote, a quotation, a startling statement, a fact, etc. . . . Ask your teacher or tutor for more help with these introductory techniques. Next, we will show you the anecdote. In addition to the opening technique, your first paragraph must contain your original thesis statement. Below is an example of an introduction for our literary analysis essay.

## Sample Introduction

A young boy born into a dysfunctional family grows up and makes a few poor choices in life and winds up in jail. His freedom is taken away. In prison, he learns the error of his ways, works with a mentor, and finds peace and calmness even behind bars. He is now free. This idea of experiencing freedom in a state of physical hardship and seeming despair can be a reality and is a theme well expressed in the literature of our most talented writers. James A. Honey's "The World's Reward" and Maya Angelou's "Caged Bird" present this truth: spiritual freedom is possible even in the midst of physical enslavement.

As you can see, our writing satisfies all of the requirements of a quality introduction. There is an attention grabber—in the form of an anecdote—background on the essay topic, and a very strong thesis statement. Thanks to all the HARD WORK we did with reading and prewriting, we were able to breeze through this part of the literary analysis task. Now, let's turn our attention to the body.

## Sample Body

As you write the body paragraphs of your essay, it is imperative that you keep three items in mind:

    a.  You must have a clearly written topic sentence for each paragraph,

    b.  You must use appropriate quotations from the texts, and

    c.  You must use transitional words, phrases, and sentences in order to organize and structure the body portion of your essay.

Let's first address the issue of topic sentences. After many years of teaching English, we find that most students struggle in this area. It's not that students do not "know" what a topic sentence is; it's more of a problem of appropriately using it in actual essay writing.

Let's look at the body of our essay on freedom in James A. Honey's "The World's Reward" and Maya Angelou's "Caged Bird." A topic sentence is just what it says: It's a sentence that tells what the paragraph is about. That's simple enough, and, we are actually one step ahead of the game. Remember our prewriting chart and our outline? Well, take a look back at it. Our topic sentences are simply the sub-themes in the boxes of our graphic organizer and letters "A" and "B" in our outline. So, look at the chart below. Here are the topic sentences throughout the entire body of our literary analysis task:

| Mini-themes | Topic Sentences |
|---|---|
| Physical and Spiritual Enslavement | In "The World's Reward" and "Caged Bird," the physical enslavement of the main characters is a symbolic representation of their spiritual degradation. First, in "The World's Reward," James A. Honey presents to the reader a fantastical world of suffering and freedom. |
| Physical and Spiritual Freedom | In "The World's Reward" and "Caged Bird" the physical freedom of the main actors is a symbolic representation of their spiritual well-being. To begin, in "The World's Reward," James A. Honey shows the reader that freedom is achievable through deep and meaningful connections to culture, to the past, and to each other. |

As you can see through these examples, the topic sentences are clear and very direct. There is no uncertainty or ambiguity about the purpose of the paragraph. The second sentence in each of the samples above is designed to show you how to transition smoothly in your first analysis of text.

There is absolutely no getting out of any English class in our country without hearing a million times from your teacher, "You must use quotations from the text to support your work." Well, the PARCC is no different. Let us show you exactly how to incorporate quotations into your body paragraphs by building upon our sample topic sentences in our sample body of the literary analysis essay:

In "The World's Reward" and "Caged Bird," the physical enslavement of the main characters is a symbolic representation of their spiritual degradation. First, in "The World's Reward," James A. Honey presents to the reader a fantastical world of suffering and freedom. The enslavement in the story begins before the story even begins, as the dog spends an entire lifetime serving his master. Immediately, the narrator informs the reader that "the dog had served him very faithfully when he was still young, but ingratitude is the world's reward, and the man now wanted to dispose of him." Physically, the dog and his animal companions are locked away through their servitude to their masters. Spiritually, on the inside, they lost their ability to fly—meaning, they lost their freedom, and the dog will be discarded like trash. Their nightmarish imprisonment continues in their captivity within the confines of these relationships. As the animals search for freedom, they "came to a house and through the open door they saw a table spread with all kinds of nice food, of which some robbers were having their fill. It would help nothing to ask for admittance, and seeing that they were hungry, they must think of something else." Even in their quest for freedom, they are roadblocked by circumstance. Once again, the dog and the other slaves' physical abuse and imprisonment mirrors the loss of freedom that they feel on the inside.

Similarly, in Maya Angelou's poem, we also see the horrors of enslavement and what it does on the inside. In "Caged Bird," the poet presents to us two birds: one locked up, and one free. The locked-up bird is characterized in these lines: "The caged bird sings / with a fearful trill / of things unknown / but longed for still." Said differently, the "caged bird" sings of freedom. The bird is spiritually hurt, as well as physically behind bars. Just like in Hamilton's folktale, the outside and the inside reflect each other. In both works, however, there is an alternative to this pain, and it involves the courage to be free.

In "The World's Reward" and "Caged Bird" the physical freedom of the main actors is a symbolic representation of their spiritual well-being. To begin, in "The World's Reward," James A. Honey shows the reader that freedom is achievable through deep and meaningful connections to culture, the past, and each other. During the height of their escape, the band of animals attempts to find refuge in a new house that they find along their travels. They are able to achieve freedom through a spiritual connection to their past by understanding the injustices burdened upon them by their masters. They are free on the outside now that they are free on the inside.

Likewise, we also see the connection between the spiritual and the physical in Maya Angelou's poem. In "Caged Bird," Angelou contrasts the darkness of imprisonment of the "enslaved" (or jailed) bird with the freedom of the free bird: "The free bird thinks of another breeze / and the trade winds soft through the sighing trees / and the fat worms waiting on a dawn bright lawn / and he names the sky his own." Of notice in this passage are the references to nature—such as the breeze, the sighing trees, the fat worm, and the dawn bright lawn. These images of the beauty of nature reflect the spiritual freedom felt on the inside of the bird. In summary, the bird's physical freedom is a representation of its spiritual freedom.

Now that we have completed the sample body of the literary analysis essay, our hope is that you can see how successful you can be if you are willing to invest the time by interacting with the text and by prewriting. The benefits of both will be shown in your actual essay writing. For now, though, let's turn your attention to two critical elements of a body of a literary analysis essay.

## Transitions

One of the undeniable aspects of quality essay writing—for the PARCC and for *all* other situations—is a writer's ability to successfully use transitional words, phrases, and sentences. To illustrate this point, the body paragraphs we wrote about in our sample essay appear below. However, we deleted all of the sentences and only show those words and phrases and sentences that are the transitions:

- **First**, in "The World's Reward," James A. Honey presents to the reader a fantastical world of suffering and freedom.

- **Immediately**, the narrator informs the reader that "the dog had served him very faithfully when he was still young, but ingratitude is the world's reward, and the man now wanted to dispose of him."

- **Physically**, the dog and his animal companions are locked away through their servitude to their masters.

- **Spiritually, on the inside**, they lost their ability to fly—meaning, they lost their freedom, and the dog will be discarded like trash.

- **Similarly**, in Maya Angelou's poem, we also see the horrors of enslavement and what it does on the inside.

- **In both works, however**, there is an alternative to this pain, and it involves the courage to be free.

- **To begin**, in "The World's Reward," James A. Honey shows the reader that freedom is achievable through deep and meaningful connections to culture, the past, and each other.

- **Likewise**, we also see the connection between the spiritual and the physical in Maya Angelou's poem.

- **In summary**, the bird's physical freedom is a representation of its spiritual freedom.

As you can see above, transitions can be thought of as the "glue" that binds the paragraph together. These words and phrases allow the reader to easily and fluidly follow the writer's train of thought. Without these transitions, the paragraphs would seem disjointed, thrown together, and even sloppy.

To help you in your literary analysis writing, we include a list of transitions that you might wish to consider using in your writing. The idea here is not to overload your essay with a transition for every sentence, but to use these terms when it is wise and appropriate to do so.

| Types of Transitions | Transitional Words/Phrases |
| --- | --- |
| Similarity | also, in the same way, just as . . . so too, likewise, similarly |
| Exception/Contrast | but, however, in spite of, on the one hand . . . on the other hand, nevertheless, nonetheless, notwithstanding, in contrast, on the contrary, still, yet |
| Sequence/Order | first, second, third, . . . next, then, finally |
| Time | after, afterward, at last, before, currently, during, earlier, immediately, later, meanwhile, now, recently, simultaneously, subsequently, then |
| Example | for example, for instance, namely, specifically, to illustrate |
| Emphasis | even, indeed, in fact, of course, truly |
| Place/Position | above, adjacent, below, beyond, here, in front, in back, nearby, there |
| Cause and Effect | accordingly, consequently, hence, so, therefore, thus |
| Additional Support or Evidence | additionally, again, also, and, as well, besides, equally important, further, furthermore, in addition, moreover, then |
| Conclusion/Summary | finally, in a word, in brief, briefly, in conclusion, in the end, in the final analysis, on the whole, thus, to conclude, to summarize, in sum, to sum up, in summary |

## Writing Conclusions

So, what makes a good conclusion? In many years of teaching, we have often asked our students this question, and the overwhelming answer is, "Restate your thesis." Well, we don't completely agree with this approach. For one, simply restating your thesis is a pretty boring way to end. Second, restating the thesis does not address the "So What?" question. While we believe that restating the thesis statement in some way is appropriate for a conclusion, simply doing so will not ensure that your reader feels satisfied about the essay you wrote. Instead of just restating the thesis, we recommend that you answer the "So What?" question. What is the "So What?" question? Glad you asked. It addresses these issues:

- What is it about this essay that I have written that is really important?
- What should a reader of my essay learn about human nature?
- Why is my essay, on which I spent all this time and energy writing, important?
- What is my call to action?

So, let's practice what we preach by writing a conclusion for our sample literary analysis essay. Remember, our thesis statement was: *James A. Honey's "The World's Reward" and Maya Angelou's "Caged Bird" present this truth about freedom: even in the most difficult of times, spiritual freedom is possible even in the midst of physical enslavement.*

## Sample Conclusion

Being in jail, locked up behind bars, and without freedom is a terrible consequence. Imagine, however, the horrors of slavery where innocent people lost their lives while committing no crime other than being alive. It is absolutely amazing, under such harsh conditions, that the human soul can still find the strength to sing. James A. Honey's folktale and Maya Angelou's poem show how such a thing is possible: that spiritual freedom is possible even under the harshest of conditions. These authors' works are testament to the power and beauty of the human drive — especially the African American drive — for freedom and dignity.

As you read our sample conclusion, two properties of the writing should be clear to you.

1. The thesis statement of the essay is "reworked" but it is definitely not "repeated" word-for-word, and

2. the author clearly and directly answers the "So What?" question, stating that human freedom is possible even in the midst of slavery.

The conclusion is really done well and it is a good model for you to follow.

## Final Thoughts on the Literary Analysis Task

Before you practice with your own literary analysis tasks, we want to emphasize the major points learned in this chapter.

1) The better and harder that you read, the better and easier your essay will be.

2) Prewriting is NOT optional; it is mandatory.

3) The use of graphic organizers, like the ones in this chapter, will help you write a very successful literary analysis essay.

4) The literary analysis essay can be mastered with enough practice.

Please. It is critical that you keep these points in mind. As you practice on your own, we have the graphic organizers for you to use. Please fill them in as you progress through each stage of the reading and writing process. Talk with your teacher and/or your tutor about the strengths and areas of improvement for your essay.

# Practice Literary Analysis Task #1

| CCSS Alignment | |
|---|---|
| RL.1 | Cite strong and textual evidence. |
| RL.2 | Determine two or more themes. |
| RL.3 | Analyze the impact of the author's choices. |
| RL.5 | Analyze how an author's choices contribute to its overall structure. |
| RL.9 | Demonstrate knowledge of foundational works of American literature, including how two or more texts from the same period treat similar themes and topics. |
| L.1 | Demonstrate command of the conventions of standard English grammar and usage when writing. |
| L.3 | Apply knowledge of language to understand how language functions in different contexts. |
| L.5 | Demonstrate understanding of figurative language, word relationships, and nuances in word meanings. |
| W.3 | Write narratives to develop real or imagined experiences. |
| W.5 | Develop and strengthen writing as needed by planning, revising, editing, and rewriting. |
| W.6 | Use technology to produce, publish, and update individual writing products. |

[ELA TASK GENERATION MODEL: 8A.2PBA]

For your first literary analysis task, we have for you an excerpt from a book written by Mark Twain, and a poem written by Robert Frost. As you read and interact with each text, the themes that are similar between each text should become vividly clear to you.

## Text #1: Chapter 9 of *The Adventures of Tom Sawyer* by Mark Twain

| Excerpt from *The Adventures of Tom Sawyer* | My Thought Processes |
|---|---|
| AT half-past nine, that night, Tom and Sid were sent to bed, as usual. They said their prayers, and Sid was soon asleep. Tom lay awake and waited, in restless impatience. When it seemed to him that it must be nearly daylight, he heard the clock strike ten! This was despair. He would have tossed and fidgeted, as his nerves demanded, but he was afraid he might wake Sid. So he lay still, and stared up into the dark. Everything was dismally still. By and by, out of the stillness, little, scarcely perceptible noises began to emphasize themselves. The ticking of the clock began to bring itself into notice. Old beams began to crack mysteriously. The stairs creaked faintly. Evidently spirits were abroad. A measured, muffled snore issued from Aunt Polly's chamber. And now the tiresome chirping of a cricket that no human ingenuity could locate, began. Next the ghastly ticking of a death-watch in the wall at the bed's head made Tom shudder—it meant that somebody's days were numbered. Then the howl of a far-off dog rose on the night air, and was answered by a fainter howl from a remoter distance. Tom was in an agony. At last he was satisfied that time had ceased and eternity begun; he began to doze, in spite of himself; the clock chimed eleven, but he did not hear it. And then there came, mingling with his half-formed dreams, a most melancholy caterwauling. The raising of a neighboring window disturbed him. A cry of "Scat! you devil!" and the crash of an empty bottle against the back of his aunt's woodshed brought him wide awake, and a single minute later he was dressed and out of the window and creeping along the roof of the "ell" on all fours. He "meow'd" with caution once or twice, as he went; then jumped to the roof of the woodshed and thence to the ground. Huckleberry Finn was there, with his dead cat. The boys moved off and disappeared in the gloom. At the end of half an hour they were wading through the tall grass of the graveyard. | |

*(continued)*

| Excerpt from *The Adventures of Tom Sawyer* | My Thought Processes |
|---|---|
| It was a graveyard of the old-fashioned Western kind. It was on a hill, about a mile and a half from the village. It had a crazy board fence around it, which leaned inward in places, and outward the rest of the time, but stood upright nowhere. Grass and weeds grew rank over the whole cemetery. All the old graves were sunken in, there was not a tombstone on the place; round-topped, worm-eaten boards staggered over the graves, leaning for support and finding none. "Sacred to the memory of" So-and-So had been painted on them once, but it could no longer have been read, on the most of them, now, even if there had been light. | |
| A faint wind moaned through the trees, and Tom feared it might be the spirits of the dead, complaining at being disturbed. The boys talked little, and only under their breath, for the time and the place and the pervading solemnity and silence oppressed their spirits. They found the sharp new heap they were seeking, and ensconced themselves within the protection of three great elms that grew in a bunch within a few feet of the grave. | |
| Then they waited in silence for what seemed a long time. The hooting of a distant owl was all the sound that troubled the dead stillness. Tom's reflections grew oppressive. He must force some talk. So he said in a whisper: | |
| "Hucky, do you believe the dead people like it for us to be here?" | |
| Huckleberry whispered: | |
| "I wisht I knowed. It's awful solemn like, *ain't* it?" | |
| "I bet it is." | |
| There was a considerable pause, while the boys canvassed this matter inwardly. Then Tom whispered: | |
| "Say, Hucky—do you reckon Hoss Williams hears us talking?" | |

*(continued)*

| Excerpt from *The Adventures of Tom Sawyer* | **My Thought Processes** |
|---|---|
| "O' course he does. Least his sperrit does." | |
| Tom, after a pause: | |
| "I wish I'd said Mister Williams. But I never meant any harm. Everybody calls him Hoss." | |
| "A body can't be too partic'lar how they talk 'bout these-yer dead people, Tom." | |
| This was a damper, and conversation died again. | |
| Presently Tom seized his comrade's arm and said: | |
| "Sh!" | |
| "What is it, Tom?" And the two clung together with beating hearts. | |
| "Sh! There 'tis again! Didn't you hear it?" | |
| "I—" | |
| "There! Now you hear it." | |
| "Lord, Tom, they're coming! They're coming, sure. What'll we do?" | |
| "I dono. Think they'll see us?" | |
| "Oh, Tom, they can see in the dark, same as cats. I wisht I hadn't come." | |
| "Oh, don't be afeard. I don't believe they'll bother us. We ain't doing any harm. If we keep perfectly still, maybe they won't notice us at all." | |
| "I'll try to, Tom, but, Lord, I'm all of a shiver." | |
| "Listen!" | |
| The boys bent their heads together and scarcely breathed. A muffled sound of voices floated up from the far end of the graveyard. | |
| "Look! See there!" whispered Tom. "What is it?" | |
| "It's devil-fire. Oh, Tom, this is awful." | |

*(continued)*

| Excerpt from *The Adventures of Tom Sawyer* | My Thought Processes |
|---|---|
| Some vague figures approached through the gloom, swinging an old-fashioned tin lantern that freckled the ground with innumerable little spangles of light. Presently Huckleberry whispered with a shudder:<br><br>"It's the devils sure enough. Three of 'em! Lordy, Tom, we're goners! Can you pray?"<br><br>"I'll try, but don't you be afeard. They ain't going to hurt us. 'Now I lay me down to sleep, I—'" | |

**Thematic Messages**

## Text #2: "The Road Not Taken," by Robert Frost

| "The Road Not Taken" | My Thought Processes |
|---|---|
| Two roads diverged in a yellow wood,<br>And sorry I could not travel both<br>And be one traveler, long I stood<br>And looked down one as far as I could<br>To where it bent in the undergrowth;<br><br>Then took the other, as just as fair,<br>And having perhaps the better claim,<br>Because it was grassy and wanted wear;<br>Though as for that the passing there<br>Had worn them really about the same,<br><br>And both that morning equally lay<br>In leaves no step had trodden black.<br>Oh, I kept the first for another day!<br>Yet knowing how way leads on to way,<br>I doubted if I should ever come back.<br><br>I shall be telling this with a sigh<br>Somewhere ages and ages hence:<br>Two roads diverged in a wood, and I—<br>I took the one less traveled by,<br>And that has made all the difference. | |

| Thematic Messages |
|---|
| |

Literary Analysis #1 Writing Prompt

Student Directions

80 Minutes

Use what you have learned by reading Mark Twain's excerpt from *The Adventures of Tom Sawyer* and Robert Frost's "The Road Not Taken" to write an essay that analyzes how both texts use symbolism to create meaning in reference to the idea of making choices.

Develop your essay by providing textual evidence from both sources. Be sure to follow the conventions of Standard English.

## Prewriting

| Use of Symbolism | |
|---|---|
| **"The Adventures of Tom Sawyer"** | **"The Road Not Taken"** |
| Mini-theme #1 (fill in):<br><br><br>Quotations (fill in): | Mini-theme #1 (fill in):<br><br><br>Quotations (fill in): |
| Mini-theme #2 (fill in):<br><br><br>Quotations (fill in) | Mini-theme #2 (fill in):<br><br><br>Quotations (fill in) |

*(continued)*

Thesis Statement:

| Mini-themes | Topic Sentences |
|---|---|
|  |  |
|  |  |

Write your essay on loose-leaf paper or in a notebook.

# Practice Literary Analysis Task #2

For your second literary analysis task, we have two poems for you: one written by William Butler Yeats and the other written by Emily Dickinson. The theme that ties the two works together is the idea of imagination versus reality.

## Text #1: "The Song of Wandering Aengus," by William Butler Yeats

| "The Song of Wandering Aengus" | My Thought Processes |
|---|---|
| I went out to the hazel wood<br>Because a fire was in my head,<br>And cut and peeled a hazel wand,<br>And hooked a berry to a thread;<br>And when white moths were on the wing,<br>And moth-like stars were flickering out,<br>I dropped the berry in a stream<br>And caught a little silver trout.<br><br>When I had laid it on the floor<br>I went to blow the fire a-flame,<br>But something rustled on the floor,<br>And someone called me by my name:<br>It had become a glimmering girl<br>With apple blossom in her hair<br>Who called me by my name and ran<br>And faded through the brightening air.<br><br>Though I am old with wandering<br>Through hollow lands and hilly lands,<br>I will find out where she has gone,<br>And kiss her lips and take her hands;<br>And walk among long dappled grass,<br>And pluck till time and times are done<br>The silver apples of the moon,<br>The golden apples of the sun. | |

*(continued)*

Thematic Messages

## Text #2: "The Railway Train," by Emily Dickinson

| "The Railway Train" | My Thought Processes |
|---|---|
| I like to see it lap the miles,<br>And lick the valleys up,<br>And stop to feed itself at tanks;<br>And then, prodigious, step<br><br>Around a pile of mountains,<br>And, supercilious, peer<br>In shanties by the sides of roads;<br>And then a quarry pare<br><br>To fit its sides, and crawl between,<br>Complaining all the while<br>In horrid, hooting stanza;<br>Then chase itself down hill<br><br>And neigh like Boanerges;<br>Then, punctual as a star,<br>Stop — docile and omnipotent —<br>At its own stable door. | |

*(continued)*

Thematic Messages

# Literary Analysis Writing Prompt

| CCSS Alignment | |
|---|---|
| RL.1 | Cite strong and textual evidence. |
| RL.2 | Determine two or more themes. |
| RL.3 | Analyze the impact of the author's choices. |
| RL.5 | Analyze how an author's choices contribute to its overall structure. |
| RL.9 | Demonstrate knowledge of foundational works of American literature, including how two or more texts from the same period treat similar themes and topics. |
| L.1 | Demonstrate command of the conventions of standard English grammar and usage when writing. |
| L.3 | Apply knowledge of language to understand how language functions in different contexts. |
| L.5 | Demonstrate understanding of figurative language, word relationships, and nuances in word meanings. |
| W.3 | Write narratives to develop real or imagined experiences. |
| W.5 | Develop and strengthen writing as needed by planning, revising, editing, and rewriting. |
| W.6 | Use technology to produce, publish, and update individual writing products. |

[ELA TASK GENERATION MODEL: 7A.5PBA]

## Literary Analysis Writing Prompt

Student Directions

80 Minutes

Use what you have learned by reading "The Song of Wandering Aengus," by William Butler Yeats, and "The Railway Train," by Emily Dickinson, to write an essay that analyzes how both texts define the importance of imagination versus reality.

Develop your essay by providing textual evidence from both sources. Be sure to follow the conventions of Standard English.

## Prewriting

| Importance of Imagination versus Reality | |
|---|---|
| "The Song of Wandering Aengus" | "The Railway Train" |
| Mini-theme #1 (fill in):<br><br><br>Quotations (fill in): | Mini-theme #1 (fill in):<br><br><br>Quotations (fill in): |
| Mini-theme #2 (fill in):<br><br><br>Quotations (fill in) | Mini-theme #2 (fill in):<br><br><br>Quotations (fill in) |

(continued)

Thesis Statement:

| Mini-themes | Topic Sentences |
| --- | --- |
|  |  |
|  |  |

Write your essay on loose-leaf paper or in a notebook.

## CHAPTER 5

# The Research Simulation Task

 **Introduction**

(Performance-Based Assessment)

Now that we have worked through the narrative and literary analysis tasks, we will begin working closely with the Research Simulation Task (RST).

Before we start with the specifics of writing the Research Simulation Task, we want to stress the following point to you: When you take the PARCC, you will encounter numerous multiple-choice items before you get to the Research Simulation Task. Our purpose in this chapter is to concentrate on the skills necessary to successfully complete the Research Simulation Task. If you need a refresher on multiple-choice items, please refer back to Chapter 2. In this chapter, we are focusing on the larger writing task (which requires intensive reading as well), also known as the prose-constructed response.

To begin, we will look at a sample RST question. In doing so, we will introduce you to a step-by-step system to addressing the task, and we will walk you through the reading and analysis process of each of the question's sources from which you can extract information to support your essay's points. This chapter's goal is to get you familiar with the structure of the task, especially the brainstorming and preparation piece, before you begin writing your essay. We will not compose full-blown practice RST essays until Chapters 6, 7, 8, and 9.

The following activities align with the Common Core standards, as detailed below:

| CCSS Alignment | |
|---|---|
| RL.1 | Cite strong and textual evidence. |
| RL.5 | Analyze how an author's choices contribute to its overall structure. |
| RI.7 | Integrate and evaluate multiple sources of information presented in different media or formats (e.g., visually, quantitatively) as well as in words in order to address a question or solve a problem. |
| L.1 | Demonstrate command of the conventions of standard English grammar and usage when writing. |
| L.3 | Apply knowledge of language to understand how language functions in different contexts. |
| L.5 | Demonstrate understanding of figurative language, word relationships, and nuances in word meanings. |
| W.1 | Write arguments to support claims in an analysis of substantive topics or texts, using valid reasoning and relevant and sufficient evidence. |
| W.2 | Write informative/explanatory texts to examine and convey complex ideas, concepts, and information clearly and accurately through the effective selection, organization, and analysis of content. |
| W.5 | Develop and strengthen writing as needed by planning, revising, editing, and rewriting. |
| W.6 | Use technology to produce, publish, and update individual writing products. |

As we work through the following exercises, keep these eight steps in mind:

| Step #1 | Read through the question carefully. Make sure to decipher if the question is asking you to convey an opinion, or to convey information/research objectively. |
|---|---|
| Step #2 | In the upper right-hand corner of your paper, simplify what the question is asking you to do. Put the question/task into your own words. |
| Step #3 | Circle the minimum amount of sources that need to be addressed. |

| Step #4 | Take notes with each of the sources. Address the source's main points. Underline actively. |
|---|---|
| Step #5 | After you've addressed and highlighted the main point of the source, make separate notes on the reliability of these sources. Is the source reliable in general? Is it slanted in any way? Do logical fallacies or "holes in argument" exist? |
| Step #6 | You've read through your sources. Choose the sources that you are most comfortable with, and put a star (*) in the upper right-hand corner of each source that you will be using in your research simulation task. |
| Step #7 | In your source chart, copy your notes from the sources into each. |
| Step #8 | Now, look at the relationships of your sources. Do they agree with each other? Do they disagree? Use your source-relationship chart to begin thinking about how you will have your sources begin conversing with one another. |

On the next page, we will begin looking at our first RST. Then, we will look at a series of sources that will help us in supporting our points with information. Let's move through this process together.

| Step #1 | Read through the question carefully. Make sure to decipher if the question is asking you to convey an opinion, or to convey information/research objectively. |
|---|---|

In the research simulation task that follows next, we have two sources under each main source. For example, there are two sources under Source A, two under Source B, and so on. We have set up this RST this way for one important reason. We want to model for you how to tackle the reading for the RST prompt about "The Truth Behind Cheating." We will show you how to interact with Source 1, and then you will practice independently for Source 2. We have done this to emphasize that good writing absolutely starts with good reading.

We want you to become familiar with what the PARCC labels as the "anchor text." The anchor text for the RST is a text that serves as the "grounding point" or "orientation" for the topic introduced by the RST. For instance, in the RST that follows, the anchor text is found in Source A, in this case entitled, "One Third of Students Use Cellphones to Cheat in School" and also, "Cheating in Schools." For ease in navigating this test-prep book, we will assume that *all* sources in Source A of the sample research simulation tasks will serve as the anchor text.

Let's begin. Here is our first sample RST:

## Sample RST Question: The Truth Behind Cheating

85 minutes

Today, students are more savy than ever before. They know more about technology than their teachers, and can ultimately use that technology to their advantage. With virtually every answer to every question at a student's fingertips, the ease of searching for information is a widely known convenience for students. This has, however, become a concern for school districts, as many students have used many means to unfortunately participate in cheating and plagiarism.

You have reviewed four sources regarding cheating/plagiarism in our schools. These four pieces provide information to begin drafting your own informational essay.

- **Source A:** "One Third of Students Use Cellphones to Cheat in School" (1) / "Cheating in Schools" (2)

- **Source B:** Academic Dishonesty Graph (1) / Scenario/Perception Graph (2)

- **Source C:** Multimedia Video Clips — "Ethics: Cheating and Plagiarism" (1) / "What is Academic Integrity?" (2)

- **Source D:** Image (1) / Image (2)

What measures should be taken in order to help decrease cheating and plagiarism issues in our schools? Write a persuasive piece that addresses the question and supports your position with evidence from at least three of the four sources. Be sure to acknowledge competing views. You may give examples from past and current events or issues to illustrate and clarify your position. You may refer to the sources by their titles (Source A, Source B, Source C, Source D).

At this point, we have read through the question thoroughly before even moving on to the reading of our sources. This question is asking us to come up with an opinion, and support that opinion with information from our sources. We know what our objective is at this point.

So, let's move to Step #2:

| Step #2 | In the upper right-hand corner of your paper, simplify what the question is asking you to do. Put the question/task into your own words. |
|---|---|

We know that the question is asking: What should be done to discourage cheating on tests?

| Step #3 | Circle the minimum amount of sources that need to be addressed. |
|---|---|

We know that the question is asking us to use at least **three** of the four sources. This is important to note before we begin.

| Step #4 | Take notes with each of the sources. Address the source's main points. Underline actively. |
|---|---|
| Step #5 | After you've addressed and highlighted the main point of the source, make separate notes on the reliability of these sources. Is the source reliable in general? Is it slanted in any way? Do logical fallacies or "holes in argument" exist? |

Now, let's work through Steps #4 and #5 together. We are looking first at the source's main points and listing those appropriately. Then, when we talk about logical fallacies, we are looking to see if any "holes" or lapses exist in the source's reliability. Is the information slanted or biased in any way? Let's start with Source A:

## SOURCE A — Traditional Text

| Source A: "One-Third of Students Use Cellphones to Cheat in School" | How Should We Analyze? |
|---|---|
| Forget passing handwritten notes underneath desks or inking your arm with essential math formulas before a killer test. If students today want to cheat, they have a more insidious tool at their disposal: cellphones. More than one-third of teens with cellphones admit to having stored information on them to look at during a test or texting friends about answers, a new survey finds. | Step #4: <br> • The modes in which students use to cheat have far surpassed those methods of the past. |
| And teens' parents, while realistic about the frequency of cheating in schools, might need to overcome their own blind spots: More than 75 percent of parents responding to the survey say that cellphone cheating happens at their children's school, but only 3 percent believe their own teen is using a cellphone to cheat. | • Parents' perception of their own children's experience with cheating may be warped. |
| "I believe my kids' consciences would prevent them from doing it, as they are good kids deep down," one parent said in an interview for the nationwide online poll, conducted by Common Sense Media, a San Francisco-based education company. | • Students' parents and families need to take a reality check. No student is perfect and cheating is an epidemic that is more widespread than ever before. |
| "The results should be a wake-up call for educators and parents," says James Steyer, CEO and founder of Common Sense Media. "These versatile technologies have made cheating easier. The call to action is clear." | |
| That action, Steyer says, should consist of parents and teachers educating themselves on how kids use technology to cheat and then helping students understand that the consequences for online or electronic cheating are just as serious as those for old-fashioned cheating. | • Technology's effect on the ease of cheating. |
| But first, adults will have to leap another hurdle. Nearly 1 in 4 students thinks that accessing notes on a cellphone, texting friends with answers, or using a phone to search the Internet for answers during a test isn't cheating. | • What exactly is cheating? How can this be communicated to all parents and students alike? |

*(continued)*

| Source A: "One-Third of Students Use Cellphones to Cheat in School" | How Should We Analyze? |
|---|---|
| Some students say that the lack of person-to-person contact in new 21st-century methods of cheating makes it harder for them to feel as if they're doing something wrong. Others see texting during tests simply as helping one another, as opposed to looking at someone else's paper during an exam, which they consider cheating.<br><br>Madeline Jones, a recent graduate of Baylake Pines School in Virginia Beach, Va., says that for papers or online tests, students might use the Web to copy and paste text from other published reports. And for regular in-class exams, she says sneaky students can easily take advantage of the iPhone and its wireless Internet access, as one of her classmates typically did.<br><br>Two thirds of responders to the poll—which surveyed 1,013 teens in late May and early June—say others in their school have cheated with cellphones. More than half admit to using the Internet to cheat.<br><br>But even as teens advance their electronic cheating strategies, educators are beginning to fight back with their own anticheating technologies, such as text-matching software, biometric equipment, virtual students, and cheatproof tests, experts say.<br><br>At the University of Central Florida, for instance, business students now take their tests on cheat-resistant computers in a supersecure testing center. UCF students report much less cheating than students at other campuses.<br><br>"We've scared the living daylights out of them," explains Taylor Ellis, associate dean for undergraduate programs and technology at UCF's college of business. | • There is a large difference between helping each other with work, and cheating.<br><br><br><br>• Internet and cellphone usage has obviously made cheating a widespread problem.<br><br><br><br><br><br>• How can these scare tactics used by colleges work at the high school level, however? |

*(continued)*

| Source A: "One-Third of Students Use Cellphones to Cheat in School" | How Should We Analyze? |
|---|---|
| Researchers at Common Sense Media and school administrators say that parents should not assume that kids know what to do or how to behave ethically when it comes to tests on their own. Families should establish open communication about the use of technology in school—including a strict set of guidelines for kids to follow—and understand that kids are cheating.<br><br>Experts also say that if teachers hold open discussions, issue warnings, and present guidelines for taking tests and writing papers, kids will be more hesitant about cheating.<br><br>Jack Lorenz, principal of Ridgewood High School in New Jersey, doesn't think restricting cellphones is the answer.<br><br>"I think it's a little bit naive to think that that's going to solve the problem," he said in an interview with CBS News. "If you have a culture in your school where . . . there is an expectation that students are honest about their academic achievements, where students and the administration promote it, I think you decrease the opportunities for students to cheat." | • What do school administrators do?<br><br>• Is there a possible solution?<br><br>**Step #5**:<br><br>In regards to reliability, this seems like an article based on survey-related research. What is most interesting and worthy of questioning is students' admittance to cheating, yet the idea of cheating is confusing for students. What is declared as cheating? And if students are not aware of this definition, how can they admit to it in the first place? This would be worth looking at again. |

# Research Simulation Essay Practice

Now that we have looked at a traditional text together, it is time for you to try out your own analysis as it relates to a similar informational text. Be sure to underline the passage and jot down notes in the appropriate area. Interacting with these sources will, most likely, be the easiest and most comfortable for you, especially since you have worked with very similar texts in your own classrooms throughout your years of being a student.

| Step #4 | Take notes with each of the sources. Address the source's main points. Underline actively. |
|---|---|
| Step #5 | After you've addressed and highlighted the main point of the source, make separate notes on the reliability of these sources. Is the source reliable in general? Is it slanted in any way? Do logical fallacies or "holes in argument" exist? |

## SOURCE A — Traditional Text

| Source A: "Cheating in Schools" (A Student Blog Post) | Analysis: |
|---|---|
| I look around me every day, and I see my peers cheating. It has become the norm, even in the eighth grade. I'll be honest, I am a participant, and I am using the blog to finally confess.<br><br>If my teachers knew, I think that they would be really disappointed. Good thing this blogpost is anonymous, huh?<br><br>While I don't use cheat sheets during classroom tests (this has only happened once or twice, because soccer practice ran late and I didn't have the time to study), it is the daily routine to copy the homework of my peers. I even share my homework with my friends. I'd like to think of this as helping, rather than cheating. I think I know, though, that helping is just a nicer way to say that I'm cheating – just like everyone else.<br><br>Eighth grade is really stressful. I blame a lot of our cheating on stress. We want to do better, especially now, because we know that these grades count for high school. I want to be in Honors English and Honors Social Studies, but I need the grades for this sort of placement! | Step #4: |

| Source A: "Cheating in Schools" (A Student Blog Post) | Analysis: |
|---|---|
| When I think about how often we cheat, I do feel guilty, but then again, I think we have to consider the consequences that are involved with cheating. We rarely get caught, and if we do get caught, we lie to cover it up. We even lie to each other to cover it up! Most of our teachers don't even know how technology works, so if we take a picture of a test on our cell phones, send it out to our friends, the teacher will never have a clue.<br><br>So, in thinking about cheating, I think it is even more important to think about how to stop it. I can only imagine how widespread cheating will be once we get into the high school! But what if we get caught? What if our parents find out? I think schools need to make these types of things happen.<br><br>I know if something was actually done, then I might think twice next time about cheating. Until then, I'll do what's easiest.<br><br>What do you all think? | **Step #5:** |

| | |
|---|---|
| Step #4 | Take notes with each of the sources. Address the source's main points. Underline actively. |
| Step #5 | After you've addressed and highlighted the main point of the source, make separate notes on the reliability of these sources. Is the source reliable in general? Is it slanted in any way? Do logical fallacies or "holes in argument" exist? |

## SOURCE B — Visual Graph

| Source B: Academic Dishonesty (Graph) |
| --- |

In two high profile colleges, the following graph illustrates the number of cases of academic dishonesty reviewed by college disciplinary committees.

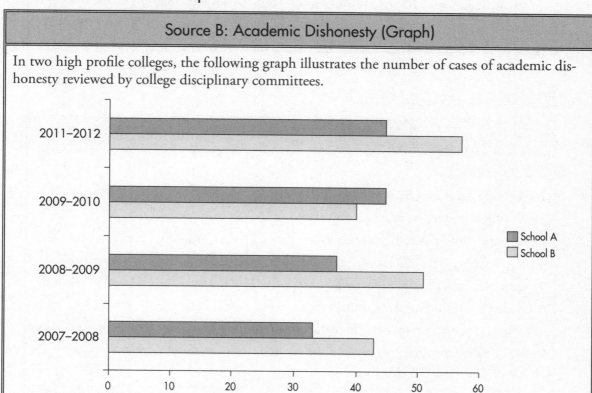

## How Should We Analyze?

<u>Step #4</u>:

- On the very surface, these numbers are shocking!

- We are looking at statistics related to two of the top universities in the country!

- What about the cases that we don't know about? What about the students who are never caught? What conclusions could be made then?

<u>Step #5</u>:

- For clarity purposes, what do the numbers on the bottom side of the graph mean? Number of cases? Percentages? While we believe it is the number of cases, one can easily argue that 50, at most, are certainly not a lot of academic dishonesty cases compared to the overall student enrollment.

- Information from Yale/Harvard disciplinary committees is reliable.

| Step #4 | Take notes with each of the sources. Address the source's main points. Underline actively. |
| --- | --- |

| Step #5 | After you've addressed and highlighted the main point of the source, make separate notes on the reliability of these sources. Is the source reliable in general? Is it slanted in any way? Do logical fallacies or "holes in argument" exist? |
| --- | --- |

## SOURCE B — Visual Graph

| Source B: Scenario/Perception Graph (Graph) |
| --- |

The scenarios:

1. Skipping a day of school to take a test later

2. Writing acronyms or notes on your hand to look at during a test

3. Asking a student who has already taken the test "what I should know"

4. Reading Maxnotes® literature guide for its analysis to finish English homework

5. Taking advantage of a teacher who guides students to the answer instead of restating

6. Students working together on take-home worksheets or packets

7. A student is playing on his phone during a test. Do you assume that he was cheating?

8. You see a student glancing around the room during a test and it looks suspicious. Do you assume that he/she was cheating?

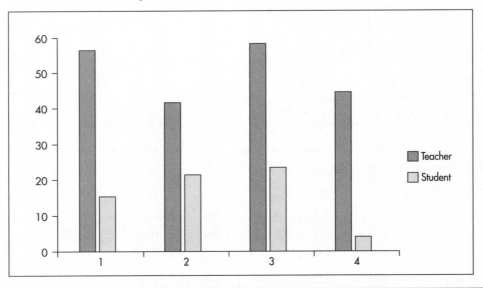

*(continued)*

Analysis:

Step #4:



Step #5:

| Step #4 | Take notes with each of the sources. Address the source's main points. Underline actively. |
|---------|---|
| Step #5 | After you've addressed and highlighted the main point of the source, make separate notes on the reliability of these sources. Is the source reliable in general? Is it slanted in any way? Do logical fallacies or "holes in argument" exist? |

## SOURCE C — Multimedia Video Clip

## Ethics: Cheating and Plagiarism:
## Summary of the video clip — for your convenience:

*The author argues that one of the reasons cheating is such a hot issue today is because of the Internet. Some students cheat because they say they must in order to keep ahead. Some students cheat because they have to stay on top. Some cheat because they simply do not have the time. The video's author argues that some students do not know what cheating and plagiarism actually are. At Bergen Academies, in Hackensack, N.J., students are required to take a course on ethics and cheating. In this course, students had to role-play as being part of the school's plagiarism board, and they had to decide whether each case presented to them violated the school's cheating and plagiarism policy. The video ultimately argues that each school should conduct a similar course in order to inform students about ethics and plagiarism.*

| Source C: Video<br>http://teacherTube.com/viewVideo.php?video_id=264679 | How Should We Analyze? |
|---|---|
| *http://teachertube.com/viewVideo.php?video_id=264679* | **Step #4:**<br><br>• Students may be confused of what cheating/plagiarism really is.<br><br>• The teacher showcased in this video provides students with the opportunity to work through scenarios dealing with plagiarism. This sort of activity should be done in all schools today!<br><br>• Students have the opportunity to analyze and discuss these scenarios openly with the class.<br><br>• The rationale from the students could be used to help discuss the further enforcement of such policies in our essay!<br><br>**Step #5:**<br><br>• This information is directly from a current student who provides information directly from his friends. This is seen as reliable. |

| Step #4 | Take notes with each of the sources. Address the source's main points. Underline actively. |
|---|---|
| Step #5 | After you've addressed and highlighted the main point of the source, make separate notes on the reliability of these sources. Is the source reliable in general? Is it slanted in any way? Do logical fallacies or "holes in argument" exist? |

## SOURCE C — Multimedia Video Clip

### What Is Academic Integrity?

*In this video, Northern Arizona University students describe what academic integrity means to them. The video begins by one student arguing, "Academic integrity is doing the right thing when nobody is looking." Another student, an early childhood education major argues that in college, plagiarism will "get you nowhere." Another student argues that academic integrity is not "lying to your teacher in order to get a better grade." Next, another student argues that cheating and plagiarism means that she "would not be getting her money's worth for her education." In addition, a journalism student argues, "Academic integrity is knowing when to cite sources that you've used in your work." Moreover, an anthropology student claims that academic integrity "consists of being intellectually honest with what you do know and what you do not."*

| Source C: Video http://www.youtube.com/ watch?v=AZVmpXcCd6o | How Should We Analyze? |
|---|---|
| *http://www.youtube.com/watch?v=AZVmpXcCd6o* | Step #4:<br><br><br><br>Step #5: |

| | |
|---|---|
| Step #4 | Take notes with each of the sources. Address the source's main points. Underline actively. |
| Step #5 | After you've addressed and highlighted the main point of the source, make separate notes on the reliability of these sources. Is the source reliable in general? Is it slanted in any way? Do logical fallacies or "holes in argument" exist? |

## SOURCE D — Visual/Image/Artwork/Advertisement

| Source D: Image |
| --- |

**Analysis:**

<u>Step #4:</u>

• The student looks frustrated and bored.

• This could raise a concern regarding our students' true love of learning.

• Where does the fault lie? Family values? Teaching practices?

<u>Step #5:</u>

• With regard to reliability, the facial expression we see above shows boredom. We can take this at face value alone.

| Step #4 | Take notes with each of the sources. Address the source's main points. Underline actively. |
| --- | --- |

| Step #5 | After you've addressed and highlighted the main point of the source, make separate notes on the reliability of these sources. Is the source reliable in general? Is it slanted in any way? Do logical fallacies or "holes in argument" exist? |
|---|---|

## SOURCE D — Visual/Image/Artwork/Advertisement

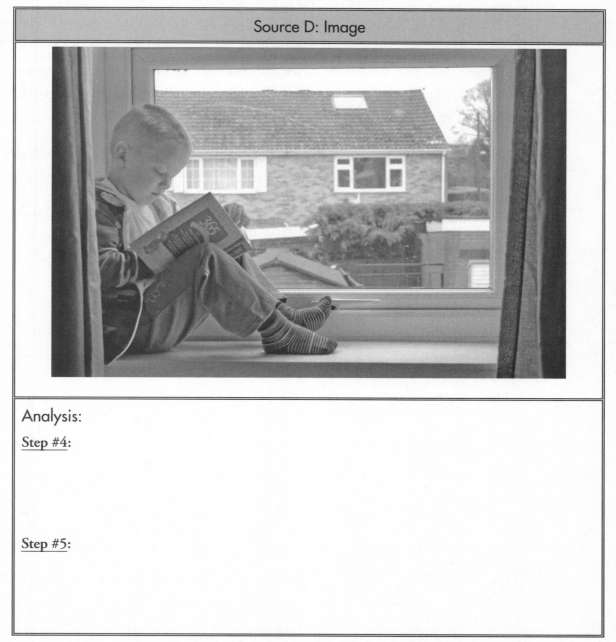

Source D: Image

**Analysis:**

<u>Step #4:</u>

<u>Step #5:</u>

| Step #6 | You've read through your sources. Choose the sources that you are most comfortable with, and put a star (*) in the upper right-hand corner of each source that you will be using in your research simulation task. |
| Step #7 | In source chart, copy your notes from your sources into each. |
| Step #8 | Now, look at the relationships of your sources. Do they agree with each other? Do they disagree? Use your source-relationship chart to begin thinking about how you will have your sources begin conversing with one another. |

At this point, you have been able to see our rationale and our thinking as we analyzed the sources provided. You also could see how we looked at each source's possible reliability of information. You have taken the time to practice these skills as well.

Look at the following charts to continue organizing your thoughts before we tackle the writing of your responses in the following chapters. Use the information you have collected from these sources to organize in the graphic organizer on the next page.

| | | Source A |
| --- | --- | :-: |
| | | Source B |
| | | Source C |
| | | Source D |

Now, look at the relationships between the sources. How do they relate to one another?

Use this graphic organizer to begin these conversations between and among your sources. This will help you as you integrate this information into your RST essays in the following chapters.

## Source Relationships

| Source _____ | How does _____ interact with _____? | Source _____ |
|---|---|---|
| | →  | |
| Source _____ | How does _____ interact with _____? | Source _____ |
| | →  | |

# The Research Simulation Task: English

 ## Introduction
(Performance-Based Assessment)

The Research Simulation Task (RST) represents a tough challenge for three primary reasons:

1. You will have to balance three or more separate sources as you consider your essay topic,

2. You will have to deal with various media-type sources; for instance, the research simulation task might present to you with an article, a video, and a graph, and

3. Perhaps most difficult of all, you will have to "synthesize" at least two of the three sources into a thesis-driven essay.

On top of this, you will be tested on how well you can read and write in relation to a particular academic subject, such as English, history, or science. Does this sound tough? Yes, it certainly is, *but not if you are prepared*. With a little practice and a little know-how, the RST is not as difficult as it sounds.

The goal of this chapter is simple: We will show you, step-by-step, how to do very well on the RST. We will give you a sample essay response to a RST prompt that will provide a model for you to follow as you practice further on in the chapter. Also, we will consider what a RST question looks like, specifically, in the content area of English.

# Writing the Research Simulation Essay for English

Let's get started. Our first RST deals with the topic of space exploration, our inspiration for using this topic comes from the famous science fiction novel, *A Wrinkle in Time*, by Madeleine L'Engle. Those lucky enough to have read this book will appreciate the topic very much. One last thing before we give you the writing prompt: *A Wrinkle in Time* appears on the Common Core State Standards reading list. Be sure to ask your teacher or tutor about the reading list, and get yourself a copy of *A Wrinkle in Time*.

| CCSS Alignment | |
|---|---|
| RL.1 | Cite strong and textual evidence. |
| RL.5 | Analyze how an author's choices contribute to its overall structure. |
| RI.7 | Integrate and evaluate multiple sources of information presented in different media or formats (e.g., visually, quantitatively) as well as in words in order to address a question or solve a problem. |
| L.1 | Demonstrate command of the conventions of standard English grammar and usage when writing. |
| L.3 | Apply knowledge of language to understand how language functions in different contexts. |
| L.5 | Demonstrate understanding of figurative language, word relationships, and nuances in word meanings. |
| W.1 | Write arguments to support claims in an analysis of substantive topics or texts, using valid reasoning and relevant and sufficient evidence. |
| W.2 | Write informative/explanatory texts to examine and convey complex ideas, concepts, and information clearly and accurately through the effective selection, organization, and analysis of content. |
| W.5 | Develop and strengthen writing as needed by planning, revising, editing, and rewriting. |
| W.6 | Use technology to produce, publish, and update individual writing products. |

[ELA TASK GENERATION MODEL: 6B2PBA]

Here's the prompt:

## RST #1: Space Exploration

85 Minutes

Look up in the night sky and you will see only a fraction of the billions of stars and planets in our galaxy, the Milky Way. Humankind has always dreamed of traveling to the stars, and since the 1950s, the United States government has funded its space program with tax dollars. There are those, however, who view space exploration as a colossal waste of money.

You have reviewed four sources regarding the benefits and drawbacks of space exploration. These four pieces provide information to begin drafting your own argument.

- **Source A:** New York Times, Peter Edelman: Poverty in America: Why Can't We End It? (opinion piece): *www.nytimes.com/2012/07/29/opinion*

- **Source B:** Forbes.com: The Cost Of Space Exploration (opinion piece): *www.forbes.com*, search "apollo moon landing anniversary 2009"

- **Source C:** NASA.gov: NASA's Innovation Impacts Across the U.S.: *www.nasa.gov/offices/oct/partnership/economic_impacts.html*

- **Source D:** Wall Street Journal: Space Tourism Could Be a Reality in 2012: *http://live.wsj.com/video*

Should the American people continue to fund space exploration? Write a persuasive piece that addresses the question and supports your position with evidence from at least two of the four sources. Be sure to acknowledge competing views. You may give examples from past and current events or issues to illustrate and clarify your position. You may refer to the sources by their titles (Source A, Source B, Source C, Source D).

As we have shown you throughout this book, the makers of the PARCC view reading and writing as connected activities. Therefore, to begin, we will show you, as in Chapter 2, how you should interact with the sources in the RST prompt in a meaningful manner. Here are some questions that will guide us as we view and read the texts:

- What is the main idea the author wishes to convey?

- What statistics seem to be important, especially when I have to write the essay?

- What type of bias does the author have in writing the piece?

- Can the information be interpreted in a way different from the way the author presents it?

- How can I use the arguments given to further my opinion on the matter?

To begin, here is the first source in our quest to answer the question, "Should the American people continue to fund space exploration?" "Source A," is an opinion piece, and we give you a graphic organizer that is an effective tool to use when interacting with text. As you read the opinion piece on the left, look at the notes we have recorded in the right side of the chart. As discussed at length in Chapter 2, these notes represent the type of mental actions our minds are required to make when interacting with on the PARCC.

## Source A

| Poverty in America: Why Can't We End It? | Our Thoughts |
|---|---|
| **Poverty in America: Why Can't We End It?**<br><br>By PETER EDELMAN<br><br>RONALD REAGAN famously said, "We fought a war on poverty and poverty won." With 46 million Americans—15 percent of the population—now counted as poor, it's tempting to think he may have been right. | • 15% of the population is poor |

(continued)

| Poverty in America: Why Can't We End It? | Our Thoughts |
|---|---|
| Look a little deeper and the temptation grows. The lowest percentage in poverty since we started counting was 11.1 percent in 1973. The rate climbed as high as 15.2 percent in 1983. In 2000, after a spurt of prosperity, it went back down to 11.3 percent, and yet 15 million more people are poor today. | • 15 million more are poor today than in 2000 |
| At the same time, we have done a lot that works. From Social Security to food stamps to the earned-income tax credit and on and on, we have enacted programs that now keep 40 million people out of poverty. Poverty would be nearly double what it is now without these measures, according to the Center on Budget and Policy Priorities. To say that "poverty won" is like saying the Clean Air and Clean Water Acts failed because there is still pollution. | • Social programs keep 40 million out of poverty.<br><br>• Center on Budget and Policy Priorities: Poverty would be double without social programs. |
| [...] | |
| The first thing needed if we're to get people out of poverty is more jobs that pay decent wages. There aren't enough of these in our current economy. The need for good jobs extends far beyond the current crisis; we'll need a full-employment policy and a bigger investment in 21st-century education and skill development strategies if we're to have any hope of breaking out of the current economic malaise. | • Americans stuck in low-income jobs<br>• more single-parent households |
| This isn't a problem specific to the current moment. We've been drowning in a flood of low-wage jobs for the last 40 years. Most of the income of people in poverty comes from work. According to the most recent data available from the Census Bureau, 104 million people—a third of the population—have annual incomes below twice the poverty line, less than $38,000 for a family of three. They struggle to make ends meet every month. | • better-paying jobs needed to get people out of poverty |

(continued)

| Poverty in America: Why Can't We End It? | Our Thoughts |
|---|---|
| Half the jobs in the nation pay less than $34,000 a year, according to the Economic Policy Institute. A quarter pay below the poverty line for a family of four, less than $23,000 annually. Families that can send another adult to work have done better, but single mothers (and fathers) don't have that option. Poverty among families with children headed by single mothers exceeds 40 percent. | • Low-wage jobs are the status quo for the last 40 years. |
| Wages for those who work on jobs in the bottom half have been stuck since 1973, increasing just 7 percent. | • 104 million Americans live below twice the poverty line ($38,000 for a family of three)<br>• Half the jobs in America pay only $34,000.<br>• A ¼ of jobs pay below the poverty line for a family of 4, less than 23,000 |
| It's not that the whole economy stagnated. There's been growth, a lot of it, but it has stuck at the top. The realization that 99 percent of us have been left in the dust by the 1 percent at the top (some much further behind than others) came far later than it should have—Rip Van Winkle and then some. It took the Great Recession to get people's attention, but the facts had been accumulating for a long time. If we've awakened, we can act. | • Wages for the lowest income workers have stagnated since 1973.<br>• 1% of the population doing very, very well |
| Low-wage jobs bedevil tens of millions of people. At the other end of the low-income spectrum we have a different problem. The safety net for single mothers and their children has developed a gaping hole over the past dozen years. This is a major cause of the dramatic increase in extreme poverty during those years. The census tells us that 20.5 million people earn incomes below half the poverty line, less than about $9,500 for a family of three—up eight million from 2000. | • safety net for single mothers has a "gaping hole"<br>• 20.5 million people earn incomes below the poverty line: $9,500 for a family of three |
| [...] | |
| One result: six million people have no income other than food stamps. Food stamps provide an income at a third of the poverty line, close to $6,300 for a family of three. It's hard to understand how they survive. | • Demise of welfare |

*(continued)*

| Poverty in America: Why Can't We End It? | Our Thoughts |
|---|---|
| At least we have food stamps. They have been a powerful antirecession tool in the past five years, with the number of recipients rising to 46 million today from 26.3 million in 2007. By contrast, welfare has done little to counter the impact of the recession; although the number of people receiving cash assistance rose from 3.9 million to 4.5 million since 2007, many states actually reduced the size of their rolls and lowered benefits to those in greatest need.<br><br>Race and gender play an enormous part in determining poverty's continuing course. Minorities are disproportionately poor: around 27 percent of African-Americans, Latinos and American Indians are poor, versus 10 percent of whites. Wealth disparities are even wider. At the same time, whites constitute the largest number among the poor. This is a fact that bears emphasis, since measures to raise income and provide work supports will help more whites than minorities. But we cannot ignore race and gender, both because they present particular challenges and because so much of the politics of poverty is grounded in those issues.<br><br>We know what we need to do — make the rich pay their fair share of running the country, raise the minimum wage, provide health care and a decent safety net, and the like. But realistically, the immediate challenge is keeping what we have. Representative Paul Ryan and his ideological peers would slash everything from Social Security to Medicare and on through the list, and would hand out more tax breaks to the people at the top. Robin Hood would turn over in his grave.<br><br>We should not kid ourselves. It isn't certain that things will stay as good as they are now. The wealth and income of the top 1 percent grows at the expense of everyone else. Money breeds power and power breeds more money. It is a truly vicious circle.<br><br>[...] | • 6 million people have no income other than food stamps.<br><br>• 46 million people today live on food stamps, up from 26.3 million in 2007.<br><br><br><br>• Minorities are disproportionately poor.<br><br>• 27% of minorities compared to 10% per whites |

(continued)

| Poverty in America: Why Can't We End It? | Our Thoughts |
|---|---|
| But history shows that people power wins sometimes. That's what happened in the Progressive Era a century ago and in the Great Depression as well. The gross inequality of those times produced an amalgam of popular unrest, organization, muckraking journalism and political leadership that attacked the big—and worsening—structural problem of economic inequality. The civil rights movement changed the course of history and spread into the women's movement, the environmental movement and, later, the gay rights movement. Could we have said on the day before the dawn of each that it would happen, let alone succeed? Did Rosa Parks know?<br><br>We have the ingredients. For one thing, the demographics of the electorate are changing. The consequences of that are hardly automatic, but they create an opportunity. The new generation of young people—unusually distrustful of encrusted power in all institutions and, as a consequence, tending toward libertarianism—is ripe for a new politics of honesty. Lower-income people will participate if there are candidates who speak to their situations. The change has to come from the bottom up and from synergistic leadership that draws it out. When people decide they have had enough and there are candidates who stand for what they want, they will vote accordingly.<br><br>I have seen days of promise and days of darkness, and I've seen them more than once. All history is like that. The people have the power if they will use it, but they have to see that it is in their interest to do so.<br><br>Peter Edelman is a professor of law at Georgetown University and the author, most recently, of "So Rich, So Poor: Why It's So Hard to End Poverty in America." | • Inequality produces popular unrest and therefore, change.<br><br><br><br><br><br>• Lower-income people will participate in the change process if there are candidates who speak to them. |

The chart above is an excellent example of how to take notes on an opinion piece published in a major newspaper. But, you might be asking, "What does this poverty piece have to do with space exploration?" The answer might not seem obvious at first, especially if you didn't read the text as carefully as we did. This is where we have to think about the purpose of the opinion piece and why the makers of the PARCC placed it in a research simulation task about the viability of funding space exploration. Looking at some of the shocking statistics about poverty in America, the answer becomes simple: "Why should we pay for the cost of space exploration when so many Americans at home, in our own country, are hurting financially and drowning in poverty?" So, it seems our first source is against using tax dollars for space exploration.

So, now that we have all these statistics at our disposal, it is still early to take a side in the question, "Should the American people continue to fund space exploration?" Let's look at our next source, written by the famous theoretical physicist Michio Kaku. His opinion piece is entitled, "The Cost Of Space Exploration." Be sure to read the text carefully and to pay attention to our thinking in the right column.

## Source B

| The Cost of Space Exploration, by Michio Kaku | Our Thoughts |
| --- | --- |
| Michio Kaku, 07.16.09, 5:00 PM ET<br><br>We will always remember July 20, 1969, as a glorious moment, when humanity stood on the brink of an exciting new era. For the first time in human history, humans walked on the surface of another extraterrestrial body. | |
| It was a technological tour de force. Scientists talked knowingly about setting their sights on Mars and beyond. The universe seemed within our grasp. | • Much excitement over the early days of the space program |
| But historians will also recognize the irony of this magnificent feat. Today, in 2009, we are actually behind where we were back then. | • We are "behind" where we were back then. Maybe financially or technologically? |

*(continued)*

| The Cost of Space Exploration, by Michio Kaku | Our Thoughts |
|---|---|
| Back then, we had a huge industrial infrastructure designed to send astronauts to the moon. We had a fleet of colossal Saturn booster rockets emerging from our factories. We had a cadre of fiercely loyal, dedicated and highly skilled engineers intensely focused on one mission. We had a public mesmerized and unified by the space age.<br><br>Today, all of that is gone. Only ghosts of that era remain, mainly in museums and dusty history books. Now, we are haunted by these memories as we painfully try to reach for the moon once again—in 2020, 60 years after the first moon landing.<br><br>What went wrong? Part of the reason is that the space race was ill-conceived from the start.<br><br>Back in the mid-1950s, President Dwight Eisenhower actually laid down a sober and methodical timetable for space exploration. He envisioned a fleet of robotic probes that would scout out the moon and beyond. Astronauts would join them later, launched on small, fast space planes. Like fighter pilots, our astronauts would be able to blast into space at the drop of a hat.<br><br>But when Sputnik's launch was splashed over every front page in October 1957, all of that changed. Suddenly, the race to the moon was all about proving the superiority of capitalism over communism. Arthur C. Clarke, the British author of 2001: A Space Odyssey, once commented that he would have never imagined there would be a push to put men on the moon if it hadn't became the focus of competition between two nations.<br><br>At the height of the Cold War, the superpowers spared no expense in funding the latest space spectacular. Dazzling stunts in space, not cost-cutting, were the order of the day. No one bothered to read their price tag. | • Public was "mesmerized" by the space program, creating a sense of national unity.<br><br><br><br><br>• The space program turned political after the Soviet's launch of Sputnik.<br><br><br><br>• During the Cold War, America was not concerned with the financial costs of the space program, a fact which is NOT TRUE today. |

*(continued)*

| The Cost of Space Exploration, by Michio Kaku | Our Thoughts |
|---|---|
| But after 1969, the Soviets dropped out of the race to the moon and, like a cancer, the land war in Asia began to devour the budget. The wind gradually came out of the sails of the space program; the Nielsen ratings for each moon landing began to fall. The last manned mission to the moon was Apollo 17, in 1972.<br><br>As Isaac Asimov once commented, we scored a touchdown, then took our football and went home.<br><br>After all is said and done about what went wrong, the bottom line is simple: money. It's about $10,000 to put a pound of anything into a near-earth orbit. (Imagine John Glenn, the first American to orbit the earth, made of solid gold, and you can appreciate the enormous cost of space travel.) It costs $500 to $700 million every time the shuttle flies. Billionaire space tourists have flown to the space station at a reputed price of $20 million per head.<br><br>And to put a pound of anything on the moon costs about 10 times as much. (To reach Mars, imagine your body made of diamonds.) We are 50 years into the space age, and yet space travel is just as expensive as it always was.<br><br>We can debate endlessly over what went wrong; there is probably no one correct answer. But a few observations can be made.<br><br>The space shuttle, the workhorse of the space program, proved to be somewhat of a disappointment, with large cost overruns and long delays. It was bloated and probably did not need to have seven astronauts on board. (The Soviet copy of the space shuttle, a near-clone called the Buran, actually flew into outer space fully automated, without any astronauts whatsoever.) | • America had interests other than space. Sounds very familiar, especially since reading the previous article, "Poverty in America: Why Can't We End It?"<br><br>• $10,000 per pound to put anything into orbit<br><br>• $500–$700 million every flight of the now-retired Space Shuttle<br><br>• Private industry has flown into space at $20 million per person; this "fact" suggests that the commercial space industry is much more cost-effective.<br><br>• Space Shuttle program was bloated in terms of cost and people. |

*(continued)*

| The Cost of Space Exploration, by Michio Kaku | Our Thoughts |
|---|---|
| An alternative to the space shuttle was the original space plane of the Eisenhower era. It was to be small and compact, but provide easy access to space on a moment's notice, instead of the long months to prepare each shuttle launch. It was to take off and land like a plane, but soar into outer space like a rocket. President Ronald Reagan called one version of it the "Orient Express." (Ironically, now there will be a hiatus as the space shuttle is mothballed next year. Instead of fast and cheap access to space, for five years we will have no access to space at all. We'll have to beg the Europeans and Russians to piggy-back off their rockets.) | • America is not dependent on other countries to get into space. |
| One of the primary missions of NASA should have been to drive down the cost of space travel. Instead of spending half a billion dollars on each shuttle mission, it should have diverted some of the funds to make research and development a primary focus. New materials, new fuels and innovative concepts, which would make space exploration less expensive, should have been prioritized. (Today, some of that entrepreneurial spirit still lives in the commercial sector, as it tries to nourish a fledgling space tourism industry.) | • NASA misspent money. Should have invested in research and development. |
| The space station costs upward of $100 billion, yet its critics call it a "station to nowhere." It has no clearly defined scientific purpose. Once, President George H.W. Bush's science adviser was asked about the benefits of doing experiments in weightlessness and microgravity. His response was, "Microgravity is of microimportance." Its supporters have justified the space station as a terminal for the space shuttle. But the space shuttle has been justified as a vehicle to reach the space station, which is a completely circular and illogical argument. | • Space station costs $100 billion per year! Considering the amount of people living in poverty, this cost is STAGGERING.<br><br>• The space station is justified as a terminal for the space shuttle; while the space shuttle has been justified as a way to reach the space station! This argument is completely illogical; it makes absolutely no sense. Perhaps the $100 billion could be spent elsewhere? Maybe to help Americans get back to work? |

*(continued)*

| The Cost of Space Exploration, by Michio Kaku | Our Thoughts |
|---|---|
| Now, NASA is painfully reconstructing the infrastructure that it dismantled back in the 1970s as it prepares to send astronauts to the moon via the Orion crew vehicle and the Ares launch rocket in 2020. This time, though, there could be a traffic jam on the moon, since China, India and Japan have all publicly announced that by then they too will have sent astronauts to the moon. (Please see story, "A Traffic Jam On The Moon?") | |
| Let's hope someone will map out a methodical plan for space exploration, like the one Eisenhower drew up, instead of wasting time and money with more fits-and-starts. Then, at the next milestone anniversary, we won't have to ask ourselves, "What if?" | |
| *Michio Kaku, professor of theoretical physics at the City University of New York, is the author of Physics of the Impossible: A Scientific Exploration into the World of Phases, Teleportation and Time Travel.* | |

Now that we have read our second piece, we are beginning to gain a better perspective of the topic, and we might start to form our own opinion on the question, "Should the American people continue to fund space exploration?" Professor Michio Kaku does not paint a pretty picture of NASA and its use of American tax dollars. When the Space Shuttle was active, for instance, each flight cost somewhere between $500–$700 million. By any estimate, that is a ton of money! In addition, NASA doesn't even have a way to fly to the $100 billion space station that it primarily built (without the help of other countries). Professor Michio Kaku argues that NASA is incredibly inefficient with the massive funds it receives from the federal government—that is, the taxpayers (us)!

As you can tell, we are leaning toward answering the RST question in the negative—that America should **not** continue to fund space exploration. However, we still have two pieces to go; maybe something in the next two texts will change our mind. Keep your eyes open and try to receive and process the new information with an open mind.

The next text comes from NASA itself, so we know that, like the two pieces before, there will be a bias in terms of pro-space exploration. This fact is not necessarily a "bad" or "good" thing. Remember our job! We have to gather information to support whether or not America should continue to fund space exploration.

The title of NASA's text is "NASA's Innovation Impacts Across the U.S." What's interesting and pretty cool about this resource is that the website is not just "text"; it is interactive and allows us to point and click is a hundred different places. This website is a little like space exploration! Since NASA's website is interactive in nature, we will use a two-row graphic organizer instead of a two-column. Remember, we want to keep the graphic organizers simple yet effective for our purposes. You are not going to have endless time on the PARCC to create crazily complicated graphic organizers. Ours below will suit us just fine:

## Source C

| NASA's Innovation Impacts Across the U.S.<br>www.nasa.gov/offices/oct/partnership/economic_impacts.html |
|---|
| **Video Notes**<br><br>• NASA has developed partnerships with private corporations in order to create innovations "in areas such as health and medicine, consumer goods, transportation, renewable energy, and manufacturing." Hmmm. This fact sheds a new light for us on NASA and the money used to fund the space program. If NASA can help businesses, then perhaps the tax dollars we spend on it are like an investment.<br><br>— NASA designed plane wings that saved the airline industry billions of dollars.<br><br>— NASA designed technology to increase fuel efficiency in tractor-trailers by 15%; great for the environment!<br><br>— NASA has developed technology to reduce groundwater contamination.<br><br>— NASA has developed technology to purify water.<br><br>— NASA partnered with Warwick Mills, Inc. to create better body armor for police. |
| • Small Business Research/Small Business Technology Transfer<br><br>— Partners with local small business, especially minority owned, to research and develop new technologies and innovations (such as the items above)<br><br>— $238 million in 247 California companies; $1.2 billion nationwide<br><br>— $80 million in the state of New York |

Wow! Talk about a game-changer. This NASA website gives an entirely new spin on the monies spent on space exploration. It seems that, by partnering with locally owned companies throughout America, NASA is actually (a) placing tax dollars back into the states' economies, and (b) putting local people back to work. Compared to the negativity in the two articles above, this website places a positive spin on the funding of space exploration.

So, what point are we at now? The first two pieces—which we must keep in mind, were opinions—painted a pretty grim picture of the amount of money and waste spent on NASA's space exploration programs. The third piece, however, shows a more benevolent NASA that gives back to the American people. Our position on the RST question, "Should the American people continue to fund space exploration?" will depend on the fourth and final source. This should be our mindset going into the fourth piece: "Will the information in this article help me answer the RST question positively or negatively?" We have to keep a sharp eye on the information presented.

The fourth, and final, piece of our RST is a video from *The Wall Street Journal*, entitled, "Space Tourism Could Be a Reality in 2012." At this point, you might be wondering, "What on earth does this video have to do with our RST topic?" Well, let's keep an open mind while we view and take notes. As you watch the video, be sure to flip back to our graphic organizer. Watch carefully the thought process that goes into critically viewing a video. Just as a refresher, we placed our "critical thinking questions," discussed previously, below:

- What is the main idea the author wishes to convey?

- What statistics seem to be important, especially when I have to write the essay?

- What type of bias does the author have in writing the piece?

- Can the information be interpreted in a way different than the way the author presents it?

- How can I use the arguments presented to further my opinion on the matter?

## Source D

## Wall Street Journal: Space Tourism Could Be a Reality in 2012

*In this video, Wall Street Journal reporter Ben Rooney interviews the CEO of Virgin Galactic, George Whitesides, about his company's quest to develop and achieve a space tourism program.*

*Mr. Whitesides informs the audience that close to 500 people have put deposits down for space flight tickets with Virgin Galactic—that number equals the total number of people in human history who have traveled in space. A ticket on the space ship costs $200,000, which, when compared to the current $65 million it currently costs to get into space with the Russian government, represents a good deal. Mr. Whitesides predicts that the cost of the ticket will go down over time. The time of the space trip will be around 2 hours, with 5 minutes of that time actually spent in space.*

---

**Title of Video: Wall Street Journal: Space Tourism Could Be a Reality in 2012**
*http://live.wsj.com/video*

**Our Thought Processes:**

• Virgin Galactic: Commercial Space Exploration, founded by Richard Branson, UK entrepreneur

• $300 million invested of private money in the business

• Meant partially for tourism; 500 people signed up

• Meant partially for the development of scientific and technological advances

• $200,000 per ticket compared to $65 million dollars with the Russians!

— Wow! This fact suggests that private business is MUCH BETTER at cost effectiveness than government.

— Over time, the price will go down.

— Space flight lasts two hours, only 5 minutes of which is actually spent in space!

---

So, what do you think? This *Wall Street Journal* piece makes a great case that private entrepreneurship is much more cost-effective and efficient in designing and developing space travel technology. Notice the fact cited above: On Virgin Galactic, a cost of a ticket is "only" $200,000 compared to the $65 million per flight cost for the Russian spacecraft, which, not incidentally, is the only way to get to space now. America does not currently have a vehicle capable of going into space. The downfall of Virgin Galactic seems to be that only 5 minutes of the two-hour flight is actually spent in space. With time and technological advancement, however, this number can be expected to increase.

All right. Now we are at the critical moment to make a decision about our position on the question, "Should the American people continue to fund space exploration?" We have the first two pieces obviously against funding a governmental space exploration program. Our third piece touts the partnerships NASA has created with local businesses, and a third piece that suggests private business is much more efficient at space travel. Based upon all this data, we have to ask, "What position could we take that would be best supported by the articles?" The answer is clear: "Yes, the American people should fund space exploration as long as the government partners with private business."

Now that we have our thesis decided upon, let's refer back to the writing prompt (reproduced below):

## RST #1: Space Exploration

### 85 Minutes

Look up in the night sky and you will see only a fraction of the billions of stars and planets in our galaxy, the Milky Way. Humankind has always dreamed of traveling to the starts. Since the 1950s, the United States government has funded its space program with tax dollars. There are those, however, who view space exploration as a colossal waste of money.

You have reviewed four sources regarding the benefits and drawbacks of space exploration. These four pieces provide information to begin drafting your own argument.

- **Source A:** New York Times, Peter Edelman: Poverty in America: Why Can't We End It? (opinion piece): *www.nytimes.com/2012/07/29/opinion*

- **Source B:** Forbes.com: The Cost Of Space Exploration (opinion piece): *www. forbes.com*, search "apollo moon landing anniversary 2009"

- **Source C:** NASA.gov: NASA's Innovation Impacts Across the U.S.: *www.nasa.gov/offices/oct/partnership/economic_impacts.html*

- **Source D:** Wall Street Journal: Space Tourism Could Be a Reality in 2012: *http://live.wsj.com/video/space-tourism-could-be-a-reality-in-2012*

Should the American people continue to fund space exploration? Write a persuasive piece that addresses the question and supports your position with evidence from at least two of the four sources. Be sure to acknowledge competing views. You may give examples from past and current events or issues to illustrate and clarify your position. You may refer to the sources by their titles (Source A, Source B, Source C, Source D).

At this point, we should be very ready to tackle this essay topic, but let's take a closer look at what the prompt is actually asking of us. In our many years of teaching, we have seen too many students do poorly on an assessment because they either (a) didn't understand the prompt, or (b) didn't do exactly what the prompt required. On the PARCC, we cannot afford to make these mistakes. Below are eleven specific steps you can take to ensure success.

# The 11 Steps for Success on the RST

## Before Writing Begins

Step #1: Read through the question carefully. Make sure to decipher if the question is asking you to convey an opinion, or to convey information/research objectively.

- *The question is asking us to convey an opinion.*

Step #2: Simplify what the question is asking you to do. Put the question/task into your own words.

- *The prompt is asking this: "Do I think American tax dollars should be spent on space exploration?"*

**Step #3:**  Circle the minimum amount of sources that NEED to be addressed.

- *Two sources*

**Step #4:**  Take notes with each of the sources. Address the source's main points. Underline actively.

- *We completed this activity extensively in our two-column approach and when we took notes on the video.*

**Step #5:**  After you've addressed and highlighted the main point of the source, make separate notes on the reliability of these sources. Is the source reliable in general? Is it slanted in any way? Do logical fallacies or "holes in argument" exist?

- *We took notes on the reliability of sources in our active reading. All the pieces, in one way or another have a bias. Source A, for example, argues that poverty in America is on the rise. Source B criticizes NASA for using tax money inefficiently. Source C is from NASA itself, so we know that it is biased. Lastly, Source D is the closest thing we have to an unbiased source. It is more of a report. In writing our essay, we will acknowledge these biases so that we can strengthen our own argument.*

**Step #6:**  You've read through your sources. Choose the sources that you are most comfortable with, and put an asterisk (*) next to them.

- *With this particular RST, we are in a position where ALL of the sources will be useful in writing our essay. Therefore, we placed an asterisk next to all of them.*

## Writing the RST

**Step #7:**  Copy the arguments—textual evidence—you will use in your essay into the prewriting chart. (Shown below.)

**Step #8:**  Now, look at the relationships of your sources. Do they agree with each other? Do they disagree? Use your source-relationship chart to begin thinking about how you will have your sources begin conversing with one another. (Shown below.)

Step #9:   Compose a quick outline of your essay. (Shown below.)

Step #10: Complete your essay using the framework/outline as a guide. (Shown below.)

Step #11: After you have completed your essay, go back to check that your sources have a conversation, and replace the verbs you've used to integrate these sources with the action verbs from the sheet provided. (Shown below.)

## Getting Your Sources Talking to Each Other

Now that we have completed Steps 1–6, it is time for us to really start writing. For the RST, we have designed a graphic organizer for you to use to structure the writing process. We feel that this organizer is important because it serves one critical aspect of the RST writing task: Getting your sources "talking to each other." This skill of getting your sources "talking" is a key feature of the RST and is used in all good writing that compares information. What do we actually mean about getting your sources "talking to each other?" Well, the answer is simple enough to explain but much more difficult to acquire.

When we have taught our students to write synthesis essays, here's what we learned: When you prewrite and organize your essay, be sure to organize the body paragraphs by **theme**, not by the text. For example, imagine that you are writing an essay on *A Wrinkle in Time* and a Ray Bradbury short story called "All Summer in a Day." Your thesis statement might be something like, *A Wrinkle in Time* and "All Summer in a Day" both embody the idea that we are not alone in the universe. Now, an uninformed student would say, "Great. I can just write about *A Wrinkle in Time* for my first body paragraph and "All Summer in a Day" for my second body paragraph." *Wrong!* A synthesis essay (or RST) requires that you set a theme for each of your body paragraphs and that you utilize *both* sources under that theme. For instance, you could develop a theme such as "alien life" in our *A Wrinkle in Time* and "All Summer in a Day" paper. Then, both stories would be explored in that body paragraph about "alien life."

If all of this sounds complicated to you, DO NOT worry. In our sample RST that follows, we will show you exactly how to get your sources "talking to each other."

Let's look at our prewriting chart:

## Topic: Should the American people continue to fund space exploration

**My Thesis Statement:** Yes, the American people should continue to fund space exploration as long as the government partners with private business.

| Source A | Source B | Source C | Source D |
|---|---|---|---|
| Poverty in America: Why Can't We End It? | The Cost of Space Exploration | NASA's Innovation Impacts Across the U.S. | Space Tourism Could Be a Reality in 2012 |
| better paying jobs needed to get people out of poverty | Public was "mesmerized" by the space program, creating a sense of national unity. | NASA has developed partnerships with private corporations in order to create innovations "in areas such as health and medicine, consumer goods, transportation, renewable energy, and manufacturing." Hmmm. This fact sheds a new light for us on NASA and the money used to fund the space program. If NASA can help businesses, then perhaps the tax dollars we spend on it are like an investment. | Virgin Galactic: Commercial Space Exploration, founded by Richard Branson, UK entrepreneur |
| 104 million Americans live twice below the poverty line (38,000 for a family of three) | $500–700 million every flight of the now-retired Space Shuttle | | meant partially for tourism; 500 people signed up |
| half the jobs in America pay only $34,000 | Private industry has flown into space at $20 million per person; this "fact" suggests that the commercial space industry is much more cost-effective | | meant partially for the development of scientific and technological advances |
| Wages for the lowest income workers have stagnated since 1973. | | In 2011, NASA pumped $1.1 billion into California's state economy. | $200,000 per ticket compared to 65 million dollars with the Russians! |
| 20.5 million people earn incomes below the poverty line: $9,500 for a family of three | America is now dependent on other countries to get into space. | NASA designed plane wings that saved the airline industry billions of dollars. | |
| 6 million people have no income other than food stamps | Space station $100 billion per year! Considering the amount of people living in poverty, this cost is STAGGERING. | NASA designed technology to increase fuel efficiency in tractor trailers by 15%; great for the environment! | Wow! This fact suggests that private business is MUCH BETTER at cost effectiveness than government. |
| 46 million people today live on food stamps, up from 26.3 million in 2007 | | NASA has developed technology to reduce ground water contamination. | Over time, the price will go down. |
| Minorities are disproportionately poor. | | NASA has developed technology to purify water. | Space flight lasts two hours, only 5 minutes of which is actually spent in space! |
| 27% of minorities compared to 10% per whites | | NASA partnered with Warwick Mills, Inc., to create better body armor for police. | |
| | | Small Business Research/Small Business Technology Transfer | |
| | | Partners with local small business, especially minority owned, to research and develop new technologies and innovations such as the items above. | |
| | | $238 million in 247 California companies; $1.2 billion nationwide $80 million in the state of New York | |

(continued)

### Exactly how do the sources talk with each other?

The four sources above are like a story waiting to be told. Source A, the New York Times opinion piece, makes a hard case against spending more money on a space program when "104 million Americans live twice below the poverty line ($38,000 for a family of three)" and "Wages for the lowest income workers have stagnated since 1973." These disturbing facts and made even more sharp by the reality that, as noted in Source B, the space shuttle cost anywhere between 500 to 700 million dollars PER FLIGHT into space and that the space station cost a mind-blowing $100 billion to create, and this figure does not take into account the maintenance of the flying space facility. Despite these statistics, NASA, when partnered with states and local businesses, can do a lot to help people rise out of poverty.

According to Source D, NASA, in California, for example, pumped $238 million into 247 local companies to develop and create new technologies. These funds — which are taxpayers' dollars — are actually being used to create jobs and to make advances in technologies that benefit the whole public. Through a program called "Small Business Research/Small Business Technology Transfer," NASA and small businesses have designed new plane wings that increase efficiency, designed new trucks that have a 15% increase in fuel efficiency, developed water filtration technologies, and developed technologies that help clean contaminated work sites. These facts support the notion that when partnered with business, NASA actually gives back to the American people in terms of jobs and technology.

Finally, Source D, which discusses Virgin Galactic's new "space tourism," strongly suggests that business is much more efficient in terms of monetary cost at sending individuals into space. This fact supports the thesis that America's space future lies with business partnerships. Considering the financial uncertainty of the last 5 years, we cannot and should not fund NASA solely by government. As Source C and D show us, NASA can continue to function when partnered with private business.

As you can see, we have tackled steps 7 and 8. The amount of prewriting we completed with these steps will be of great benefit to us as we compose a response to the RST. For now, however, we must move on to Step 9: Making an Outline. Please note that our outline need not be "formal" or overly detailed. We just need to do enough in order to provide structure and organization to our own writing. Look at our sample below:

 # Sample Outline for Space Exploration RST

I. Introduction

    a. Attention grabber: Shocking Statement

    b. Thesis statement: Yes, the American people should continue to fund space exploration as long as the government partners with private business.

II. Body

    a. Argument A: Rampant Poverty and Government Inefficiency

    b. Argument B: NASA and Business Partnership

III. Conclusion

    a. Reworking of thesis

    b. Answering the So What? Question (What is really important about the thesis of this paper?)

 # Step 10: Writing the Essay

Now that we have completed all the necessary steps for the RST, it is time to actually do the essay writing. What we want you to note at this point in the process is that a majority of the work of our writing has already been completed. The actual writing of the RST essay should be quite easy. Here is our sample below.

According to statistics published in *The New York Times*, 104 million Americans living in a family of three live TWICE below the poverty line (Source A). As shocking as this is, here's another: Six million people in our great country have no source of income other than the food stamps that they receive from the Federal government (Source A). Moreover, turn on the news and you will find that the United States' economy is still struggling to right itself. In the midst of all this heartache and economic misery, it *seems* ridiculous that the American people should lavish funds on its space exploration program. One might ask, "Why should we spend money on space travel when so many are living below the poverty level?" The answer is simple: Space exploration — when our money is spent and invested wisely — is not only good for our economy; it is good for the health of our nation. Therefore, the American people should continue to fund space exploration as long as the government creates successful partnerships with private business.

There is an old saying that goes something like this: "Big government spends money wastefully. Business and private enterprise are much more efficient." Historically speaking, one need look no further than the federal government's funding of the space program to see that this axiom is true. During the 1980s and 90s, when the United States had a space shuttle program, it cost the American taxpayer 500 to 700 million dollars to blast the rocket ship into space (Source B). As staggering as that sum is, consider the following statistic: The place that the space shuttle flew to — the International Space Station — funded partly by the United States cost an approximate 100 billion dollars (Source B). These numbers are very hard to fathom. Proof of the excess and wastefulness of this spending can be found in the private business community's newfound passion to space exploration. Consider the company, Virgin Galactic. In its fledgling space travel program, it cost a mere 200,000 dollars a ticket for a tourist to take a ride into outer space (Source D). Compare this $200,000 cost in Source D with the staggering sum of $500 to $700 million price tag the American people paid each time the space shuttle flew into outer space (Source B). It seems, and it is true, that the private business community knows how to make space travel much more cost effective.

Should America, then, give up its publically funded space program? The answer is an absolute, "No!" NASA, when partnered with private business, can actually keep space travel costs down by benefitting the local economies of the states in our great country. Take, for example, the case of California. Through a program called "Small Business Research/Small Business Technology Transfer," NASA pumped 1.1 billion dollars into the local economy of the state, creating partnerships with small businesses to create technological advances in science that NASA can use in outer space (Source C). $238 million of that money went directly to partnerships with 247 local companies (Source C). The implications of these statistics are amazing. Part of the poverty noted in Source A, comes in large part due to the low-paying jobs that most Americans have. In the case of "the Small Business Research/Small Business Technology Transfer," people who are struggling can regain some dignity and self-worth with hire-paying jobs, funded, in part, by NASA's partnership. These businesses, in turn, create technologies that not only make NASA function more efficiently — it also benefits our economy. Here's just a partial list of what NASA and the business community have created: more efficient planes, more efficient trucks, better water-filtration systems, and innovations in cleaning up environmental contamination. When partnered with private business, funding NASA is a win-win situation for all.

Consider the fact that in America 46 million people today live on food stamps, up from 26.3 million in 2007 (Source A). America should be ashamed of itself for having this many people struggling to provide the bare basics of life, such as feeding oneself and one's family. There is no dignity in poverty. When the U.S. government spends its money wisely, it can help these poor people lift themselves out of poverty. By having NASA partner with local business, we can have the best of both worlds: First and foremost, we can create well-paying jobs and give people dignity by putting them back to work; second, we can continue our noble goal of space travel and space exploration by making ever-more advances in technology. It seems that America can keep its space travel programs and pump life into its ailing economy!

# Step 11: Looking at the Verbs

Now that we have completed the essay, it is time to consider our last step, number 11: the use of active verbs. After many years in education, we have learned that the key to quality writing is contained within the verbs. Using precise, descriptive action verbs is a sure way to improve the value of what you have written. This list is given to you in Appendix A. Look back through the sample essay. Did the author do an adequate job with the action verbs? Which ones would you change?

# Analysis of Sample Essay

You may have been wondering through this entire process, "How will the PARCC grade my essay?" Well, we're glad you asked the question. In terms of the writing you will complete on the test, the PARCC has defined quality written expression in four categories:

1.  Development of Ideas,
2.  Organization,
3.  Clarity of Language, and
4.  Knowledge of Language and Conventions.

By "Development of Ideas," the makers of the PARCC refer to the ways in which arguments are developed and maintained throughout the course of the essay. Some questions might be: "Did the author use evidence from the text?" "Did this evidence come from more than one source?" "Did the author successfully have the two sources interact with each other?" As you can see, these questions are quite difficult and will take time for you to master. However, you can see these principles in action if you read carefully our sample essay above. We did cite evidence from both sources. We did have the two sources interact with each other. For example, let's take a closer look at this position of the essay:

The place that the space shuttle flew to — the International Space Station — funded partly by the United States cost an approximate 100 billion dollars (Source B). These numbers are very hard to fathom. Proof of the excess and wastefulness of this spending can be found in the private business community's newfound passion to space exploration. Consider the company, Virgin Galactic. In its fledgling space travel program, it cost a mere 200,000 dollars a ticket for a tourist to take a ride into outer space (Source D). Compare this $200,000 cost in Source D with the staggering sum of $500 to $700 million price tag the American people paid each time the space shuttle flew into outer space (Source B).

and

$238 million of that money went directly to partnerships with 247 local companies (Source C). The implications of these statistics are amazing. Part of the poverty noted in Source A, comes in large part due to the low-paying jobs that most Americans have. In the case of "the Small Business Research/Small Business Technology Transfer," people who are struggling can regain some dignity and self-worth with hire-paying jobs, funded, in part, by NASA's partnership.

In the first excerpt, Sources B and D are used in conjunction with each other. In the second, Sources C and A talk with each other. These two excerpts exemplify what we mean about having the sources talk to each other.

Second, the PARCC will look at the organization of your writing. This, in fact, should come as no surprise at all. Organization is a key facet of all good writing, regardless of where it is done. Since we carefully followed our outline, we organized our work. The three main parts of the essay are clearly present: Introduction, body, and conclusion.

The next criterion, "clarity of language," will look at your writing style and the effectiveness of that style. "What is writing style?" It deals with the author's ability to effectively use vocabulary, including content-specific words, to use vivid and proper description, and to appropriately use transitional words throughout the piece. (Check our Appendix B for transitional words.) Style, then, is nothing more than the writer's identity on paper. What the PARCC cares about most is simple: Is your style clear, concise, and to the point? There is nothing worse than reading an essay that lacks clarity and is difficult to read because the writer lacks a command of language.

Looking at our sample essay: What would you say of the style? Look back at our choice of vocabulary: Did we use vocabulary terms that were appropriate to research and statistics? Were our descriptions of the research sources clear? Was any of the wording ambiguous and difficult to comprehend? Could something we wrote have been written more clearly? All of these questions are great starting points when looking at style.

Finally, the PARCC will consider your knowledge of language and conventions. This is where your knowledge of grammar, mechanics, and usage will come to play. Were there any mistakes in these three categories? Did the author go back and edit the work? Does the work read effortlessly? Does poor grammar become a distraction or a nuisance? Our sample essay, we believe, does pretty well in this area, and gives you an RST essay that is free of grammatical issues and reads as thought it were edited (which it was!).

In order to assist you in the skill of evaluating writing, we have included a checklist for you based upon PARCC writing standards and the PARCC rubric in the back of the book. You might wish to score our sample essay using the rubric.

##  Summary of the RST in English

We have covered a great many skills and issues in this chapter concerning the RST, including the skills involved, the necessary steps in terms of reading and prewriting, and the structure and organization of a model essay. We are under no delusions that this task is easy, but we are absolutely certain that the more closely you follow our 11 steps and the more you practice getting your sources "talking," the better you will be at the RST task.

In the interest of helping you achieve success on the RST in English, we will give you three sample essay prompts with the accompanying graphic organizers for you to use. You are about to venture on a highly productive journey. Refer back often to our model essay and when you first start, try not to skip any of the 11 steps.

One last thing:

We have said this numerous times in this book: Your ability to write well depends upon your ability to read well. Make sure you read and understand the texts before you begin any of the writing work.

| CCSS Alignment | |
|---|---|
| RL.1 | Cite strong and textual evidence. |
| RL.5 | Analyze how an author's choices contribute to its overall structure. |
| RI.7 | Integrate and evaluate multiple sources of information presented in different media or formats (e.g., visually, quantitatively) as well as in words in order to address a question or solve a problem. |
| L.1 | Demonstrate command of the conventions of standard English grammar and usage when writing. |
| L.3 | Apply knowledge of language to understand how language functions in different contexts. |
| L.5 | Demonstrate understanding of figurative language, word relationships, and nuances in word meanings. |
| W.1 | Write arguments to support claims in an analysis of substantive topics or texts, using valid reasoning and relevant and sufficient evidence. |
| W.2 | Write informative/explanatory texts to examine and convey complex ideas, concepts, and information clearly and accurately through the effective selection, organization, and analysis of content. |
| W.5 | Develop and strengthen writing as needed by planning, revising, editing, and rewriting. |
| W.6 | Use technology to produce, publish, and update individual writing products. |

[ELA TASK GENERATION MODEL: 7B5PBA]

## RST #2: Native American Contributions

85 Minutes

As the first known inhabitants of North America, Native Americans established a culture rich in literature, song, and art. In particular, a variety of Native American tribes in the United States have made great contributions to American society and culture.

For this writing task, you have reviewed four sources regarding the contributions of Native Americans to our land called America. These four texts provide information to begin drafting your own argument.

- **Source A:** Excerpt, "The North American Indian" (Edward S. Curtis)
- **Source B:** "The Lynx and Hare" (A Chippewa Fable)
- **Source C:** Photograph, "Navajo Family" (Edward S. Curtis)
- **Source D:** "Untold Stories of The Second World War: The Navajo (Part 1)" http://www.youtube.com/watch?v=LN2oKqa1o04

What is the significance of Native American contributions to American society and culture? Write an informative piece that addresses and analyzes the question and supports your position with evidence from at least three of the four sources. Be sure to acknowledge competing views. You may give examples from past and current events or issues to illustrate and clarify your position. You may refer to the sources by their titles (Source A, Source B, Source C, Source D).

## SOURCE A

| Excerpt, "The North American Indian" | My Thought Processes |
|---|---|
| Since known to history, the many bands of Apache have occupied the mountains and plains of southern Arizona and New Mexico, northern Sonora and Chihuahua, and western Texas—an area greater than that of the states of New York, Pennsylvania, New Jersey, Connecticut, Massachusetts, Vermont, Maine, Ohio, North Carolina, South Carolina, and West Virginia. They were always known as "wild" Indians, and indeed their early warfare with all neighboring tribes, as well as their recent persistent hostility toward our Government, which precipitated a "war of extermination," bear out the appropriateness of the designation. An admission of fear of anything is hard to elicit from the weakest of Indian tribes, but all who lived within raiding distance of the Apache, save the Navaho, their Athapascan cousins, freely admit that for generations before their subjugation the Apache were constantly held in mortal terror. | |

*(continued)*

| Excerpt, "The North American Indian" | My Thought Processes |
|---|---|
| Through the constant depredations carried on against the Mexican settlements in northern Sonora and Chihuahua, under the leadership of Juan José, an Apache chief educated among the Mexicans, those two states were led, in 1837, to offer a bounty for Apache scalps. The horror of this policy lay in the fact that the scalp of a friendly Indian brought the same reward as that of the fiercest warrior, and worse still, no exception was made of women or children. Nothing could have been more effective than this scalp bounty in arousing all the savagery in these untamed denizens of the mountains, and both Mexico and the United States paid dearly in lives for every Apache scalp taken under this barbarous system. Predatory warfare continued unabated during the next forty years in spite of all the Mexican government could do. With the consummation of the treaty of Guadalupe Hidalgo, in 1848, the Apache problem became one to be solved by the United States as well.<br><br>In 1864, under General James H. Carleton, the "war of extermination" was begun in a most systematic manner. On April 20 this officer communicated a proposal of co-operation to Don Ignacio Pesqueira, Governor of Sonora, saying: "If your excellency will put a few hundred men into the field on the first day of next June, and keep them in hot pursuit of the Apaches of Sonora, say for sixty or ninety days, we will either exterminate the Indians or so diminish their numbers that they will cease their murdering and robbing propensities and live at peace."<br><br>This request was met. The settlers in Arizona, under agreement, placed a force in the field provisioned with army supplies. Several hundred Pima, Papago, and Maricopa Indians also were supplied with guns, ammunition, and clothing, and pressed into service; but a year's effort netted the combined forces little gain. Although two hundred Apache were killed and many head of stolen stock recovered, practically no advance toward the termination of hostilities was accomplished. | |

*(continued)*

| Excerpt, "The North American Indian" | My Thought Processes |
|---|---|
| In April, 1865, Inspector-General Davis arranged a conference at the Copper Mines in New Mexico with Victorio, Nané, Acosta, and other chiefs, among whom were Pasquin, Cassari, and Salvador, sons of Mangas Coloradas, through which he learned of the existence of dire destitution among the Apache and a desire for peace on condition that they be permitted to occupy their native haunts. But the Government had adopted a policy of removal by which the Arizona Apache desiring peace should join the Mescaleros at the Bosque Redondo in New Mexico. To this they flatly refused to agree, and the warfare continued. | |

## SOURCE B

| "The Lynx and Hare" (A Chippewa Fable) | My Thought Processes |
|---|---|
| A lynx almost famished, met a hare one day in the woods, in the winter season, when food was very scarce. The hare, however, stood up on a rock, and was safe from its enemy.<br><br>"Wabose," said the lynx, in a very kind manner, "come here, my little white one, I wish to talk to you."<br><br>"Oh no," replied the hare, "I am afraid of you, and my mother told me never to go and talk to strangers."<br><br>"You are very pretty," answered the lynx, "and a very obedient child to your parents, but you must know that I am a relative of yours. I wish to send some word to your lodge. Come down and see me."<br><br>The hare was pleased to be called pretty, and when she heard that it was a relative, she jumped down from the place where she stood, and was immediately torn in pieces by the lynx. | |

## SOURCE C

### "Navajo Family," by Edward S. Curtis

My Thought Process:

## SOURCE D

## Untold Stories of The Second World War: The Navajo

This short documentary video chronicles the critical role the Navajo Indian people played as "code talkers" in World War II.

*One hundred years before World War II, the Navajo people were fighting the U.S. government. The United States, during that time period, was in the midst of "relocating" Native American peoples, forcing them to live on reservations. Children on the reservations were forced to speak English only, to give up their Navajo language. Talking Navajo was actually on offense that was reported to superiors at school.*

*After Pearl Harbor, as the United States was rebuilding its Pacific navy, the U.S. government found that the Japanese were able to decipher the codes the U.S. used to communicate. That's when the United States turned to young male Navajo Indians to use their native language as "code talkers." This language that the Japanese government was never able to interpret or to "crack"—was the language that helped the U.S. government win World War II in the Pacific. Ironically, the United States Marines had turned to the Navajo people to use their language so that the Japanese could no longer break their codes.*

| "Untold Stories of the Second World War: The Navajo (Part 1)" |
| :---: |
| *http://www.youtube.com/watch?v=LN2oKqa1o04* |

**My Thought Processes**

## Prewriting

RST Graphic Organizer

Topic:

My Thesis Statement:

| Source A | Source B | Source C | Source D |
|---|---|---|---|
| | | | |

Exactly how do the sources talk with each other?

## Space for your Outline:

Write your essay on loose-leaf paper or in a notebook. Review your work using the Scoring Checklist and Scoring Rubric for Analytic Writing in the back of the book.

| CCSS Alignment | |
|---|---|
| RL.1 | Cite strong and textual evidence. |
| RL.5 | Analyze how an author's choices contribute to its overall structure. |
| RI.7 | Integrate and evaluate multiple sources of information presented in different media or formats (e.g., visually, quantitatively) as well as in words in order to address a question or solve a problem. |
| L.1 | Demonstrate command of the conventions of standard English grammar and usage when writing. |
| L.3 | Apply knowledge of language to understand how language functions in different contexts. |
| L.5 | Demonstrate understanding of figurative language, word relationships, and nuances in word meanings. |
| W.1 | Write arguments to support claims in an analysis of substantive topics or texts, using valid reasoning and relevant and sufficient evidence. |
| W.2 | Write informative/explanatory texts to examine and convey complex ideas, concepts, and information clearly and accurately through the effective selection, organization, and analysis of content. |
| W.5 | Develop and strengthen writing as needed by planning, revising, editing, and rewriting. |
| W.6 | Use technology to produce, publish, and update individual writing products. |

[ELA TASK GENERATION MODEL: 8B1PBA]

## RST #3: African American Literary Experience

85 Minutes

The African American influence on American literature is omnipresent in our society today. Even before "The Harlem Renaissance," a rebirth of African American art and culture located in New York City, many African American speakers and writers have expressed the African American experience in simple, yet beautiful ways.

You have reviewed three texts from various African American contributors. These three texts provide information you can use to formulate your argument,

- **Source A:** Excerpt from *Up from Slavery: An Autobiography* (Booker T. Washington)

- **Source B:** "O, Pity the Slave Mother" (William Wells Brown)

- **Source C:** "Malcolm X: Life and Death" (video): *http://watchmojo.com/video/id/9207/*

Consider the ideas and arguments that these three texts use in their characterization of how the African American speakers, writers, and leaders have contributed to African American literature experience as a whole. Write an informative piece that addresses the question and supports your position with evidence from at least two of the three sources. Be sure to acknowledge competing views. You may give examples from past and current events or issues to illustrate and clarify your position. You may refer to the sources by their titles (Source A, Source B, Source C).

## SOURCE A

| Excerpt from *Up from Slavery: An Autobiography* (Booker T. Washington) | My Thought Process |
|---|---|
| In those days, and later as a young man, I used to try to picture in my imagination the feelings and ambitions of a white boy with absolutely no limit placed upon his aspirations and activities. I used to envy the white boy who had no obstacles placed in the way of his becoming a Congressman, Governor, Bishop, or President by reason of the accident of his birth or race. I used to picture the way that I would act under such circumstances; how I would begin at the bottom and keep rising until I reached the highest round of success. | |

*(continued)*

| Excerpt from *Up from Slavery: An Autobiography* (Booker T. Washington) | My Thought Process |
|---|---|
| In later years, I confess that I do not envy the white boy as I once did. I have learned that success is to be measured not so much by the position that one has reached in life as by the obstacles which he has overcome while trying to succeed. Looked at from this standpoint, I almost reached the conclusion that often the Negro boy's birth and connection with an unpopular race is an advantage, so far as real life is concerned. With few exceptions, the Negro youth must work harder and must perform his tasks even better than a white youth in order to secure recognition. But out of the hard and unusual struggle through which he is compelled to pass, he gets a strength, a confidence, that one misses whose pathway is comparatively smooth by reason of birth and race.<br><br>From any point of view, I had rather be what I am, a member of the Negro race, than be able to claim membership with the most favoured of any other race. I have always been made sad when I have heard members of any race claiming rights or privileges, or certain badges of distinction, on the ground simply that they were members of this or that race, regardless of their own individual worth or attainments. I have been made to feel sad for such persons because I am conscious of the fact that mere connection with what is known as a superior race will not permanently carry an individual forward unless he has individual worth, and mere connection with what is regarded as an inferior race will not finally hold an individual back if he possesses intrinsic, individual merit. Every persecuted individual and race should get much consolation out of the great human law, which is universal and eternal, that merit, no matter under what skin found, is, in the long run, recognized and rewarded. This I have said here, not to call attention to myself as an individual, but to the race to which I am proud to belong. | |

## SOURCE B

| "O, Pity the Slave Mother"<br>(William Wells Brown) | My Thought Process |
|---|---|
| **O, PITY THE SLAVE MOTHER.**<br><br>I pity the slave mother, careworn and weary,<br>  Who sighs as she presses her babe to her breast;<br>I lament her sad fate, all so hopeless and dreary,<br>  I lament for her woes, and her wrongs unredressed.<br>O who can imagine her heart's deep emotion,<br>  As she thinks of her children about to be sold;<br>You may picture the bounds of the rock-girdled<br>    ocean,<br>  But the grief of that mother can never be known.<br>The mildew of slavery has blighted each blossom,<br>  That ever has bloomed in her path-way below;<br>It has froze every fountain that gushed in her bosom,<br>  And chilled her heart's verdure with pitiless woe;<br>Her parents, her kindred, all crushed by oppression;<br>  Her husband still doomed in its desert to stay;<br>No arm to protect from the tyrant's aggression—<br>  She must weep as she treads on her desolate way.<br>O, slave mother, hope! see—the nation is shaking!<br>  The arm of the Lord is awake to thy wrong!<br>The slave-holder's heart now with terror is quaking,<br>  Salvation and Mercy to Heaven belong!<br>Rejoice, O rejoice! for the child thou art rearing,<br>  May one day lift up its unmanacled form,<br>While hope, to thy heart, like the rain-bow so<br>    cheering,<br>  Is born, like the rain-bow, 'mid tempest and storm. | |

## SOURCE C

*The following video highlights the significant events that made up the life and death of Malcolm X. Being a proponent of black pride, Malcolm X was heavily involved in groups that were often viewed as extremist. Conversing with the Islamic group's leader, Malcolm X stressed that it was most important for black Americans to stand up for their rights, and to fight at all costs. Quickly moving through the Islamic ranks, Malcolm X became very persuasive in expanding its membership. Especially when speaking to college students, Malcolm X proclaimed that his race, the black race, was the supreme race. He shared his passion for change throughout his travels around the world. While speaking in Manhattan, he was shot him to death by Islamic members. He is still remembered today as a prominent African American activist.*

| "Malcolm X: Life and Death" (video): *http://watchmojo.com/video/id/9207/* |
| --- |
| **Video Notes:** |

# Prewriting

**RST Graphic Organizer**

Topic:

My Thesis Statement:

| Source A | Source B | Source C |
|---|---|---|
| | | |

Exactly how do the sources talk with each other?

**Space for your Outline:**

Write Your Essay Response on loose-leaf paper or in a notebook.
Then, check it with the Scoring Checklist and Scoring Rubric for
Analytic Writing that are found at the back of the book.

| CCSS Alignment | |
|---|---|
| RL.1 | Cite strong and textual evidence. |
| RL.5 | Analyze how an author's choices contribute to its overall structure. |
| RI.7 | Integrate and evaluate multiple sources of information presented in different media or formats (e.g., visually, quantitatively) as well as in words in order to address a question or solve a problem. |
| L.1 | Demonstrate command of the conventions of standard English grammar and usage when writing. |
| L.3 | Apply knowledge of language to understand how language functions in different contexts. |
| L.5 | Demonstrate understanding of figurative language, word relationships, and nuances in word meanings. |
| W.1 | Write arguments to support claims in an analysis of substantive topics or texts, using valid reasoning and relevant and sufficient evidence. |
| W.2 | Write informative/explanatory texts to examine and convey complex ideas, concepts, and information clearly and accurately through the effective selection, organization, and analysis of content. |
| W.5 | Develop and strengthen writing as needed by planning, revising, editing, and rewriting. |
| W.6 | Use technology to produce, publish, and update individual writing products. |

[ELA TASK GENERATION MODEL: 6B10PBA]

## RST #4: Bullying

85 Minutes

Recent events in America have raised the level of concern about bullying, especially in middle school.

You have reviewed four sources regarding the causes and effects of bullying and what could be done to prevent it from happening in the middle school. These four texts provide information to begin drafting your own argument.

- **Source A:** "Bullying: From a Teacher's Perspective" (excerpt from article, Dennis M. Fare)

- **Source B:** "Bullying: Prevention and Tips" *http://watchmojo.com/video/ id/7327/*

- **Source C:** Cyber Bullying Statistics, *www.bullyingstatistics.org/content/cyber-bullying-statistics.html*

- **Source D:** Sample Anti-Bullying School Policy Introduction

What should be done to stop bullying in middle school? Write an informative piece that addresses the question and supports your position with evidence from at least three of the four sources. Be sure to acknowledge competing views. You may give examples from past and current events or issues to illustrate and clarify your position. You may refer to the sources by their titles (Source A, Source B, Source C, Source D).

## SOURCE A

| "Bullying: From a Teacher's Perspective" (excerpt from article by Dennis M. Fare) | My Thought Processes |
|---|---|
| I stand in the hallways sometimes, waiting for my students to arrive to their next class. I often wonder what goes on through their heads as they pile into narrow doorways like herded cattle. How do they make it through their days? <br><br> And I stand in front of them, discussing grammar and literature and social issues, when in reality, how can I expect them to care at all sometimes? | |

*(continued)*

| "Bullying: From a Teacher's Perspective" (excerpt from article by Dennis M. Fare) | My Thought Processes |
|---|---|
| With Facebook, Instagram, Twitter, and every other form of social media, teenagers need to be heard. What happens, though, when their status update isn't liked? Or their tweet isn't re-tweeted? As an adult, we still rely on such self-validation that I cannot begin to imagine what my former teenage-self would have done or felt in a similar world. | |
| I once saw a student poking another. Not the virtual Facebook-kind, but rather, one student actually putting his finger repeatedly on the back of the head of a classmate. The look on their faces remained quite similar, ironically—both uncomfortable—the former trying to avoid the poke, and the other trying to be "cool" in doing so in the first place. | |
| And when I asked them to stop, neither looked relieved. They have somehow become accustomed to putting on this exterior just to get through their every day existence. | |
| Maybe I take this too much to heart, but I've been there. And while I wouldn't ever, ever want to go back, I feel like I'm there every day being back in the classroom even so many years later. | |
| As adults, we take for granted how strong our American students actually are. We constantly knock them for their lack of work ethic, or their absence of intrinsic care, but what about their will just to get by in a day and age where it might be so hard to do so in the first place? | |
| I think our students deserve a little more credit. | |

## SOURCE B

### Bullying: Prevention and Tips

*This video, published by WatchMojo, looks closely at the variety of forms of bully-ing, from verbal, physical or emotional abuse, but no matter how bullying manifests, this interview makes note that it is harmful to the victim. Further, this video also discusses how a student can manage and deal with these types of bullying.*

| "Bullying: Prevention and Tips" *http://watchmojo.com/video/id/7327/* |
|---|
| My Thought Processes |

## SOURCE C

| Cyber Bullying Statistics<br>*www.bullyingstatistics.org* | My Thought Processes |
|---|---|
| Cyber bullying statistics refers to Internet bullying. Cyber bullying is a form of teen violence that can do lasting harm to young people. Bullying statistics show that cyber bully-ing is a serious problem among teens. By being more aware of cyber bullying, teens and adults can help to fight it.<br><br>Cyber bullying affects many adolescents and teens on a daily basis. Cyber bullying involves using technology, like cell phones and the Internet, to bully or harass another person. Cyber bullying can take many forms: | |

*(continued)*

| Cyber Bullying Statistics<br>*www.bullyingstatistics.org* | **My Thought Processes** |
|---|---|
| • Sending mean messages or threats to a person's email account or cell phone<br><br>• Spreading rumors online or through texts<br><br>• Posting hurtful or threatening messages on social networking sites or web pages<br><br>• Stealing a person's account information to break into their account and send damaging messages<br><br>• Pretending to be someone else online to hurt another person<br><br>• Taking unflattering pictures of a person and spreading them through cell phones or the Internet<br><br>• Sexting, or circulating sexually suggestive pictures or messages about a person<br><br>Cyber bullying can be very damaging to adolescents and teens. It can lead to anxiety, depression, and even suicide. Also, once things are circulated on the Internet, they may never disappear, resurfacing at later times to renew the pain of cyber bullying.<br><br>Many cyber bullies think that bullying others online is funny. Cyber bullies may not realize the consequences for themselves of cyber bullying. The things teens post online now may reflect badly on them later when they apply for college or a job. Cyber bullies can lose their cell phone or online accounts for cyber bullying. Also, cyber bullies and their parents may face legal charges for cyber bullying, and if the cyber bullying was sexual in nature or involved sexting, the results can include being registered as a sex offender. Teens may think that if they use a fake name they won't get caught, but there are many ways to track some one who is cyber bullying. | |

*(continued)*

| Cyber Bullying Statistics<br>*www.bullyingstatistics.org* | My Thought Processes |
|---|---|
| Despite the potential damage of cyber bullying, it is alarmingly common among adolescents and teens. According to Cyber bullying statistics from the i-SAFE foundation:<br><br>• Over half of adolescents and teens have been bullied online, and about the same number have engaged in cyber bullying.<br><br>• More than 1 in 3 young people have experienced cyber threats online.<br><br>• Over 25 percent of adolescents and teens have been bullied repeatedly through their cell phones or the Internet.<br><br>• Well over half of young people do not tell their parents when cyber bullying occurs.<br><br>The Harford County Examiner reported similarly concerning cyber bullying statistics:<br><br>• Around half of teens have been the victims of cyber bullying<br><br>• Only 1 in 10 teens tells a parent if they have been a cyber bully victim<br><br>• Fewer than 1 in 5 cyber bullying incidents are reported to law enforcement<br><br>• 1 in 10 adolescents or teens have had embarrassing or damaging pictures taken of themselves without their permission, often using cell phone cameras<br><br>• About 1 in 5 teens have posted or sent sexually suggestive or nude pictures of themselves to others<br><br>• Girls are somewhat more likely than boys to be involved in cyber bullying<br><br>The Cyberbullying Research Center also did a series of surveys that found these cyber bullying statistics:<br><br>• Over 80 percent of teens use a cell phone regularly, making it the most popular form of technology and a common medium for cyber bullying | |

*(continued)*

| Cyber Bullying Statistics<br>www.bullyingstatistics.org | My Thought Processes |
|---|---|
| • About half of young people have experienced some form of cyber bullying, and 10 to 20 percent experience it regularly<br><br>• Mean, hurtful comments and spreading rumors are the most common type of cyber bullying<br><br>• Girls are at least as likely as boys to be cyber bullies or their victims<br><br>• Boys are more likely to be threatened by cyber bullies than girls<br><br>• Cyber bullying affects all races<br><br>• Cyber bullying victims are more likely to have low self esteem and to consider suicide<br><br>Parents and teens can do some things that help reduce the cyber bullying statistics:<br><br>• Talks to teens about cyber bullying, explaining that it is wrong and can have serious consequences. Make a rule that teens may not send mean or damaging messages, even if someone else started it, or suggestive pictures or messages or they will lose their cell phone and computer privileges for a time.<br><br>• Encourage teens to tell an adult if cyber bullying is occurring. Tell them if they are the victims they will not be punished, and reassure them that being bullied is not their fault.<br><br>• Teens should keep cyber bullying messages as proof that the cyber bullying is occurring.<br><br>• The teens' parents may want to talk to the parents of the cyber bully, to the bully's Internet or cell phone provider, and/or to the police about the messages, especially if they are threatening or sexual in nature.<br><br>• Try blocking the person sending the messages. It may be necessary to get a new phone number or email address and to be more cautious about giving out the new number or address. | |

*(continued)*

| Cyber Bullying Statistics<br>*www.bullyingstatistics.org* | My Thought Processes |
|---|---|
| • Teens should never tell their password to anyone except a parent, and should not write it down in a place where it could be found by others.<br><br>• Teens should not share anything through text or instant messaging on their cell phone or the Internet that they would not want to be made public—remind teens that the person they are talking to in messages or online may not be who they think they are, and that things posted electronically may not be secure.<br><br>• Encourage teens never to share personal information online or to meet someone they only know online.<br><br>• Keep the computer in a shared space like the family room, and do not allow teens to have Internet access in their own rooms.<br><br>• Encourage teens to have times when they turn off the technology, such as at family meals or after a certain time at night.<br><br>• Parents may want to wait until high school to allow their teens to have their own email and cell phone accounts, and even then parents should still have access to the accounts.<br><br>If teens have been the victims or perpetuators of cyber bullying they may need to talk to a counselor or therapist to overcome depression or other harmful effects of cyber bullying.<br><br>Sources:<br><br>Richard Webster, Harford County Examiner, "From cyber bullying to sexting: What on your kids' cell?" [online]<br><br>i-SAFE Inc., "Cyber Bullying: Statistics and Tips" [online]<br><br>Cyberbullying Research Center, "Summary of our cyberbullying research from 2004-2010" [online]<br><br>National Crime Prevention Council, "Cyberbullying" [online] | |

## SOURCE D

| Sample Anti-Bullying School Policy Introduction | My Thought Processes |
|---|---|
| This district has approved the first school district Anti-Bullying policy in its history. | |
| The district's Anti-Bullying Policy specifically prohibits bullying of or by any district student or employee, based on the established definition of bullying: | |
| "Bullying" means systematically and chronically inflicting physical hurt or psychological distress on one or more students or employees. | |
| As our school district goal is for protection of students and their feelings of safety and belonging, this Anti-Bullying policy will follow all relevant protocol. The policy requires teachers and staff to utilize a series of prevention and intervention activities, as per necessary and required district-wide training. | |
| All students will be made to feel safe, and as such, a chain of command for reporting such bullying incidents has been put into place to ensure that communication is shared throughout the district as a whole. | |
| Once a bullying incident is reported, an investigation will then take place, and subsequently, a judgment will be made after all evidence is presented to our Anti-Bullying committee. | |
| Our Anti-Bullying Policy was created by a community-included committee, which implemented the input from community members and parental involvement. | |

# Prewriting

**RST Graphic Organizer**

Topic:

My Thesis Statement:

| Source A | Source B | Source C | Source D |
|----------|----------|----------|----------|
|          |          |          |          |

Exactly how do the sources talk with each other?

**Space for your Outline:**

Write your Essay Response on loose-leaf paper or in a notebook. Make use of the Scoring Checklist and Scoring Rubric to go over your work.

## CHAPTER 7

# The Research Simulation Task: History

 ## Introduction

Congratulations! You have made it far in your progress on the Research Simulation Task. Chapter 6, the English RST, should have prepared you for this new-type of synthesis-based writing. You have learned how to

- take notes while you read;

- breakdown the RST prompt;

- prewrite using a graphic organizer;

- create a workable outline;

- create a high-quality essay in the RST style;

- get your sources talking to each other; and

- edit your work using vivid, action verbs.

All of these skills are no small accomplishment.

The good news is that you have all the necessary skills to perform at a high level on the PARCC's RST. Now, it's only a matter of you transferring these skills to different subjects. The rest of the book, including this chapter, will take you through the process of completing the RST in a variety of academic subjects. This chapter will focus on social studies/history.

At this point, you might be tired of hearing that the PARCC views reading and writing as a combined literacy task, but we cannot say it too often. The better you read, the easier and more effective your writing will be. Therefore, in this chapter, we will take you, step-by-step, through the completion of a RST in history. First, we will actively read the texts, using our two-column approach. Afterward, we will use the 11-step process to completing the written portion of the RST. Next, we will give you a model essay. Finally, you will do two practice RSTs in history. By the end of this chapter, you will be a pro when it comes to the RST in history.

| CCSS Alignment | |
|---|---|
| RH.1 | Cite specific textual evidence. |
| RH.5 | Analyze in detail how a complex primary source is structured, including how key sentences, paragraphs, and larger portions of the text contribute to the whole. |
| RH.8 | Evaluate an author's premises, claims, and evidence by corroborating or challenging them with other information. |
| RH.9 | Integrate information from diverse sources, both primary and secondary, into a coherent understanding of an idea or event, noting discrepancies among sources. |
| RI.7 | Integrate and evaluate multiple sources of information presented in different media or formats (e.g., visually, quantitatively) as well as in words in order to address a question or solve a problem. |
| L.1 | Demonstrate command of the conventions of standard English grammar and usage when writing. |
| L.3 | Apply knowledge of language to understand how language functions in different contexts. |
| W.1 | Write arguments to support claims in an analysis of substantive topics or texts, using valid reasoning and relevant and sufficient evidence. |
| W.6 | Use technology to produce, publish, and update individual writing products. |
| WHST.1 | Write arguments focused on discipline-specific content. |
| WHST.4 | Produce clear and coherent writing in which the development, organization, and style are appropriate to task, purpose, and audience. |

[ELA TASK GENERATION MODEL: 7B1PBA]

Let's begin with the model RST:

## RST #1: Fighting Segregation

85 Minutes

Each day in school, children across the United States repeat these words of the Pledge of Allegiance: "With liberty and justice for all." However, "liberty and justice for all" was not a reality for ALL American citizens for more than 100 years after the end of the Civil War. Segregation, or the forced separation of the races, was the law in a large portion of the United States. Many brave individuals fought to end segregation.

You have reviewed three sources regarding the segregation in America. These three pieces provide information to begin drafting your own argument.

- **Source A:** Excerpt from "My Bondage and My Freedom," by Frederick Douglass, *http://www.gutenberg.org/files/202/202-h/202-h.htm#link2HCH0008*

- **Source B:** *The Problem We All Live With,* by Norman Rockwell (1968)

- **Source C:** Jim Crow Laws: *http://www.scholastic.com/teachers/article/jim-crow-laws*

What led to the end of the legal segregation of African Americans and whites? Write an information piece that addresses and analyzes the question and supports your position with evidence from at least two of the three sources. Be sure to acknowledge competing views. You may give examples from past and current events or issues to illustrate and clarify your position. You may refer to the sources by their titles (Source A, Source B, Source C).

After reading the RST on the American Dream, you might be thinking that this is a difficult topic, and, yes, you would be right. The above prompt is difficult, in part, because of the number of sources involved. However, we will break it down for you. As you know, before we can attack the RST prompt, we must actively read our three sources. So, let's begin:

## SOURCE A

| SOURCE A: "My Bondage and My Freedom," by Frederick Douglass | Our Thought Processes |
|---|---|
| I have nothing cruel or shocking to relate of my own personal experience, while I remained on Col. Lloyd's plantation, at the home of my old master. An occasional cuff from Aunt Katy, and a regular whipping from old master, such as any heedless and mischievous boy might get from his father, is all that I can mention of this sort. I was not old enough to work in the field, and, there being little else than field work to perform, I had much leisure. The most I had to do, was, to drive up the cows in the evening, to keep the front yard clean, and to perform small errands for my young mistress, Lucretia Auld. I have reasons for thinking this lady was very kindly disposed toward me, and, although I was not often the object of her attention, I constantly regarded her as my friend, and was always glad when it was my privilege to do her a service. In a family where there was so much that was harsh, cold and indifferent, the slightest word or look of kindness passed, with me, for its full value. Miss Lucretia— as[102] we all continued to call her long after her marriage—had bestowed upon me such words and looks as taught me that she pitied me, if she did not love me. In addition to words and looks, she sometimes gave me a piece of bread and butter; a thing not set down in the bill of fare, and which must have been an extra ration, planned aside from either Aunt Katy or old master, solely out of the tender regard and friendship she had for me. Then, too, I one day got into the wars with Uncle Able's son, "Ike," and had got sadly worsted; in fact, the little rascal had struck me directly in the forehead with a sharp piece of cinder, fused with iron, from the old blacksmith's forge, which made a cross in my forehead very plainly to be seen now. The gash bled very freely, and I roared very loudly and betook myself home. The coldhearted Aunt Katy paid no attention either to my wound or my roaring, except to tell me it served me right; I had no business with Ike; it was good for me; I would now keep away *from dem Lloyd niggers.* Miss Lucretia, in this state of the case, came | • While Douglass does not mention extreme brutality, his very acceptance of being owned on a plantation should be worthy of discussion here.<br><br>• This very happiness over bread is saddening, especially for a man who is working hard on the plantation.<br><br>• Douglass is struck by a child! |

*(continued)*

| SOURCE A: "My Bondage and My Freedom," by Frederick Douglass | Our Thought Processes |
|---|---|
| forward; and, in quite a different spirit from that manifested by Aunt Katy, she called me into the parlor (an extra privilege of itself) and, without using toward me any of the hard-hearted and reproachful epithets of my kitchen tormentor, she quietly acted the good Samaritan. With her own soft hand she washed the blood from my head and face, fetched her own balsam bottle, and with the balsam wetted a nice piece of white linen, and bound up my head. The balsam was not more healing to the wound in my head, than her kindness was healing to the wounds in my spirit, made by the unfeeling words of Aunt Katy. After this, Miss Lucretia was my friend. I felt her to be such; and I have no doubt that the simple act of binding up my head, did much to awaken in her mind an interest in my welfare. It is quite true, that this interest was never very marked, and it seldom showed itself in anything more than in giving me a piece of bread when I was hungry; but this was a great favor on a slave plantation, and I was the only one of the children to whom such attention was paid.[103] When very hungry, I would go into the back yard and play under Miss Lucretia's window. When pretty severely pinched by hunger, I had a habit of singing, which the good lady very soon came to understand as a petition for a piece of bread. When I sung under Miss Lucretia's window, I was very apt to get well paid for my music. The reader will see that I now had two friends, both at important points— Mas' Daniel at the great house, and Miss Lucretia at home. From Mas' Daniel I got protection from the bigger boys; and from Miss Lucretia I got bread, by singing when I was hungry, and sympathy when I was abused by that termagant, who had the reins of government in the kitchen. For such friendship I felt deeply grateful, and bitter as are my recollections of slavery, I love to recall any instances of kindness, any sunbeams of humane treatment, which found way to my soul through the iron grating of my house of bondage. Such beams seem all the brighter from the general darkness into which they penetrate, and the impression they make is vividly distinct and beautiful. | • The treatment by those on this plantation is mixed. The idea of friendship seems to be confused.<br><br><br><br>• Douglass shares his coping habits in regards to dealing with his own hunger. |

*(continued)*

| SOURCE A: "My Bondage and My Freedom," by Frederick Douglass | Our Thought Processes |
| --- | --- |
| As I have before intimated, I was seldom whipped—and never severely—by my old master. I suffered little from the treatment I received, except from hunger and cold. These were my two great physical troubles. I could neither get a sufficiency of food nor of clothing; but I suffered less from hunger than from cold. In hottest summer and coldest winter, I was kept almost in a state of nudity; no shoes, no stockings, no jacket, no trowsers; nothing but coarse sackcloth or tow-linen, made into a sort of shirt, reaching down to my knees. This I wore night and day, changing it once a week. In the day time I could protect myself pretty well, by keeping on the sunny side of the house; and in bad weather, in the corner of the kitchen chimney. The great difficulty was, to keep warm during the night. I had no bed. The pigs in the pen had leaves, and the horses in the stable had straw, but the children had no beds. They lodged anywhere in the ample kitchen. I slept, generally, in a little closet, without even a blanket to cover me. In very cold weather. I sometimes got down the bag in which corn[104] meal was usually carried to the mill, and crawled into that. Sleeping there, with my head in and feet out, I was partly protected, though not comfortable. My feet have been so cracked with the frost, that the pen with which I am writing might be laid in the gashes. The manner of taking our meals at old master's, indicated but little refinement. Our corn-meal mush, when sufficiently cooled, was placed in a large wooden tray, or trough, like those used in making maple sugar here in the north. This tray was set down, either on the floor of the kitchen, or out of doors on the ground; and the children were called, like so many pigs; and like so many pigs they would come, and literally devour the mush—some with oyster shells, some with pieces of shingles, and none with spoons. He that eat fastest got most, and he that was strongest got the best place; and few left the trough really satisfied. I was the most unlucky of any, for Aunt Katy had no good feeling for me; and if I pushed any of the other children, or if they told her anything unfavorable of me, she always believed the worst, and was sure to whip me. | • The idea of "suffering" is described here.<br><br><br>• Fed and treated like animals. It is important to discuss the long strides the Black Americans have gained at this point. |

So, what have we learned through reading this text that will help us answer the RST question, "What led to the end of the legal segregation of African Americans and whites?" This text, "My Bondage and My Freedom" documents the physical violence African Americans had to endure when trying to endure slavery. Unfortunately, too, African Americans had to endure humiliation, as shown through the Douglass's interactions with those on the plantation; therefore, it is correct to infer that bravery was required to work towards ending segregation. This bravery, however, did not come in the form of violence; it came in the form of eventual peaceful protest. While African Americans would have been justified to fight violence with violence, they chose the more moral route through the path of escape from slavery's shackles.

Great job analyzing the first text! That didn't seem too difficult, but we are still early in the reading and writing process. We still have two sources to go! The second "text" is actually pretty exciting; it comes in the form of a famous painting. You might be wondering, "Why are they calling a painting a 'text'?" Technically speaking, you are correct that a painting is not a "text," as least not in the traditional sense. The PARCC (and we) consider a painting a "text" because you, the student, can read the painting with the same literacy skills as a traditional text. Questioning, connecting, and inferring are all similar in the interpretation of traditional text as well as art. Here are some questions that are useful when "reading" art:

- What does the title of the painting/artwork suggest? How do you know?

- What is the focal point (the item your eye first goes to) when you look at the text? What is the significance of this focal point?

- Are there any prominent colors used in the painting? What do these colors suggest? (Unfortunately, we can't see the colors here, but Google it—you see so much more!)

- What is in the foreground of the painting and why? The foreground would be "the front of the painting, or the objects in the painting that are closest to you, the viewer.

- What is in the background of the painting and why? The background being those "objects in the back" that are furthest from you, the viewer.

- Are there any small details in the painting that are significant? These would include items that are not easily noticeable upon a first glance. But, when you look at the work more closely, you get to see their significance.

Now that we are prepared with a bunch of valuable questions, let's interact with the picture. Be sure to read "Our thought processes" carefully. Compare what we write to Norman Rockwell's painting.

## SOURCE B

*The Problem We All Live With*, by Norman Rockwell (1968)

### Our Thought Process

• The young girl is the focal point of the painting. She is carrying a ruler, pen, and books, which suggests that she is being escorted to school.

• The tomatoes smashed against the wall (as well as the horrific words written on the wall; i.e. "kkk" and the "n" word) suggest that the young girl is VERY BRAVE.

• The girl is being escorted by U.S. Marshalls, suggesting that the Federal government, not the State government, is enforcing "de-segregation" in the schools.

• The title of the painting, "The Problem We All Live With" implies that racial segregation should be America's problem. In other words, segregation "impacts" us all. African Americans exhibited a great sense of bravery. Racist whites were filled with anger and rage, which is also a very negative place in which to live. Also, there are those whites who helped to end legal segregation, as shown through the men in the painting.

The question now is, "Given this new information, where do we stand in terms of answering the RST question, What led to the end of the legal segregation of African Americans and whites?" And, just as importantly, "How do Sources A and B treat the issue of ending slavery?" Let's talk about the first question first: Considering the tomatoes on the wall and the horrific language, it is very fair to say that the little girl exhibited a high degree of bravery. One must remember, she is not an adult; she's an innocent child and she is putting herself at great risk. In addition, the painting suggests that the Federal government had to intervene to help end segregation. This fact suggests that the local State government was not willing to do so. Lastly, we must also note that the threats of violence mentioned previously in the picture suggest that at least some whites were enraged about ending segregation; this fact reinforcing the topic of bravery. Now for the second question: Sources A and B both suggest that a high degree of bravery, even in the face of threats of physical violence, was required to end segregation. This bravery did not come in the form of violence, but of peace.

Great! We are doing an excellent job analyzing our sources. Now let's head to Source C, which informs us about Jim Crow laws.

## SOURCE C

| Jim Crow Laws: www.scholastic.com/teachers/article/jim-crow-laws | Our Thought Process |
|---|---|
| Jim Crow laws, named for an antebellum minstrel show character, were late-19th-century statutes passed by the legislatures of the Southern states that created a racial caste system in the American South. Although slavery had been abolished, many whites at this time believed that nonwhites were inherently inferior and to support this belief sought rationalizations through religion and science. The U.S. Supreme Court was inclined to agree with the white-supremacist judgment and in 1883 began to strike down the foundations of the post–Civil War Reconstruction, declaring the Civil Rights Act of 1875 unconstitutional. In 1896 it legitimized the principle of "separate but equal" in its ruling *Plessy v. Ferguson*. | • Jim Crow refers to actual "laws" passed by the Southern state governments. It was legal racism.<br><br>• Even the U.S. Supreme Court refused to stop these laws in the late 1800s.<br><br>• "Separate but Equal" was established in 1896. |

(continued)

| Jim Crow Laws: *www.scholastic.com/teachers/article/jim-crow-laws* | Our Thought Process |
|---|---|
| The high court rulings led to a profusion of Jim Crow laws. By 1914 every Southern state had passed laws that created two separate societies — one black, the other white. This artificial structure was maintained by denying the franchise to blacks through the use of devices such as grandfather clauses, poll taxes, and literacy tests. It was further strengthened by the creation of separate facilities in every part of society, including schools, restaurants, streetcars, health-care institutions, and cemeteries. | • By 1914 EVERY Southern state had established segregation as the law of the land.<br><br>• Like Source A, this text describes the literacy tests and the taxes. |
| The first major blow against the Jim Crow system of racial segregation was struck in 1954 by the Supreme Court's decision in *Brown v. Board of Education of Topeka, Kansas*, which declared segregation in the public schools unconstitutional. In the following decade the system slowly crumbled under the onslaught of the civil rights movement. The legal structure of segregation was finally ended by the civil rights legislation of 1964–68.<br><br>Ronald L. Lewis | • 1954: *Brown v. Board of Education of Topeka, Kansas.* This case is a direct reference to Source B, the Norman Rockwell painting. |

So where do we stand on gathering information for the RST question, "What led to the end of the legal segregation of African Americans and whites?" Source C establishes a historical perspective to this answer. From the late 1800s to 1914, ALL states in the South had enacted segregation as the legal and cultural laws of the land. It wasn't until *Brown vs. the Board of Education*, in 1954, that segregation began to crumble. Such a large time span suggests that *patience* and *dedication* were required to end segregation. Moreover, it took acts of the Federal government to overthrow the practice of segregation, as seen through the US Marshals in Source B and the Supreme Court in Source C.

To summarize, we have seen three themes emerge in answer the RST question, "What led to the end of the legal segregation of African Americans and whites?" Patience and dedication as well as bravery were required.

As you can undoubtedly tell, after reading all three sources, we are well on our way to writing a response to the RST prompt that shows "What led to the end of the legal segregation of African Americans and whites." Our three themes—bravery, patience, and dedication—will become the basis of our essay! So, it's time to begin. Let's take a look at our 11-step process:

 # The 11 Steps for Success on the RST

| Before Writing Begins | |
|---|---|
| Step #1: | Read through the question carefully. Make sure to figure out if the question is asking you to give an opinion, or to give information/research objectively. <br><br> • The question is asking us to analyze what led to the end of segregation. |
| Step #2: | Simplify what the question is asking you to do. Put the question/task into your own words. <br><br> • The prompt is asking this: "What led to the end of racial segregation?" |
| Step #3: | Circle the minimum amount of sources that need to be addressed. <br><br> • Two/Three sources |
| Step #4: | Take notes with each of the sources. Address the source's main points. <u>Underline!</u> <br><br> • We completed this activity extensively in our two-column approach and when we took notes on the piece of artwork. |
| Step #5: | After you've addressed and highlighted the main point of the source, make separate notes on the reliability of these sources. Is the source reliable in general? Is it slanted in any way? Do logical fallacies or "holes in argument" exist? <br><br> • We took notes on the sources in our active reading. |
| Step #6: | You've read through your sources. Choose the sources that you are most comfortable with, and put an asterisk (*) next to them. <br><br> • We will be able to work with all three sources in our essay. |

*(continued)*

| Writing the RST | |
|---|---|
| Step #7: | Copy the arguments—textual evidence—you will use in your essay into the pre-writing chart. (shown below) |
| Step #8: | Now, look at the relationships of your sources. Do they agree with each other? Do they disagree? Use your source-relationship chart to begin thinking about how you will have your sources begin conversing with one another. (shown below) |
| Step #9: | Compose a quick outline of your essay (shown below) |
| Step #10: | Complete your essay using the framework/outline as a guide. (shown below) |
| Step #11: | After you have completed your essay, go back to check that your sources have a conversation, and replace the verbs you've used to integrate these sources with the action verbs from the sheet provided. (shown below) |

So, let's get started on doing the prewriting for our response. We have worked through the RST graphic organizer for you.

## RST Graphic Organizer

### Topic: The End of Segregation

**Thesis Statement:** Three ideals led to the end of racial segregation: bravery, patience, and dedication.

| Source A | Source B | Source C |
|---|---|---|
| Excerpt from "My Bondage and My Freedom," by Frederick Douglass | The Problem We All Live With, by Norman Rockwell (1968) | Jim Crow Laws: www.scholastic.com/teachers/article/jim-crow-laws |
| • While Douglass does not mention extreme brutality, his very acceptance of being owned on a plantation should be worthy of discussion here. | • Young girl is the focal point of the painting. She is carrying a ruler, pen, and books, which suggests that she is being escorted to school. | • Jim Crow refers to actual "laws" passed by the Southern state governments. It was legal racism. |
| • This very happiness over bread is saddening, especially for a man who is working hard on the plantation. | • The tomatoes smashed against the wall (as well as the horrific words written on the wall; i.e. "kkk" and the "n" word) suggest that the young girl is VERY BRAVE. | • Even the U.S. Supreme Court refused to stop these laws in the late 1800s |
| • Douglass is struck by a child! | • The girls is being escorted by US Marshalls, suggesting that the federal government, not the state government is enforcing "de-segregation" in the schools | • "Separate but Equal" was established in 1896. |
| • The treatment by those on this plantation is mixed. The idea of friendship seems to be confused. | | • By 1914 EVERY Southern state had established segregation as the law of the land |
| • Douglass shares his coping habits in regards to dealing with his own hunger. | | • Like Source A, this text describes the literacy tests and the taxes. |
| • Fed and treated like animals. It is important to discuss the long strides the Black Americans have gained at this point. | | • 1954: Brown v. Board of Education of Topeka, Kansas. This case is a direct reference to Source B, the Norman Rockwell painting. |

### How can the sources talk to each other?

Since we completed all that hard work with our readings, the answer to this question, "How do the sources talk with each other" is fairly easy to answer. All three sources address three ideals in ending segregation: bravery, patience, and dedication. In the face of oppression and violence, Douglass in Source A chose to live peacefully, thereby showing a high degree of bravery in the face of physical and emotional threats and violence. Source B, moreover, clearly shows the bravery of the little girl being escorted to school. Lastly, Source C gives a historical account of segregation and Jim Crow, thus showing the years of patience on the part of African Americans.

As you can see, we did a fairly good job tackling Step 7 and Step 8. At the bottom of our chart, we prewrote a bit on how our sources share the common themes of bravery, patience, and dedication. That work will become useful as we write our essay. For now, though, we must head to Step 9, the outline. As discussed previously, we want to keep our outline brief, focusing on the major themes of the essay. Here we go:

I.   Introduction

    a.   Attention Grabber

    b.   Thesis: The American Dream is alive and well, although it is a changed dream from the past

II.  Body

    a.   Theme 1: Bravery

    b.   Theme 2: Patience and Dedication

III. Conclusion

    a.   Rework thesis statement

    b.   Answer to the *So What?* question

Let's just take brief look at our outline. Did you notice the three major themes in the body: "bravery" in the first body paragraph and "patience and dedication" in the second? This is exactly how we will organize our essay to ensure that our sources "talk with each other." What we want you to know: Our very close reading of the three texts has served us very well. We are in a good position to write an excellent response to the RST prompt because we have a high degree of knowledge about the writing topic. Please listen to this advice: The better you read, the better you will write. Here's our sample essay:

In a cell in Birmingham, Alabama, a young Baptist minister wrote on scraps of paper in a cold, dark, and damp cell something to the effect: "Just because a law is legal does not make it moral." What did Martin Luther King, Jr. mean by these words? What were these words directed at? Undoubtedly, MLK Jr. was arguing against the *Plessy v. Ferguson* ruling in 1896 that legally, but not morally, made legal the principle of "separate but equal" (Source C)—that is, the law established government-approved, institutional racism. Not until the *Brown vs. Board of Education* ruling in 1954 (Source C) did the chains of segregation begin to crack. Ultimately, three ideals led to the end of racial segregation: bravery, patience, and dedication.

Without a doubt, those who fought to end segregation were in a war—a war fought with bravery. Legally and emotionally, white supremacists actively tried to belittle and dehumanize African Americans by blocking their access to voting through the use of taxes and literacy tests, and ultimately through terrible acts of violence (Sources A & B). In the face of such danger, African Americans chose the path of peace to end segregation, not violence. African Americans bravely marched against segregation in peaceful protest. In short, to walk peacefully in the face of threats and physical violence, like the young girl in Norman Rockwell's painting (Source B) requires a tremendous amount of bravery. Bravery, however, was not the only ingredient that eventually brought down segregation.

From a historical point of view, segregation lasted from the late 1800s all the way to Civil Rights legislation that was enacted from 1964–68 (Source C). Compounded upon the fact that African Americans had endured slavery for more than 300 years, patience and dedication were key factors that finally buried segregation. The African American race, therefore, had diligently and patiently waited centuries for legalized racism to end.

MLK King Jr.'s distinction between a law that is legal vs. a law that is moral gives tremendous insight into the vast history of government-sponsored slavery, segregation, and racism enacted by the United States. This evil did not disappear overnight. Through the bravery of those who endured years upon years of slavery, only then could African Americans learn from their very tormented past (Source A), through the children affected by *Brown vs. the Board of Education* (Source B), did segregation ultimately fall. In memory of those brave souls who fought and died for freedom should we never forget the war to end racism? Recently areas in the United States have passed laws that begin again to endanger the civil rights of the poor and minorities. We must remain vigilant in the name of freedom promised by the United States of America.

## Step 11: Looking at the Verbs

Now that we have completed our written response to the RST topic, it is time to pay close attention to our verb choice. Look through the essay above and circle the verb choices. Do you find them "boring" or "tiresome?" If so, use the Vivid Verb Chart in Appendix A to find replacements.

# Analysis of Sample Essay

As we did in the previous chapter, we have given you an analysis of the sample essay according to the four criteria identified in our Scoring Checklist Chart (in the back of the book, along with the PARCC's writing rubric). Be sure to rate the sample essay using the 4-point scale.

By "Development of Ideas," the makers of the PARCC refer to the ways in which arguments are developed and maintained throughout the course of the essay. Some questions might be: "Did the author use evidence from the text?" "Did this evidence come from more than one source?" "Did the author successfully have the two sources interact with each other?" As you can see, these questions are quite difficult and will take time for you to master. However, you can see these principles in action if you read carefully our sample essay above. We did cite evidence from all four sources, and we did have the four sources interact, or "talk." For instance, check out the following excerpts from our model essay. Observe how the sources "speak as one voice" in response to topics of bravery, patience, and dedication.

> Through the children affected by *Brown vs. The Board of Education* (Source B), and through the peaceful demonstrations, and through the bravery of individual families seeking a better life, segregation fell.

> Legally and emotionally, white supremacists actively tried to belittle and dehumanize African Americans by blocking their access to voting through the use of taxes and literacy tests, blocking residence in white neighborhoods, and ultimately through wanton acts of violence (Sources A and C).

> Starting with Frederick Douglass (Source A) and on to Mrs. Rosa Parks in 1955 with her act of defiance on a segregated bus, African Americans bravely marched against segregation in peaceful protest. In short, to walk peacefully in the face of threats and physical violence, like the young girl in Norman Rockwell's painting (Source B) requires a tremendous amount of bravery.

> Through the bravery of Frederick Douglass (Source A), through the children affected by *Brown vs. the Board of Education* (Source B), and through so many acts of defiance, segregation ultimately fell.

Second, the PARCC will look at the organization of your writing. This, in fact, should come as no surprise at all for you. Organization is a key facet of all good writing, no matter where it is done. By following our outline, we organized our work. The three main parts of the essay are clearly present: Introduction, body, and conclusion.

The next criteria, "clarity of language" will look at your writing style and the effectiveness of that style. "What is writing style?" you may ask? It deals with the author's ability to effectively use vocabulary, including content-specific words, to utilize vivid and proper description, and to appropriately use transitional words throughout the piece. Style, then, is nothing more than the writer's identity on paper. What the PARCC cares about most is simple: **Is your style clear, concise, and to the point?** There is nothing worse than reading an essay that lacks clarity and is difficult to read because the writer lacks a command of language.

Looking at our sample essay: What would you say of the style? Look back at our choice of vocabulary: Did we use vocabulary terms that were appropriate to research and statistics? Were our descriptions of the research sources clear? Was any of the wording ambiguous and difficult to comprehend? Could something we wrote have been written clearer? All of these questions are great starting points when looking at style.

Lastly, the PARCC will consider your knowledge of language and conventions. This is where your knowledge of grammar, mechanics, and usage will come to play. Were there any mistakes in these three categories? Did the author go back and edit the work? Does the work read effortlessly? Does poor grammar become a distraction or a nuisance? Our sample essay, we believe, does pretty well in this area, and shows you, a RST essay that is free of grammatical issues and reads as thought it were edited (which it was!).

## Summary of the RST in History

As you know by this point in the chapter, once the skills of the RST are mastered—particularly the active reading and the 11 Steps to Success—success only becomes a matter of learning new content. In the case of Chapter 7, we have shown you how difficult texts, such as the ones on the American Dream, can become manageable when formulating a quality, written response. Can you guess the idea that we want to impress upon you the most? You got it! The better you read, the better you will write!

# Practice RSTs in History

Now, it's your turn. We will give you two sample RST tasks in history with accompanying organizers. Please be sure, as you go through this process to utilize the 11 Steps for Success, and, as always, read well; your writing depends upon it.

| CCSS Alignment | |
|---|---|
| RH.1 | Cite specific textual evidence. |
| RH.5 | Analyze in detail how a complex primary source is structured, including how key sentences, paragraphs, and larger portions of the text contribute to the whole. |
| RH.8 | Evaluate an author's premises, claims, and evidence by corroborating or challenging them with other information. |
| RH.9 | Integrate information from diverse sources, both primary and secondary, into a coherent understanding of an idea or event, noting discrepancies among sources. |
| RI.7 | Integrate and evaluate multiple sources of information presented in different media or formats (e.g., visually, quantitatively) as well as in words in order to address a question or solve a problem. |
| L.1 | Demonstrate command of the conventions of standard English grammar and usage when writing. |
| L.3 | Apply knowledge of language to understand how language functions in different contexts. |
| W.1 | Write arguments to support claims in an analysis of substantive topics or texts, using valid reasoning and relevant and sufficient evidence. |
| W.6 | Use technology to produce, publish, and update individual writing products. |
| WHST.1 | Write arguments focused on discipline-specific content. |
| WHST.4 | Produce clear and coherent writing in which the development, organization, and style are appropriate to task, purpose, and audience. |

[ELA TASK GENERATION MODEL: 8B7PBA]

## RST #2: Winston Churchill

85 Minutes

Writer, statesman, and politician, Winston Churchill was one of the defining figures of the 20th century. Faced with the threat of Nazism and the impending conquering of the British Isles, Churchill defied Hitler and led Great Britain to ultimate victory in World War II.

You have reviewed four texts about Winston Churchill that you can use to formulate your ideas and argument. These sources are:

- **Source A:** Sir Winston Churchill Biography: British Prime Minister's Life: *www.watchmojo.com/index.php?id=10820*

- **Source B:** "Blood, Toil, Tears and Sweat: Address to Parliament on May 13th, 1940."

- **Source C:** Excerpt from *An Essay on the American Contribution and the Democratic Idea* (Winston Churchill)—Project Gutenberg

- **Source D:** Excerpt from *Real Soldiers of Fortune* (Richard Harding Davis)—Project Gutenberg

What about Winston Churchill's character made him a truly outstanding leader? Consider the arguments that these three texts use in their characterization of President Roosevelt. Write an informative piece that addresses the question and supports your position with evidence from at least three of the four sources. Be sure to acknowledge competing views. You may give examples from past and current events or issues to illustrate and clarify your position. You may refer to the sources by their titles (Source A, Source B, Source C, Source D).

## SOURCE A

### Sir Winston Churchill Biography: British Prime Minister's Life

Born on November 30, 1874, Sir Winston Churchill overcame poor grades in school and a speech impediment to graduate military college in 1895. Churchill's political career began in 1900, when he won a parliamentary seat for the Conservative party. After some setbacks in politics, Churchill once again re-enlisted in the military, where he served as lieutenant colonel. Churchill's political career continued once his term of service ended. In 1919, he served as Secretary of State for War, and in 1921, he was appointed Colonial Secretary. On September 3, 1939, Britain declared war against Germany, and Churchill was appointed as First Lord of the Admiralty. On May 10, 1940, Churchill became Prime Minister of Great Britain, amidst the growing death toll of World War II. As Commander-in-Chief, Churchill refused to appease the Nazis. Ignoring ill health, Churchill traveled the world, meeting with the President of the United States, Franklin Delano Roosevelt, and the Soviet Union's Joseph Stalin. All together, these three countries formed a grand alliance to help defeat the Nazis. Despite a British victory in World War II, Churchill was not re-elected, and consequently he became the leader of the opposition. His main goal during those years was to warn of and speak against the spread of communism. In 1953, Churchill was awarded the Nobel Prize in Literature. Despite his ailing health, Churchill stayed active in politics until his death on January 24, 1965. For his leadership during World War II, and his tremendous skill as a public speaker, Winston Churchill is considered to be one of the most important leaders in world history.

| Source A: Sir Winston Churchill Biography: British Prime Minister's Life: *http://www.watchmojo.com/index.php?id=10820* |
|---|
| **My Thought Processes** |
| |

## SOURCE B

| "Blood, Toil, Tears and Sweat: Address to Parliament on May 13th, 1940." | My Thought Processes |
|---|---|
| I say to the House as I said to ministers who have joined this government, I have nothing to offer but blood, toil, tears, and sweat. We have before us an ordeal of the most grievous kind. We have before us many, many months of struggle and suffering.<br><br>You ask, what is our policy? I say it is to wage war by land, sea, and air. War with all our might and with all the strength God has given us, and to wage war against a monstrous tyranny never surpassed in the dark and lamentable catalogue of human crime. That is our policy.<br><br>You ask, what is our aim? I can answer in one word. It is victory. Victory at all costs—Victory in spite of all terrors—Victory, however long and hard the road may be, for without victory there is no survival.<br><br>I take up my task in buoyancy and hope. I feel sure that our cause will not be suffered to fail among men. I feel entitled at this juncture, at this time, to claim the aid of all and to say, "Come then, let us go forward together with our united strength." | |

## SOURCE C

| Excerpt from *An Essay on the American Contribution and the Democratic Idea* (Winston Churchill) | My Thought Processes |
|---|---|
| In fighting Germany we are indeed fighting an evil Will—evil because it seeks to crush the growth of individual and national freedom. Its object is to put the world back under the thrall of self-constituted authority. So long as this Will can compel the bodies of soldiers to do its bidding, these bodies must be destroyed. Until the Will behind them is broken, the world cannot be free. Junkerism is the final expression of reaction, organized to the highest efficiency. The war against the Junkers marks the consummation of a long struggle for human liberty in all lands, symbolizes the real cleavage dividing the world. As in the French Revolution and the wars that followed it, the true significance of this war is social. But today the Russian Revolution sounds the keynote. Revolutions tend to express the extremes of the philosophies of their times—human desires, discontents, and passions that cannot be organized. The French Revolution was a struggle for political freedom; the underlying issue of the present war is economic freedom—without which political freedom is of no account. It will not, therefore, suffice merely to crush the Junkers, and with them militarism and autocracy. Unless, as the fruit of this appalling bloodshed and suffering, the democracies achieve economic freedom, the war will have been fought in vain. More revolutions, wastage and bloodshed will follow, the world will be reduced to absolute chaos unless, in the more advanced democracies, an intelligent social order tending to remove the causes of injustice and discontent can be devised and ready for inauguration. This new social order depends, in turn, upon a world order of mutually helpful, free peoples, a league of Nations.—If the world is to be made safe for democracy, this democratic plan must be ready for the day when the German Junker is beaten and peace is declared. | |

*(continued)*

| Excerpt from *An Essay on the American Contribution and the Democratic Idea* (Winston Churchill) | My Thought Processes |
|---|---|
| The real issue of our time is industrial democracy we must face that fact. And those in America and the Entente nations who continue to oppose it will do so at their peril. Fortunately, as will be shown, that element of our population which may be designated as domestic Junkers is capable of being influenced by contemporary currents of thought, is awakening to the realization of social conditions deplorable and dangerous. Prosperity and power had made them blind and arrogant. Their enthusiasm for the war was, however, genuine; the sacrifices they are making are changing and softening them; but as yet they can scarcely be expected, as a class, to rejoice over the revelation—just beginning to dawn upon their minds—that victory for the Allies spells the end of privilege. | |

## SOURCE D

| Excerpt from *Real Soldiers of Fortune* (Richard Harding Davis) | My Thought Processes |
|---|---|
| In the strict sense of the phrase, a soldier of fortune is a man who for pay, or for the love of adventure, fights under the flag of any country. In the bigger sense he is the kind of man who in any walk of life makes his own fortune, who, when he sees it coming, leaps to meet it, and turns it to his advantage. Than Winston Spencer Churchill to-day there are few young men (sic)—and he is a very young man—who have met more varying fortunes, and none who has more frequently bent them to his own advancement. To him it has been indifferent whether, at the moment, the fortune seemed good or evil, in the end always it was good. | |

*(continued)*

| Excerpt from *Real Soldiers of Fortune* (Richard Harding Davis) | My Thought Processes |
|---|---|
| As a boy officer, when other subalterns were playing polo, and at the Gaiety Theatre attending night school, he ran away to Cuba and fought with the Spaniards. For such a breach of military discipline, any other officer would have been court-martialled. Even his friends feared that by his foolishness his career in the army was at an end. Instead, his escapade was made a question in the House of Commons, and the fact brought him such publicity that the *Daily Graphic* paid him handsomely to write on the Cuban Revolution, and the Spanish Government rewarded him with the Order of Military Merit.<br><br>At the very outbreak of the Boer War he was taken prisoner. It seemed a climax of misfortune. With his brother officers he had hoped in that campaign to acquit himself with credit, and that he should lie inactive in Pretoria appeared a terrible calamity. To the others who, through many heart-breaking months, suffered imprisonment, it continued to be a calamity. But within six weeks of his capture Churchill escaped, and, after many adventures, rejoined his own army to find that the calamity had made him a hero.<br><br>When after the battle of Omdurman, in his book on *The River War*, he attacked Lord Kitchener, those who did not like him, and they were many, said: "That's the end of Winston in the army. He'll never get another chance to criticise K. of K."<br><br>But only two years later the chance came, when, no longer a subaltern, but as a member of the House of Commons, he patronized Kitchener by defending him from the attacks of others. | |

*(continued)*

| Excerpt from *Real Soldiers of Fortune* (Richard Harding Davis) | My Thought Processes |
|---|---|
| Later, when his assaults upon the leaders of his own party closed to him, even in his own constituency, the Conservative debating clubs, again his ill-wishers said: "This *is* the end. He has ridiculed those who sit in high places. He has offended his cousin and patron, the Duke of Marlborough. Without political friends, without the influence and money of the Marlborough family he is a political nonentity." That was eighteen months ago. To-day, at the age of thirty-two, he is one of the leaders of the Government party, Under-Secretary for the Colonies, and with the Liberals the most popular young man in public life.<br><br>Only last Christmas, at a banquet, Sir Edward Grey, the new Foreign Secretary, said of him: "Mr. Winston Churchill has achieved distinction in at least five different careers—as a soldier, a war correspondent, a lecturer, an author, and last, but not least, as a politician. I have understated it even now, for he has achieved two careers as a politician—one on each side of the House. His first career on the Government side was a really distinguished career. I trust the second will be even more distinguished—and more prolonged. The remarkable thing is that he has done all this when, unless appearances very much belie him, he has not reached the age of sixty-four, which is the minimum age at which the politician ceases to be young."<br><br>Winston Leonard Spencer Churchill was born thirty-two years ago, in November, 1874. By birth he is half-American. His father was Lord Randolph Churchill, and his mother was Jennie Jerome, of New York. On the father's side he is the grandchild of the seventh Duke of Marlborough, on the distaff side, of Leonard Jerome. | |

# Prewriting

## RST Graphic Organizer

RST Graphic Organizer

Topic:

My Thesis Statement:

| | Source A | Source B | Source C | Source D |
|---|---|---|---|---|

Exactly how do the sources talk with each other?

## Space for Your Outline:

Write your essay on loose-leaf paper or in a notebook. Be sure to make use of the Scoring Rubric and Scoring Checklist in the back of the book.

| CCSS Alignment | |
|---|---|
| RH.1 | Cite specific textual evidence. |
| RH.5 | Analyze in detail how a complex primary source is structured, including how key sentences, paragraphs, and larger portions of the text contribute to the whole. |
| RH.8 | Evaluate an author's premises, claims, and evidence by corroborating or challenging them with other information. |
| RH.9 | Integrate information from diverse sources, both primary and secondary, into a coherent understanding of an idea or event, noting discrepancies among sources. |
| RI.7 | Integrate and evaluate multiple sources of information presented in different media or formats (e.g., visually, quantitatively) as well as in words in order to address a question or solve a problem. |
| L.1 | Demonstrate command of the conventions of standard English grammar and usage when writing. |
| L.3 | Apply knowledge of language to understand how language functions in different contexts. |
| W.1 | Write arguments to support claims in an analysis of substantive topics or texts, using valid reasoning and relevant and sufficient evidence. |
| W.6 | Use technology to produce, publish, and update individual writing products. |
| WHST.1 | Write arguments focused on discipline-specific content. |
| WHST.4 | Produce clear and coherent writing in which the development, organization, and style are appropriate to task, purpose, and audience. |

[ELA TASK GENERATION MODEL: 7B9PBA]

85 Minutes

April 15th, 1912, marks one of the modern era's greatest maritime tragedies: The sinking of the Titanic. It is fair to say that just about everyone knows that the Titanic sank because it hit an iceberg, but what fewer people know are the stories of bravery that helped 702 people of the 2,224 aboard the ship survive.

You have reviewed four sources regarding the Titanic. These four pieces provide information to begin drafting your own argument.

- **Source A:** The Sinking of the Titanic: A Timeline: *www.watchmojo.com/video/id/9401/*

- **Source B:** Special Dispatch to The North American/"Woman in Wilmington Tells of the Disaster" (Miss Emily Rugg), April 19, 1912—Library of Congress

- **Source C:** Titanic Survivors: *www.youtube.com/watch?v=4n4Cf2OSnBI*

- **Source D:** Excerpt from *Sinking of the Titanic* (edited by Logan Marshall)—Project Gutenberg (2009)

Write a persuasive piece that analyzes the issue of bravery in the disaster of the Titanic. You must use three of the four sources, as well as textual support, in your analysis. You may refer to the sources by their titles (Source A, Source B, Source C, Source D).

# SOURCE A

## The Sinking of the Titanic: A Timeline

Considered by many to be unsinkable, its failure resulted in a massive loss of life. Construction of the Titanic began on March 30, 1909, in Belfast, Ireland. The finances for the ship came from American banker, JP Morgan. Upon completion, the Titanic became the world's largest passenger ship, with a capacity of 3,547 people. The ship was the most luxurious and lavish during that time period. Prior to setting sail, the Titanic was equipped with 20 life boats, which was more than the number required by law, but only enough to save one-third of the ship's passengers. On April 10, 1912, the Titanic set sail from Southampton, England, to New York City with 2,223 people on board. The first few days of the journey ran smoothly, but the captain began receiving information about icebergs in the ship's path. At 11:40 PM, Sunday April 14th, the lookout spotted an iceberg directly in the ship's path, and it ripped into Titanic's side, rupturing the hull. By 12:00 AM, lifeboats were being prepared and calls for help were broadcast to ships in the area. The closest ship, the Carpathia, was four hours away. The temperature of the water was so cold that hypothermia would kill within 15 minutes. Because the electricity still worked on the ship, and because the ship remained relatively level while sinking, many people thought it safe to stay aboard the Titanic, and numerous lifeboats were launched practically empty. By 2:20 AM, the Titanic broke in half due to the pressure of the water and both parts sank to the bottom of the ocean. The Carpathia arrived approximately 2 hours after the sinking of the Titanic. Only 700 passengers made it aboard the Carpathia, meaning over 1,500 people perished in the disaster.

| The Sinking of the Titanic: A Timeline: www.watchmojo.com/video/id/9401/ |
| --- |
| My Thought Processes |
|  |

## SOURCE B

| Special Dispatch to *The North American* "Woman in Wilmington Tells of the Disaster" (Miss Emily Rugg), April 19, 1912 | **My Thought Processes** |
| --- | --- |
| WILMINGTON, Del., April 19—Miss Emily Rugg, 20 years old, of the Isle of Guernsey, England, one of the survivors of the Titanic, arrived in this city today, and told a graphic story of the sinking.<br><br>Miss Rugg, who was one of the second-class passengers, was met in New York last night by her uncle, F. W. Queripell, a grocer. The young woman was on her way to visit relatives here.<br><br>She was asleep when the ship struck the berg, and the jar aroused her. Looking out she saw a mass of ice. Throwing a coat about her, she went on deck and saw lifeboats being lowered. Returning to the cabin, she dressed, and then went to an adjoining cabin and aroused two women friends.<br><br>Following this Miss Rugg ran up on deck and was taken in charge by some of the crew, who dragged her toward a lifeboat. She was lifted into the third boat from the last to leave the ship.<br><br>She said that there seemed to be nearly seventy-five persons in the boat and that it was very much crowded. In the meantime a panic had started among those who remained on the Titanic. An Italian jumped from the steerage deck and fell into a lifeboat, landing upon a woman who had a baby in her arms.<br><br>Miss Rugg saw the Titanic go down and declares but for the horror of it all, it might have been termed one of the grandest sights she ever saw. The boat seemed to have broken in half, and with all the lights burning brightly, the stern arose into the air, the lights being extinguished as it did so. A moment later the ship plunged beneath the surface. | |

## SOURCE C

### Titanic Survivors

This video is a historical reenactment of people who survived the sinking of the Titanic. Various individuals are being interviewed and speaking in the character of the person who survived. Most of the individuals being interviewed expressed disbelief that the ship was actually sinking, and one woman, Mrs. Mary Smith, reassured there was no danger, took her time getting changed when the captain called all people to the deck. Fireman Walter Hurst describes some of the ensuing chaos on board the sinking ship. He recalls a crewman on the Titanic firing warning shots into the air so as not to have people charge toward the rescue boats. Mr. Hurst also recalls that many people jumped to their deaths into the frigid cold Atlantic. Second Officer, C.H. Lightoller describes swimming in the icey-cold Atlantic as having a thousand knives stuck into the body at once. He survived the ordeal. Mrs. Mary Smith recalls sitting some distance away in the lifeboat, listening to the cries of the people in the ocean, and thinking to herself that the "poor captain" would have to go down with the ship.

| Titanic Survivors: *http://www.youtube.com/watch?v=4n4Cf2OSnBl* |
|---|
| My Thought Processes |
|  |

## SOURCE D

| Excerpt from *Sinking of the Titanic* (edited by Logan Marshall) | My Thought Processes |
|---|---|
| STORY OF HAROLD BRIDE, THE SURVIVING WIRELESS OPERATOR OF THE TITANIC, WHO WAS WASHED OVERBOARD AND RESCUED BY LIFE-BOAT—BAND PLAYED RAGTIME AND "AUTUMN"<br><br>ONE of the most connected and detailed accounts of the horrible disaster was that told by Harold Bride, the wireless operator. Mr. Bride said:<br><br>"I was standing by Phillips, the chief operator, telling him to go to bed, when the captain put his head in the cabin.<br><br>" 'We've struck an iceberg,' the captain said, 'and I'm having an inspection made to tell what it has done for us. You better get ready to send out a call for assistance. But don't send it until I tell you.'<br><br>"The captain went away and in ten minutes, I should estimate the time, he came back. We could hear a terrific confusion outside, but there was not the least thing to indicate that there was any trouble. The wireless was working perfectly.<br><br>" 'Send the call for assistance,' ordered the captain, barely putting his head in the door.<br><br>" 'What call shall I send?' Phillips asked.<br><br>" 'The regulation international call for help. Just that.'<br><br>"Then the captain was gone Phillips began to send 'C. Q. D.' He flashed away at it and we joked while he did so. All of us made light of the disaster.<br><br>"The Carpathia answered our signal. We told her our position and said we were sinking by the head. The operator went to tell the captain, and in five minutes returned and told us that the captain of the Carpathia, was putting about and heading for us. | |

*(continued)*

| Excerpt from *Sinking of the Titanic* (edited by Logan Marshall) | My Thought Processes |
|---|---|
| **GREAT SCRAMBLE ON DECK**<br><br>"Our captain had left us at this time and Phillips told me to run and tell him what the Carpathia had answered. I did so, and I went through an awful mass of people to his cabin. The decks were full of scrambling men and women. I saw no fighting, but I heard tell of it.<br><br>"I came back and heard Phillips giving the Carpathia fuller directions. Phillips told me to put on my clothes. Until that moment I forgot that I was not dressed.<br><br>"I went to my cabin and dressed. I brought an overcoat to Phillips. It was very cold. I slipped the overcoat upon him while he worked.<br><br>"Every few minutes Phillips would send me to the captain with little messages. They were merely telling how the Carpathia was coming our way and gave her speed.<br><br>"I noticed as I came back from one trip that they were putting off women and children in life-boats. I noticed that the list forward was increasing.<br><br>"Phillips told me the wireless was growing weaker. The captain came and told us our engine rooms were taking water and that the dynamos might not last much longer. We sent that word to the Carpathia.<br><br>"I went out on deck and looked around. The water was pretty close up to the boat deck. There was a great scramble aft, and how poor Phillips worked through it right to the end I don't know.<br><br>"He was a brave man. I learned to love him that night and I suddenly felt for him a great reverence to see him standing there sticking to his work while everybody else was raging about. I will never live to forget the work of Phillips for the last awful fifteen minutes. | |

*(continued)*

| Excerpt from *Sinking of the Titanic* (edited by Logan Marshall) | My Thought Processes |
|---|---|
| "I thought it was about time to look about and see if there was anything detached that would float. I remembered that every member of the crew had a special life-belt and ought to know where it was. I remembered mine was under my bunk. I went and got it. Then I thought how cold the water was.<br><br>"I remembered I had an extra jacket and a pair of boots, and I put them on. I saw Phillips standing out there still sending away, giving the Carpathia details of just how we were doing.<br><br>"We picked up the Olympic and told her we were sinking by the head and were about all down. As Phillips was sending the message I strapped his life-belt to his back. I had already put on his overcoat. Every minute was precious, so I helped him all I could." | |

# Prewriting

## RST Graphic Organizer

**RST Graphic Organizer**

Topic:

My Thesis Statement:

| | Source A | Source B | Source C | Source D | |
|---|---|---|---|---|---|
| | | | | | |

Exactly how do the sources talk with each other?

## Space for Your Outline:

Write your essay on loose-leaf paper or in a notebook. Review your writing by using the Scoring Checklist and the Scoring Rubrics at the back of the book.

## CHAPTER 8

# The Research Simulation Task: Science

##  Introduction

You've done some great work so far with your work through the research simulation task, as you have worked through the English and history-based questions! You have continued to learn how to take notes while you read; to breakdown the RST prompt; to pre-write in the form of a graphic organizer; to create a workable outline; to execute a high-quality essay in the RST style; to get your sources talking to each other; and to edit your work using vivid, action verbs. Remember that mastering these skills is no small accomplishment.

We will now focus on how we can use these same skills to tackle the science RST. Read through the following research simulation task question and its accompanying sources. While you have to think about scientific pieces of this question, you may also (and often) have to address the social implications of these scientific topics as well. Keep both in mind as you work through these RSTs in this chapter.

As we have done in the previous three chapters, we will take you, step-by-step, through the completion of an RST in science. First, we will actively read the texts, using our two-column approach. Afterward, we will utilize the 11-step process to completing the written portion of the RST. Next, we will provide you with a model essay. Finally, you will be presented with two practice RSTs in science. By the end of this chapter, you will be that much more prepared when it comes to the RST in science.

| CCSS Alignment | |
|---|---|
| RH.1 | Cite specific textual evidence. |
| RH.5 | Analyze in detail how a complex primary source is structured, including how key sentences, paragraphs, and larger portions of the text contribute to the whole. |
| RST.8 | Evaluate the hypotheses, data, analysis, and conclusions in a science or technical text, verifying the data when possible and corroborating or challenging conclusions with other sources of information. |
| RST.9 | Synthesize information from a range of sources (e.g., texts, experiments, simulations) into a coherent understanding of a process, phenomenon, or concept, resolving conflicting information when possible. |
| RI.7 | Integrate and evaluate multiple sources of information presented in different media or formats (e.g., visually, quantitatively) as well as in words in order to address a question or solve a problem. |
| L.1 | Demonstrate command of the conventions of standard English grammar and usage when writing. |
| L.3 | Apply knowledge of language to understand how language functions in different contexts. |
| W.1 | Write arguments to support claims in an analysis of substantive topics or texts, using valid reasoning and relevant and sufficient evidence. |
| W.6 | Use technology to produce, publish, and update individual writing products. |
| WHST.1 | Write arguments focused on discipline-specific content. |
| WHST.4 | Produce clear and coherent writing in which the development, organization, and style are appropriate to task, purpose, and audience. |

[ELA TASK GENERATION MODEL: 7B7PBA]

Let's begin with the model RST:

## RST #1: Anti-Antibiotic?

85 minutes

Antibiotics are substances that inhibit the growth of or destroy bacteria that cause infection. At an everyday doctor's appointment, antibiotics are prescribed on a regular basis to patients. Oftentimes, patients demand the usage of antibiotics even for viral infections, which resist antibiotics. Many feel that doctors over-prescribe antibiotics for viral infections, which may ultimately mutate bacteria that eventually can resist the effects of antibiotics, rendering antibiotics useless. Others feel that the usage of antibiotics is necessary in order to feel better.

You have reviewed three sources regarding antibiotics and possible antibiotic resistance. These three pieces provide information to begin drafting your own argument.

- **Source A:** "In Praise of Antibiotics," *http://dwb.unl.edu/Teacher/NSF/C10/ C10Links/www.asmusa.org/memonly/asmnews/may99/feature6.html*

- **Source B:** Antibiotic Resistance Infographic, *http://www.medicinenet.com/ antibiotic_resistance/page4.htm*

- **Source C:** Reasons for Antibiotics Infographic, *http://infographiclist.com/ 2012/03/03/reasons-for-antibiotics-infographic/*

Write a well-written essay discussing either your support of the use of antibiotics or your position against the use of antibiotics. In this argumentative piece, address the question and support your position with evidence from at least two of the three sources. Be sure to acknowledge competing views. You may give examples from past and current events or issues to illustrate and clarify your position. You may refer to the sources by their titles (Source A, Source B, Source C).

After reading the RST on antibiotics and possible antibiotic resistance, you might be thinking that this particular topic has a lot of layers, and you're right, it absolutely does. The above prompt is difficult, in part, because you not only have to address the use of antibiotics, but you also must look closely at the concerns regarding the possibility of antibiotic resistance. We will break this task down for you, though. As you know, before we can attack the RST prompt, we must actively read our three sources. So, let's begin:

## SOURCE A

| "In Praise of Antibiotics" (Julian Davies) | Our Thought Processes |
|---|---|
| **In Praise of Antibiotics**<br><br>**These "wonder drugs" revolutionized the treatment of infectious diseases-but they cannot be taken for granted**<br><br>The use of antibiotics, often considered one of the wonders of the modern world, has had dramatic effects on the practice of medicine, the pharmaceutical industry, and microbiology. Prior to the discovery of antibiotics, the treatment of infectious diseases was empirical, at best. Various types of antimicrobial agents, including extracts of plants, fungi, and lichens, were employed for thousands of years in primitive populations without any scientific knowledge of what was being used. Even in the early part of the twentieth century, therapy for infectious diseases was based essentially on patient isolation and chicken soup.<br><br>However, the seminal work of Joseph Lister, Louis Pasteur, Robert Koch, and others-identifying microbes as agents of disease and devising means for avoiding infections by the use of disinfectants and antiseptics-made possible rational approaches to the treatment of infectious diseases.<br><br>[…] | • Antibiotics are often viewed as "wonder drugs."<br><br><br>• Antibiotics have had a huge impact on modern medicine! |

*(continued)*

| "In Praise of Antibiotics" (Julian Davies) | Our Thought Processes |
|---|---|
| Surprisingly, no infectious disease has been eliminated by the use of antibiotics, even though vaccines against viruses such as those causing smallpox, polio, and measles have proved very successful. Many of the bacteria that caused human suffering pre-1950 are still making people sick, and we have come to the woeful realization that the use of antibiotics has even contributed to the recent phenomenon of emerging infections. | • No infectious disease has been eliminated by the usage of antibiotics. |
| **Penicillin Marks True Start of Antibiotic Era** | |
| Penicillin really changed the way that medicine was practiced. Starting in the mid-1940s, antibiotic therapy and prophylaxis became the norm in medical practice, and, ever since, several generations of physicians, surgeons, and their patients have relied on antibiotics. Their use has become pervasive in all types of disease treatment for one reason or another, rightly or wrongly. | • Antibiotics have been used often and have a regular role in the medical and pharmaceutical world. |
| [...] | |
| From the point of view of human benefit, never was a Nobel Prize so justifiably awarded as was the award to Selman Waksman for the discovery of streptomycin and other antibiotics produced from *Streptomyces* spp. Waksman and his talented team (many of whom went on to make important antibiotic discoveries in their own right) developed the concept of systematic screening of microbial culture products for biological activity, a technology which has provided the foundation of the antibiotic industry, and for this alone his name should rank high in any pantheon of microbiology. | |
| **Antibiotics Influenced Pharmaceutical Industry Developments** | |
| The well-known pharmaceutical companies such as Squibb, Merck, Lederle, and Eli Lilly have a long history, but there is little doubt that a decisive event in their evolution into "big pharma" was the discovery that low-molecular-weight products of microbes have potent antibacterial activity. | |

(continued)

| "In Praise of Antibiotics" (Julian Davies) | Our Thought Processes |
|---|---|
| The introduction of fermentation methods to the industry was also a milestone; the recognition that microbes could be employed as biosynthetic factories on a large scale to generate not only antibiotics and other biologicals, but also a variety of useful products such as enzymes, amino acids, and vitamins, was the genesis of the biotechnology industry.<br><br>[…]<br><br>The discovery of antibiotics and the maturation of the antibiotic industry illustrates well the marriage of basic and applied science in the development of industrial microbiology. The birth and growth of this field are linked to the production of antibiotics by the pharmaceutical industry on a large scale, while the massive production of antibiotics by fermentation processes would not have been possible without extensive basic research in microbial genetics, physiology, and engineering.<br><br>[…]<br><br>**Antibiotics Influence Medicine, Public Health Perceptions**<br><br>The use of antibiotics has certainly changed public perceptions of infectious disease and its treatment. This change has not been an entirely positive development in the sense that some people regard antibiotics as a panacea, employing them for so many different purposes. Through the use of antibiotics in nonhuman applications such as agriculture and aquaculture, antibiotic-resistant microbes are near-ubiquitous.<br><br>The widespread distribution of such microorganisms has many implications, not only in terms of the maintenance of the resistance gene pool, but also in contributing to the spread of antibiotic-resistant organisms in the food chain. The recent spate of cases of human infection by animal-derived antibiotic-resistant strains of *Salmonella typhimurium* DT104 and glycopeptide-resistant enterococci attest to this. | • Antibiotics have sparked further research and influence on other forms of medicine.<br><br><br><br>• Advancements in microbiology are largely due to antibiotics. |

*(continued)*

| "In Praise of Antibiotics" (Julian Davies) | Our Thought Processes |
|---|---|
| Likewise, and in no small measure, the concepts of "Give me an antibiotic, doc" and "Take two of these and call me in the morning" have contributed to inappropriate and unnecessary use with coincident development of antibiotic resistance, perhaps not killing, but certainly threatening, the goose that lays the golden eggs. | • Many people see antibiotics as a cure-all.<br><br>• As a result, more and more antibiotic-resistant bacteria are becoming prevalent. |
| **Countering Antibiotic Resistance**<br><br>There have been numerous proposals suggesting ways to counteract this trend toward antibiotic resistance and thus to ameliorate the public health crisis that threatens us. One answer lies in the discovery of new antibiotics by chemical synthesis or by natural product screening. Indeed, traditional approaches for identifying and developing antibiotic agents are now being supplemented by newer approaches, including the systematic genetic and chemical manipulation of biosynthetic pathways. | • New approaches are being investigated to combat the further creation of antibiotic-resistant bacteria. |
| Moreover, the genomic sequences of many bacterial pathogens are being determined, bringing great expectations that sophisticated bioinformatic analyses will provide new target reactions for the screening of potential inhibitors that may become new classes of antibiotics, which will be unaffected by the resistance mechanisms now present in bacterial pathogens.<br><br>[…] | • Despite the existence of antibiotic-resistant bacteria, the world of antibiotics is far from over. |
| Could we instead be facing the end of the golden age of antibiotics? I think not. Increasingly effective diagnostic methods and the institution of reliable early warning systems (with appropriately rapid responses) will aid in containing the problems of antibiotic resistance that we can expect to encounter in the immediate future.<br><br>[…] | • This writer looks at the changes in antibiotics to be the beginning of a new antibiotic "era." |

(continued)

| "In Praise of Antibiotics" (Julian Davies) | Our Thought Processes |
|---|---|
| Ironically, the use of antibiotics and subsequent development of antibiotic resistance have played a highly significant role in the development of the modern biotechnology industry. The discovery that antibiotic resistance is genetically transmissible, in the form of extrachromosomal elements (R plasmids), led Herbert Boyer and Stanley Cohen to transform *E. coli*, thereby demonstrating the underlying principles of genetic engineering. R plasmids served as vectors in their original recombinant DNA studies and continue to be used extensively for such purposes. Furthermore, the dominant selective markers used in the majority of horizontal gene transfer studies are largely derived from antibiotic-resistant bacterial pathogens. Even the dark cloud of antibiotic resistance has a small silver lining! | |
| Key signs indicate that we are at a critical point in the history of antibiotic use. However, rather than being the beginning of the end, with a threat of returning to the pre-antibiotic era, this period can be taken as the end of the beginning, setting the stage for a new antibiotic era. To succeed, this new era needs to be based on creative approaches to the discovery and development of novel therapeutic agents, and it should be administered in an intellectual climate of better understanding of microbial pathogens and the diseases they cause and of procedures for treating those diseases. In addition, newer knowledge of the pathogens and their interactions with their hosts is likely to lead to the development of novel and more effective vaccines. | Reliability:<br><br>• By the tone and information in this article, the writer has a sense of credibility. We can tell, however, that this writer is an immediate supporter for antibiotics. |
| Only time will tell if these applications of the science of microbiology can enable humankind to maintain parity with our microbial adversaries. | |

As you can see through our notes in the right column, this piece, by Julian Davies, looks at how antibiotics may not always be the answer. It highlights the idea that antibiotics are almost viewed as a cure-all when patients are sick. This is, however, a very common misconception. Davies makes another important point. It is crucial to change patients' perspectives and approaches when making considerations for medications. Overall, looking at this source by itself, we would use it to address the need to continue in the usage of antibiotics, especially since they do have a place in medical changes, but we need to be mindful of more precautions. In particular, though, the main focus of this article is on the wonderment and advancement of antibiotics, and although the writer acknowledges the pitfalls of the possibility in creating antibiotic-resistant bacteria, the pros, to this writer, outweigh the cons. Keep this in mind as we move forward. We still have two sources to go! Here's our second:

## SOURCE B

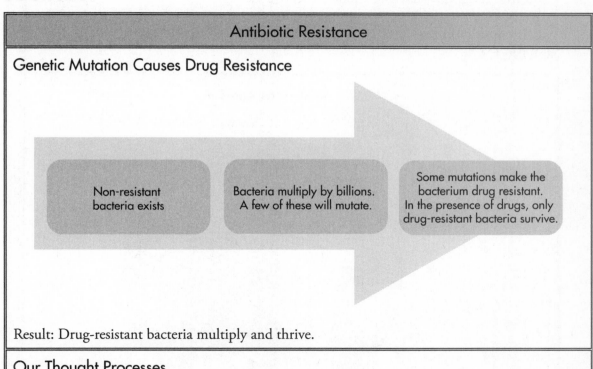

**Antibiotic Resistance**

**Genetic Mutation Causes Drug Resistance**

Non-resistant bacteria exists

Bacteria multiply by billions. A few of these will mutate.

Some mutations make the bacterium drug resistant. In the presence of drugs, only drug-resistant bacteria survive.

Result: Drug-resistant bacteria multiply and thrive.

### Our Thought Processes

- Bacteria multiply excessively, while some mutate in DNA.
- These mutations make the bacteria drug resistant to antibiotics.
- As a result, the more drug-resistant bacteria that exist, the more of a chance these bacteria will multiply and thrive.

Compared to Source A, this infographic takes a quick look at the process of how bacteria become resistant, which is just a visual representation of the description in Source A. How do we use it then? Now that we know that not all information provided is going to be entirely reliable, it is important to sort through our data to use it to our advantage. The chart refers to a very simplistic way to look at how a bacterium becomes resistant. Regardless, though, this works heavily towards the anti-antibiotic side of the argument. The visual itself shows how the bacteria multiply and thrive in the last illustration, depicting the overwhelming ways in which bacteria can become regularly resistant, and we must, as we craft our own arguments, be mindful of the implications of this occurrence.

With this mind, let's take a look at Source C.

## SOURCE C

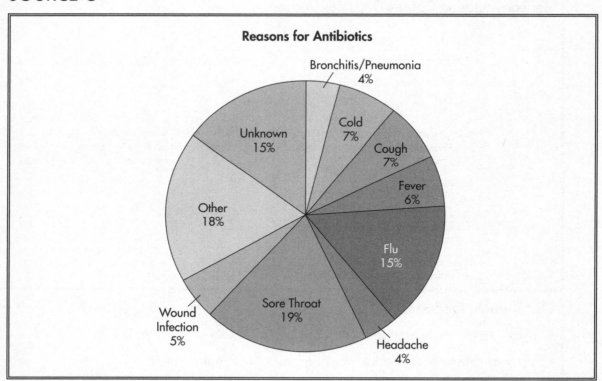

*(continued)*

---

## Our Thought Processes

• It is obvious, according to this chart, that people have used antibiotics for very common ailments. We must make note that some of the reasons people take antibiotics are not legitimate. Headache? Cold?

**Reliability:**

• In looking at the percentages, we don't know how many people these percentages are referencing. This could be a major blow to our argument when discussing these percentages as useful data to our argument. If we do, however, we must mention the possibility that this information might not be entirely accurate.

---

With our third source read, it is important to note that, again, while this source is leaning more towards the side that antibiotics should not be used, as many people use them incorrectly, much more exists than meets the eye. Arguments for benefits of antibiotics may also exist, such as the idea that antibiotics do indeed help when used properly. Keep these two perspectives in mind as we move forward.

Let's review our three sources—unlike those reviewed in our past RSTs, it is important to keep in mind that each can be used for very opposite arguments. Be careful in selecting your supporting details. In terms of responding to our RST prompt, we are leaning toward writing an essay about the importance of using antibiotics, but we also feel it is crucial to make mention that antibiotics can only be useful if used correctly.

As you can undoubtedly tell, after reading all three sources, we are well on our way to writing a response to the RST prompt that shows that antibiotics should still be administered by doctors and taken by patients, but we will focus on taking further precautions when completing each (administering and taking antibiotics). This idea can be supported by all three of the sources. So, it's time to begin. Keep in mind that when we write this model essay, while only two sources need to be used, the third source can easily be infused in our argument, or it can be referenced to make a counterargument. We'll talk about that further as we move ahead together.

Let's take a look at our 11-step process:

# The 11 Steps for Success on the RST

| | Before Writing Begins |
|---|---|
| Step #1: | Read through the question carefully. Make sure to decipher if the question is asking you to convey an opinion, or to convey information/research objectively.<br><br>• The question is asking us to convey an opinion |
| Step #2: | Simplify what the question is asking you to do. Put the question/task into your own words.<br><br>• The prompt is asking this: "Do you support the use of antibiotics or are you against their use?" |
| Step #3: | Circle the minimum amount of sources that need to be addressed.<br><br>• Two sources |
| Step #4: | Take notes with each of the sources. Address the source's main points. Underline actively.<br><br>• We completed this activity extensively in our two-column approach and when we took notes on the infographics |
| Step #5: | After you've addressed and highlighted the main point of the source, make separate notes on the reliability of these sources. Is the source reliable in general? Is it slanted in any way? Do logical fallacies or "holes in argument" exist?<br><br>• We took notes on the reliability of sources in our active reading. |
| Step #6: | You've read through your sources. Choose the sources that you are most comfortable with, and put an asterisk (*) next to them.<br><br>• We will be primarily working with Sources A, B, and C. |
| | Writing the RST |
| Step #7: | Copy the arguments—textual evidence—you will use in your essay into the prewriting chart. (shown below) |
| Step #8: | Now, look at the relationships of your sources. Do they agree with each other? Do they disagree? Use your source-relationship chart to begin thinking about how you will have your sources begin conversing with one another. (shown below) |
| Step #9: | Compose a quick outline of your essay. (shown below) |
| Step #10: | Complete your essay using the framework/outline as a guide. (shown below) |
| Step #11: | After you have completed your essay, go back to check that your sources have a conversation, and replace the verbs you've used to integrate these sources with the action verbs from the sheet provided. (shown below) |

So, let's get started on doing the prewriting for our response. On the next page we have the RST graphic organizer.

# RST Graphic Organizer

Topic: Anti-Antibiotics

My Thesis Statement: Antibiotics should continue to be used and developed, keeping in mind the necessary precautions

| Source A | Source B | Source C |
|---|---|---|
| "In Praise of Antibiotics" (Julian Davies) | Antibiotic Resistance Infographic | Reasons for Antibiotics Infographic |
| Antibiotics are often viewed as "wonder drugs." | Bacteria multiply excessively, while some mutate in DNA. | It is obvious, according to this chart, that people have used antibiotics for very common ailments. We must make note that some of the reasons people take antibiotics are not legitimate. Headache? Cold? |
| Antibiotics have had quite the impact on modern medicine! | These mutations make the bacteria drug resistant to antibiotics. | |
| No infectious diseases have been eliminated by the usage of antibiotics. | As a result, the more drug resistant bacteria that exists, the more of a chance this bacteria will multiple and thrive. | Reliability: |
| Simply, antibiotics have been used often and have a regular role in the medical and pharmaceutical world. | | In looking at the percentages, we don't know what amount of people these percentages are referencing. This could be a major problem when discussing these percentages as useful data to our argument. If we do, however, we must mention the possibility that this information might not be entirely accurate. |
| Antibiotics have sparked further research and influence on other forms of medicine. | | |
| Advancements to microbiology are largely due to antibiotics. | | |
| By the tone and information in this article, the writer has a sense of credibility. We can tell, however, that this writer is a big supporter for antibiotics, however. | | |

## How can the sources talk to each other?

At the core of each of these sources is the idea that antibiotics have changed the way patients deal with illness and the way doctors deal with treating illness. Mostly, a very natural conversation exists between Source A and Source B, looking closely at antibiotics, and the ways in which they could possible be resisted. We have already addressed the fact that Source C can easily be used for both sides of the argument. Since we are looking at the wonderment of the scientific advancements of antibiotics, Source A and B can work with ease. Source C can contribute to this conversation as well. Talking about the positive attributes of the usage of antibiotics can be done using all three sources, but it is imperative to really use the information provided at the end of Source A, and throughout Sources B and C to discuss the necessary precautions that need to be followed when talking further about the impact of antibiotics on any patient.

As you can see, we again did a fairly good job tackling Step 7 and Step 8. At the bottom of our chart, we pre-wrote a bit on how our sources share a common theme that works towards crafting our argument on the precautions and benefits of using antibiotics. That work, undoubtedly, will become useful as we write our essay. For now, though, we must head to Step 9, the outline. As discussed previously, we want to keep our outline brief, focusing on the major themes of the essay. Here we go:

    I.  Introduction

        a.  Attention Grabber

        b.  Thesis: Antibiotics should continue to be used and developed, keeping in mind the necessary precautions.

    II.  Body

        a.  Theme 1: Antibiotics / Benefits

        b.  Theme 2: Antibiotics / Necessary Precautions

    III. Conclusion

        a.  Rework thesis statement

        b.  Answer to the So What? question

As you can see in the outline above, our essays will be working through the concept of how antibiotics should still be used, and its advancements should still be pursued, but necessary precautions and measures need to be followed. What we want you to know: Our very close reading of the three texts has served us very well. We are in a good position to write an excellent response to the RST prompt because we have a high degree of knowledge about the writing topic. **Heed this advice: The better you read, the better you will write.** Here's our sample essay:

> We have often been plagued by the common cold, or the everyday sinus infection. Looking for a simple fix to at least temporarily cure these illnesses, we find comfort in taking an antibiotic to make it all just go away. What if we are doing so improperly and turning our bodies into vessels that end up resisting the very "fix" that we needed in the first place? Have our bodies become destined to be

anti-antibiotic? While necessary precautions need to be taken into consideration, antibiotic usage still remains crucial to help in resolving many of our doctor's visits.

Antibiotics are often viewed as "wonder drugs," helping to stop the nuisance and pain of such illnesses as bronchitis, pneumonia, and strep throat. Nothing feels better than the security in knowing the sickness will eventually subside. Antibiotics give us that security as patients (Source A). While Source A does not consider antibiotics an absolute cure, as it has not ever eliminated an infectious disease, its usage in temporary fulfillment keep us as patients completely and utterly satisfied. As patients, we have become so fixated on the usage of antibiotics, that we use them as a cure for anything and everything. It is nice to know that once the injection is taken or the required dosage of medication is completed, definite results will occur. In reviewing Source C, it is obvious that patients are using antibiotics to help in curing everything from the common cold to an extreme headache. This is, however, where the lines between fulfilled and reliant become completely blurred. Antibiotics are indeed helpful, but we cannot simply use this sort of medication blindly, as uninformed patients.

Necessary precautions need to be followed in order to use antibiotics wisely. Source B's illustration depicts the process by which misusing an antibiotic can cause the creation and multiplication of antibiotic-resistant bacteria. While it is clearly discussed in Source A as well that such a process is a reality, does that mean we need to be anti-antibiotic after all? Absolutely not, and this is because the usefulness of antibiotics far outweigh any of their pitfalls. It is clearly defined in Source B that once an antibiotic is misused, whether it is because a patient took an antibiotic for a viral disease, like the common cold, or whether the antibiotic was not taken through its completion, bacteria may become mutated to then eventually create antibiotic-resistant strains that can be harmful to a patient in the future. Source C supports this very real occasion where patients can easily and often misuse antibiotics. So, do we halt our taking of these medications? We become informed, and we use antibiotics the right way, as defined in Source A.

While many bacterial infections will come back to haunt us over and over again throughout our lifetime, it is comforting to know that there is a reliable way to get rid of them for the time being. An antibiotic gives us an answer, and provides us with a temporary cure. With anything, however, antibiotics are no perfect solution.

It is important to know its ramifications, and take these medications as informed patients before we pop the next series of pills because, as we've read, while the antibiotic is not always the right decision, the anti-antibiotic isn't either.

### Step 11: Looking at the Verbs

Now that we have completed our written response to the RST topic, it is time to pay close attention to our verb choice. Look through the essay above and circle the verb choices. Do you find them "boring" or "tiresome?" If so, use the Commonly Used Action Verbs chart in Appendix A to find replacements. In our experiences with holistic scoring for high-stakes tests, action verbs often acted as the tipping point between a lower score and a higher score. Keep this in mind as you revise your work.

# Analysis of Sample Essay

As we did in the previous chapter, we will provide to you an analysis of the sample essay according to the four criteria identified in our Scoring Checklist Chart at the end of the book. In addition, you might want to check out the writing rubric from the PARCC also at the back of the book. You might wish to check our sample essay against rubric, too.

## Scoring Checklist

| Development of Ideas |
| --- |
| ❏ Did the author use evidence from the text? |
| ❏ Did this evidence come from more than one source? |
| ❏ Did the author successfully have the two sources interact with each other? |

| Organization |
| --- |
| ❏ Is there a clearly expressed introduction, body, and conclusion? |
| ❏ Does the introduction have an attention-grabber and a clearly stated thesis? |
| ❏ Do each of the body paragraphs support the thesis? |
| ❏ Does the conclusion successfully answer the So What? question? |

*(continued)*

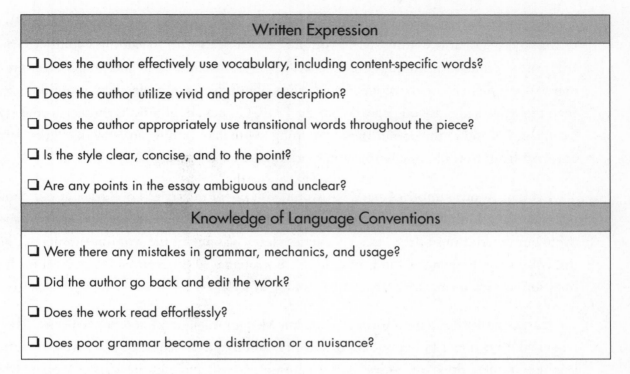

| Written Expression |
| --- |
| ❑ Does the author effectively use vocabulary, including content-specific words? |
| ❑ Does the author utilize vivid and proper description? |
| ❑ Does the author appropriately use transitional words throughout the piece? |
| ❑ Is the style clear, concise, and to the point? |
| ❑ Are any points in the essay ambiguous and unclear? |
| **Knowledge of Language Conventions** |
| ❑ Were there any mistakes in grammar, mechanics, and usage? |
| ❑ Did the author go back and edit the work? |
| ❑ Does the work read effortlessly? |
| ❑ Does poor grammar become a distraction or a nuisance? |

By "Development of Ideas," the makers of the PARCC refer to the ways in which arguments are developed and maintained throughout the course of the essay. Some questions might be: "Did the author use evidence from the text?" "Did this evidence come from more than one source?" "Did the author successfully have the two sources interact with each other?" As you can see, these questions are quite difficult and will take time for you to master. However, you can see these principles in action if you read carefully our sample essay above. We did cite evidence from two of the three sources, and we did have the three sources interact, or "talk." For instance, in the second paragraph, we looked at how Source A and Source C "interacted" or "talked" with each other as they showed the positive and negative effects of antibiotics.

Second, the PARCC will look at the organization of your writing. This, in fact, should come as no surprise at all for you. Organization is a key facet of all good writing, regardless of where it is done. By virtue of the fact that we meticulously followed our outline, we organized our work. The three main parts of the essay are clearly present: Introduction, body, and conclusion.

The next criterion, "clarity of language" will look at your writing style and the effectiveness of that style. "What is writing style?" you may ask? It deals with the author's ability to effectively use vocabulary, including content-specific words, to utilize vivid and proper description, and to appropriately use transitional words throughout the piece. Style, then, is nothing more than the writer's identity on paper. What the PARCC cares about most is simple: Is your style clear, concise, and to the point? There is nothing worse than reading an essay that lacks clarity and is difficult to read because the writer lacks a command of language.

Looking at our sample essay: What would you say of the style? Look back at our choice of vocabulary: Did we use vocabulary terms that were appropriate to research and statistics? Were our descriptions of the research sources clear? Was any of the wording ambiguous and difficult to comprehend? Could something we wrote have been written clearer? All of these questions are great starting points when looking at style.

Lastly, the PARCC will consider your knowledge of language and conventions. This is where your knowledge of grammar, mechanics, and usage will come to play. Were there any mistakes in these three categories? Did the author go back and edit the work? Does the work read effortlessly? Does poor grammar become a distraction or a nuisance? Our sample essay, we believe, does pretty well in this area, and provides to you, a RST essay that is free of grammatical issues and reads as though it were edited (which it was!). Use the PARCC rubric at the very back of the book to see how you would score our work on a scale of 4 to 1.

## Summary of the RST in Science

As you know by this point in the chapter, once the skills of the RST are mastered—particularly the active reading and the 11 Steps to Success—success only becomes a matter of learning new content. In the case of Chapter 8, we have shown you how difficult texts, such as the ones dealing with contemporary scientific-related issues, can become manageable when formulating a quality, written response. Can you guess the idea that we want to impress upon you the most? You got it! The better you read, the better you will write!

# Practice RSTs in Science

Now, it's your turn. We will present to you two sample RST tasks in science with accompanying organizers and space to write. Please be sure, as you go through this process to utilize the 11 Steps of Success, and, as always, read carefully; your writing depends upon it!

| CCSS Alignment | |
|---|---|
| RH.1 | Cite specific textual evidence. |
| RH.5 | Analyze in detail how a complex primary source is structured, including how key sentences, paragraphs, and larger portions of the text contribute to the whole. |
| RST.8 | Evaluate the hypotheses, data, analysis, and conclusions in a science or technical text, verifying the data when possible and corroborating or challenging conclusions with other sources of information. |
| RST.9 | Synthesize information from a range of sources (e.g., texts, experiments, simulations) into a coherent understanding of a process, phenomenon, or concept, resolving conflicting information when possible. |
| RI.7 | Integrate and evaluate multiple sources of information presented in different media or formats (e.g., visually, quantitatively) as well as in words in order to address a question or solve a problem. |
| L.1 | Demonstrate command of the conventions of standard English grammar and usage when writing. |
| L.3 | Apply knowledge of language to understand how language functions in different contexts. |
| W.1 | Write arguments to support claims in an analysis of substantive topics or texts, using valid reasoning and relevant and sufficient evidence. |
| W.6 | Use technology to produce, publish, and update individual writing products. |
| WHST.1 | Write arguments focused on discipline-specific content. |
| WHST.4 | Produce clear and coherent writing in which the development, organization, and style are appropriate to task, purpose, and audience. |

[ELA TASK GENERATION MODEL: 6B9PBA]

## RST #2: Life on Other Planets

85 minutes

Our society has always been fascinated with life on other planets. From famous science-fiction movies to countless news reports, curiosity pertaining to Mars and its vast possibilities are long lasting. Many feel that the exploration of life on Mars is useful only for entertainment purposes. Others feel that the possibility for life on other planets is an obvious reality.

- **Source A:** Seven Characteristics of Life, *http://academic.wsc.edu/mathsci/ hammer_m/life.htm*

- **Source B:** "Five Reasons Why Mars May Have Never Seen Life," *http://www. forbes.com/sites/brucedorminey/2012/11/15/5-reasons-mars-may-never- have-seen-life/*

- **Source C:** "Evidence of Water on Mars" (Video), *http://watchmojo.com/ video/id/7867/*

- **Source D:** "The Practical Values of Space Exploration" (Repert, 1960)

According to what you know about the characteristics of life, do you believe that life exists on other planets, like Mars? Consider the arguments that these four sources use in their observations of the possibility of life on Mars. Write an informative piece that addresses the question and supports your position with evidence from at least three of the four sources. Be sure to acknowledge competing views. You may give examples from past and current events or issues to illustrate and clarify your position. You may refer to the sources by their titles (Source A, Source B, Source C, Source D).

## SOURCE A

| Seven Characteristics of Life | My Thought Processes |
|---|---|
| According to Hickman, Roberts, and Larson (1997), any living organism will meet the following seven basic properties of life:<br><br>1) **Chemical uniqueness.** Living systems demonstrate a unique and complex molecular organization.<br><br>2) **Complexity and hierarchical organization.** Living systems demonstrate a unique and complex hierarchical organization.<br><br>3) **Reproduction.** Living systems can reproduce themselves.<br><br>4) **Possession of a genetic program.** A genetic program provides fidelity of inheritance.<br><br>5) **Metabolism.** Living organisms maintain themselves by obtaining nutrients from their environments.<br><br>6) **Development.** All organisms pass through a characteristic life cycle.<br><br>7) **Environmental reaction.** All animals interact with their environment. | |

## SOURCE B

| "Five Reasons Mars May Have Never Seen Life" | My Thought Processes |
|---|---|
| After decades of following the water, the reality that "life as we know it" may have never gotten a foothold on Mars' surface, at least, has arguably taken root within the planetary science community.<br><br>If life ever was or is lurking on the Red planet, it's been extremely coy about revealing itself. | |

(continued)

| "Five Reasons Mars May Have Never Seen Life" | My Thought Processes |
|---|---|
| The recent news that the Mars Curiosity rover has thus far detected no Methane is reminiscent of the frustration that followed the still contentious 1996 announcement that the Alan Hills Mars meteorite (ALH 84001) showed evidence of microfossils.<br><br>Thus, in the spirit of proving the negative, here are five reasons why Mars may have always been barren.<br><br>**1. No evidence of organic molecules on Mars**<br>"Barring methane [which is a hydrocarbon], there's never been a single organic molecule found on Mars," said David Catling, a planetary scientist at the University of Washington in Seattle, who stresses that he remains scientifically agnostic about the whole Mars life issue. "If life had been present, you would expect something to be left behind. If you put a bag of coal out in the rain, even in our oxygen-rich atmosphere, it's still going to stick around quite a while."<br><br>**2. Too much Carbon Monoxide (CO)—hundreds of parts per million in the Martian atmosphere**<br>"I have to work hard to invent stories where life can be on Mars and not eat that Carbon Monoxide (CO)," said Kevin Zahnle, a planetary scientist at NASA Ames Research Center. "In the presence of life, it would be eaten. There's no evidence that life on Mars, past or present, is interacting with the atmosphere."<br><br>**3. Lack of nitrates in Martian soil**<br>"We don't find nitrates in the Martian soil," said Catling. "All life on earth uses Nitrogen. In proteins, [Nitrogen] is a structural element that holds life together. Life takes Nitrogen directly out of the air and puts into the soil to form nitrates. But we don't see nitrates on Mars. That suggests that Nitrogen instead was blasted into space by [asteroidal and cometary] impacts or by Mars' low gravity."<br><br>**4. Lack of abundant liquid water and a long-lived stable environment**<br>Catling doesn't think that Mars ever had water over a large geographic area. | |

*(continued)*

| "Five Reasons Mars May Have Never Seen Life" | My Thought Processes |
|---|---|
| "Only a very small fraction of the surface of Mars has been altered by liquid water," said Catling. "Only about 3 percent of the old Noachian Martian surface has hydrous minerals; minerals that incorporated some water into their structure. The planet has been dry even when it was supposedly wet. If Mars had oceans, there's very little direct evidence for it." <br><br> And, as Zahnle points out, Mars may have only been warm briefly and locally, so that clement conditions would have been too short-lived and far between for life to connect on a planetary scale. <br><br> **5. Too much molecular Hydrogen ($H_2$) early in Mars' history** <br> New research by James Kasting, a planetary scientist at Penn State University, argues that early Mars was kept warm by a Carbon Dioxide ($CO_2$)-Hydrogen ($H_2$) atmosphere which in turn allowed for the running water thought to be needed to form Mars' valley networks. <br><br> For 20 years, Kasting has been looking for ways that early Mars could have been warm enough to form those valleys. In a paper now in peer review, Kasting posits that a combined greenhouse effect from $CO_2$ and $H_2$ could have created these warm, wet conditions, some 3.8 billion years ago. <br><br> "The presence of significant amounts of $H_2$ essentially requires that Mars was lifeless at that time," said Kasting. "Organisms would probably have eaten the hydrogen if they were present. You can't do [valleys] without a warm climate, and a warm climate is hard to produce. A $CO_2$-$H_2$ greenhouse can do it. | |

## SOURCE C

### Evidence of Water on Mars

*This video is an interview with astronomer Louie Bernstein about the implications of finding water on Mars. A satellite, known as the Mars Reconnaissance Orbiter, has scanned the Martian environment and found what seems to be land formations that could have been made by flowing water in Mars's distant past. Additionally, the Mars Reconnaissance Orbiter also seems to have identified frozen ice on the surface of Mars exposed by meteor impacts. Moreover, it is known that Mars's polar caps contain frozen water. Louie Bernstein warns, however, that the presence of frozen water on Mars does not mean that there is or once was life present on the planet. Mr. Bernstein does reason, though, that where there is water the conditions are very good that there is life. Therefore, once in its distant past, Mr. Bernstein and others assume that the conditions existed on Mars to support life. Mr. Bernstein speculates that by 2040, we will have progressed to the point where astronauts will be able to walk and live on Mars. The presence of frozen water would be key to sustaining human life on Mars.*

| Video — Evidence of Water on Mars |
|---|
| http://watchmojo.com/video/id/7867/ |
| My Thought Processes |

## SOURCE D

| "The Practical Values of Space Exploration" (Report, 1960) | My Thought Process |
|---|---|
| **"Fundamental Knowledge About Life"**<br><br>Everything learned from space exploration thus far indicates that the knowledge lying in wait for those who manage to observe the universe from outside Earth's atmosphere will be far grander than anything uncovered to date.<br><br>We may finally learn the origin of our universe and the method of its functioning. A good part of this knowledge may be no farther away than the next 3 to 5 years. Satellite telescopes now under construction are expected to elicit far more information than even the 200-inch giant at Mount Palomar. One such observatory satellite, to be launched in 1963 or before, "will permit a telescope of about 10 feet in length to point at heavenly bodies within a tenth of a second of arc for periods up to an hour. Present plans call for an orbit between 400 and 500 miles, as a lifetime of at least 6 months is required to observe the entire celestial field."<br><br>Perhaps, and sooner than we think, we shall find a clue to the destiny of all intelligent life.<br><br>Perhaps the theory advanced by a noted eastern astronomer will turn out to be true—that biological evolution on the habitable planets of the universe may be the result of contamination left by space travelers arriving from (and leaving for) other worlds. In other words, the fruition of life on the various planets of the millions of solar systems might be the product of a wandering group of astronautic Johnny Appleseeds who leave the grains of life behind them. "Space travel between galaxies has to be possible for this, but of course this needs to be only quite a rare event. In a time of about 3.3 billion years, the most advanced form of life occurring in a galaxy must be able to reach a neighboring one." | |

*(continued)*

| "The Practical Values of Space Exploration" (Report, 1960) | My Thought Process |
|---|---|
| The notion seems fantastic.<br><br>But when we look clear to the end of Earth's road (and assuming the astrophysicists are right in their theories about the evolution and ultimate death of our solar system) we know that Earth will one day become uninhabitable. Life on Earth must then perish or move elsewhere. If we further assume that mankind will not want to die with his planet and if we acknowledge that other worlds may have been through this entire cycle in eons past—perhaps the notion is not so unreasonable after all.<br><br>Whatever the truth is on this score, space exploration will certainly be of "practical" value to our descendants when that dim, far-off day arrives. | |

# Prewriting

RST Graphic Organizer

Topic:

My Thesis Statement:

| Source A | Source B | Source C | Source D |
|---|---|---|---|
| | | | |

Exactly how do the sources talk with each other?

## Your Outline:

Write your essay on loose-leaf paper or in a notebook.
Check the Scoring Checklist and the Scoring Rubric
found at the back of the book to see how you did.

| CCSS Alignment | |
|---|---|
| RH.1 | Cite specific textual evidence. |
| RH.5 | Analyze in detail how a complex primary source is structured, including how key sentences, paragraphs, and larger portions of the text contribute to the whole. |
| RST.8 | Evaluate the hypotheses, data, analysis, and conclusions in a science or technical text, verifying the data when possible and corroborating or challenging conclusions with other sources of information. |
| RST.9 | Synthesize information from a range of sources (e.g., texts, experiments, simulations) into a coherent understanding of a process, phenomenon, or concept, resolving conflicting information when possible. |
| RI.7 | Integrate and evaluate multiple sources of information presented in different media or formats (e.g., visually, quantitatively) as well as in words in order to address a question or solve a problem. |
| L.1 | Demonstrate command of the conventions of standard English grammar and usage when writing. |
| L.3 | Apply knowledge of language to understand how language functions in different contexts. |
| W.1 | Write arguments to support claims in an analysis of substantive topics or texts, using valid reasoning and relevant and sufficient evidence. |
| W.6 | Use technology to produce, publish, and update individual writing products. |
| WHST.1 | Write arguments focused on discipline-specific content. |
| WHST.4 | Produce clear and coherent writing in which the development, organization, and style are appropriate to task, purpose, and audience. |

[ELA TASK GENERATION MODEL: 8B1PBA]

## RST #3: The Safety in Science

85 minutes

Many children and teenagers still argue with the idea of sporting the well-known bulky helmet before hopping onto their bicycles. Laws have been passed making such a safety precaution a requirement when going for an everyday bike ride. What many don't always realize is that this law, many feel, is based on the reliability of science.

You have reviewed three sources regarding Newton's laws of motion and their relationship with bicycle helmets. These three pieces provide information to begin drafting your own argument.

- **Source A:** Isaac Newton's Three Laws of Motion

- **Source B:** Image — Mountain Cyclist, *http://www.publicdomainpictures.net/view-image.php?image=4387&picture=mountain-cyclist*

- **Source C:** "Pros and Cons of Wearing Bike Helmets," *http://www.livestrong.com/article/351836-pros-cons-of-wearing-bike-helmets/*

Write a well-written essay that addresses the discussion regarding the absolute necessity for wearing a bicycle helmet. Source A, Newton's Three Laws of Motion, should be central in your supporting your argument. Be sure to address the question and support your position with evidence from at least two of the three sources. Make sure to address both sides of this issue before deciding on a definitive stance. You may give examples from past and current events or issues to illustrate and clarify your position. You may refer to the sources by their titles (Source A, Source B, Source C).

## SOURCE A

| "Isaac Newton's Three Laws of Motion" | My Thought Processes |
|---|---|
| 1. Every object persists in its state of rest or uniform motion in a straight line unless it is compelled to change that state by forces impressed on it.<br><br>2. Force is equal to the change in momentum per change in time. For a constant mass, force equals mass times acceleration.<br><br>3. For every action, there is an equal and opposite reaction. | |

## SOURCE B

| Mountain Cyclist (Image) | My Thought Processes |
|---|---|
| | |

## SOURCE C

| "Pros and Cons of Wearing Bike Helmets" | My Thought Processes |
|---|---|
| Whether or not your state has a mandatory bike helmet law, all encourage their use. This recommendation pleases some, infuriates others and leads to what the Bicycle Helmet Safety Institute calls "helmet wars." Arguments regarding the general effectiveness of bike helmets and against the laws making them mandatory exist at both ends of the helmet war spectrum, making consideration of some of the pros and cons of wearing one important if you decide to choose sides. **Effectiveness** The National Highway Traffic Safety Division of the U.S. Department of Transportation states that in the event of a crash, wearing a bike helmet can reduce your risk of sustaining a serious head or brain injury by 85 to 88 percent. This is largely due, says the NHTSD, to helmet safety standards the U.S. Consumer Product Safety Division began enforcing in 1999. These standards cover helmets manufactured in the U.S. as well as helmets imported from other countries. While not directly attacking these safety estimate numbers, some, however, question the validity of impact testing and state that testing procedures fail to mimic real-world crash situations. In addition, bike helmet critics say impact testing does not provide a means to test the ability of the bike helmet to limit rotational injuries, a fact the Bike Helmet Safety Institute admits is true. Finally, Thomas A. Kunich, a writer for VehicularCyclist.com notes that helmet manufacturers conduct their own, in-house safety testing, with no third-party verification of results. **Durability** A bike helmet can easily sustain damage that renders it useless but that is also invisible to your eye. Although bike helmet manufacturers include warning labels on helmets that tell you to replace your helmet if it receives an impact due to an accident, and to avoid cleaning the helmet with chemicals such as ammonia or bleach, there is no way to know for sure if even a new helmet is really operational. | |

*(continued)*

| "Pros and Cons of Wearing Bike Helmets" | My Thought Processes |
|---|---|
| **Cost**<br><br>Cost is a factor many list as a con of bike helmets. Although helmet costs can vary widely, the price you pay is not an indication of its safety level. A helmet costing as little as $10, says the BHSI, provides the same level of protection as versions that are more expensive. An additional point is to consider the savings a helmet can provide with regard to medical expenses. The Children's Safety Network estimated in 2005 that bike helmet use rate for children age 14 and under was about 15 percent in the U.S. CSN offers a projection that if 85 percent of children in the U.S. wore a bike helmet, within a one-year period, lifetime cost savings would run between $197 and $256 million.<br><br>**Comfort**<br><br>If comfort is an argument you use to describe the cons of wearing a bike helmet, you are most likely wearing a bike helmet that does not fit correctly. Try the helmet on before you buy it, paying extra attention to fitting pads and straps. Although your helmet should feel snug, you should not feel any pressure points. If heat is a problem, look for a helmet with larger air vents and wear a separate sweatband. If you have long hair, a helmet with a ponytail port can improve the fit. | |

# Prewriting

RST Graphic Organizer

Topic:

My Thesis Statement:

| Source A | Source B | Source C |
| --- | --- | --- |
| | | |

Exactly how do the sources talk with each other?

**Your Outline:**

Write your essay on loose-leaf paper or in a notebook.
You might want to ask someone to review it for you.

## CHAPTER 9

# Research Simulation Task Practice Questions

## Introduction

The following are a series of research simulation tasks that deal with a variety of subject areas. This is your opportunity to take the lessons you have been reading and writing about, and putting those into further practice in other disciplines.

The following questions are aligned with the common core standards listed below:

| CCSS Alignment | |
|---|---|
| RL.1 | Cite strong and textual evidence. |
| RL.5 | Analyze how an author's choices contribute to its overall structure. |
| RI.7 | Integrate and evaluate multiple sources of information presented in different media or formats (e.g., visually, quantitatively) as well as in words in order to address a question or solve a problem. |
| L.1 | Demonstrate command of the conventions of standard English grammar and usage when writing. |
| L.3 | Apply knowledge of language to understand how language functions in different contexts. |
| L.5 | Demonstrate understanding of figurative language, word relationships, and nuances in word meanings. |
| W.1 | Write arguments to support claims in an analysis of substantive topics or texts, using valid reasoning and relevant and sufficient evidence. |

*(continued)*

| W.2 | Write informative/explanatory texts to examine and convey complex ideas, concepts, and information clearly and accurately through the effective selection, organization, and analysis of content. |
| W.5 | Develop and strengthen writing as needed by planning, revising, editing, and rewriting. |
| W.6 | Use technology to produce, publish, and update individual writing products. |

Keep in mind the following steps as you work through:

| Step #1 | Read through the question carefully. Make sure to decipher if the question is asking you to convey an opinion, or to convey information/research objectively. |
| Step #2 | In the upper right-hand corner of your paper, simplify what the question is asking you to do. Put the question/task into your own words. |
| Step #3 | Circle the minimum amount of sources that need to be addressed. |
| Step #4 | Take notes with each of the sources. Address the source's main points. Underline actively. |
| Step #5 | After you've addressed and highlighted the main point of the source, make separate notes on the reliability of these sources. Is the source reliable in general? Is it slanted in any way? Do logical fallacies or "holes in argument" exist? |
| Step #6 | You've read through your sources. Choose the sources that you are most comfortable with, and put a star (*) in the upper right-hand corner of each source that you will be using in your research simulation task. |
| Step #7 | In source chart, copy your notes from your sources into each. |
| Step #8 | Now, look at the relationships of your sources. Do they agree with each other? Do they disagree? Use your source-relationship chart to begin thinking about how you will have your sources begin conversing with one another. |
| Step #9 | Complete the outline for your essay. |
| Step #10 | Complete your essay, using the outline/framework as a guide. |
| Step #11 | After you have completed your essay, go back to check that your sources have a conversation, and replace the verbs you've used to integrate these sources with the action verbs from the sheet provided. |

[ELA TASK GENERATION MODEL: 8B5PBA]

# Practice RST

## Research Simulation Task — Art

85 minutes

**Rationale:**

Your school district is thinking about eliminating all funding for the arts in order to redistribute the money to what the district finds to be more worthwhile and important programs for the school, including expanding its mathematics, science, and athletic departments.

Please review the following sources as you articulate your response:

- **Source A:** "Cutting Funding for Arts Education Makes No Sense as We Struggle to Create Jobs," *www.annarbor.com/news/opinion/cutting-funding-for-arts-education-makes-no-sense-as-we-struggle-to-create-jobs/*

- **Source B:** Graphs: Trends in Math and Science Scores by Country, *http://online.wsj.com/ad/article/mathscience-rising*

- **Source C:** Excerpt from the Notebooks of Leonardo da Vinci

- **Source D:** Process of Animation (Video), *http://watchmojo.com/video/id/6131/*

Consider the perspective each source uses to demonstrate their viewpoint on art and its role in our society.

**Task**

Should funding for the arts be eliminated in order to make room for other programs that need strengthening in our school districts? Write an essay that analyzes the value, or lack thereof, of school funds being used on the arts, using at least three (3) sources. Remember to use textual evidence to support your ideas.

## Source A

| OPINION: Cutting funding for arts education makes no sense as we struggle to create jobs | My Thought Processes |
|---|---|
| September 24, 2011 | |
| I have worked as an educator in the state of Michigan since 1997. In 1994, I founded Vincent York's Jazzistry as a way to use live performance to teach the story of jazz and its role in American history and culture. Like many educators, I am confused by the mixed messages that our state government seems to be sending out: How can we create new jobs and new industries, when at the same time we are cutting funding to education and the arts? | |
| Many research studies point to the importance of the arts in developing creative thinking skills. Earlier this year, a **Michigan State University** study by the University Outreach and Engagement Center for Community and Economic Development, ArtSmarts, found that art, music, dance, and crafts are useful, valuable and essential components for the economic recovery of Michigan and the nation. The study shows that MSU Honors College graduates who majored in science, technology, engineering and math (STEM) were far more likely to have extensive arts and craft skills than the average American. Those who were involved in printmaking, composing music, metal work and other crafts as a mature adult also tended to have more patents attached to their names. I perform in elementary, middle, and high schools all around this state. I have seen with my own eyes the immensely positive effect that the arts can have on our youth and the way that appreciation for and participation in the arts can open up healthy options for a young person's future. | |
| This is changing in the wake of state budget cuts. In July 2011, the Michigan **unemployment rate** hit 10.9 percent. In this severe job crisis it's disheartening to think that the public dollars "saved" by cuts in funding for education and the arts may end up being spent later on room and board for these young people in our prison system. In light of these budget cuts Jazzistry is | |

*(continued)*

| OPINION: Cutting funding for arts education makes no sense as we struggle to create jobs | My Thought Processes |
|---|---|
| very grateful for the grant we received this year from the Michigan Council for Arts and Cultural Affairs. It, along with funds from the Ann Arbor Area Community Foundation, United Bank and Trust, Target, The Mardi Gras Fund, CS Partners, Zingerman's Community of Businesses and other supporters, enabled us to reach 5,774 young people in schools around Michigan this year.   Each year, more and more kids need Jazzistry's services as their schools cut arts programming, but each year it's getting harder for us to raise the money to reach them. I believe I speak for all of my colleagues in the art world when I say that we limit our children's future when we deny them access to the arts.<br><br>Art is not a luxury or a frill. In addition to the way art nurtures creativity and all-important STEM skills as described above, there are many other ways that art provides unique education opportunities. For example, Jazzistry embeds the arts into Michigan's required curriculum, in subjects such as history, English, and the social sciences. A live Jazzistry performance tells the story of the history, artistry, and ethnic roots of jazz. We explain how music integrated races and cultures a long time before the civil rights movement.   Jazz is this country's only indigenous art form, and its very existence testifies to the fact that the ethnic, racial, and cultural diversity of this country is a tremendous asset. Jazz—and all art—is a testimony to the resilience of the human spirit. Jazz, which was born between 1890 and 1920, thrived in adversity and raised the morale of our country during the Great Depression. Introducing today's youth to this symbol of American freedom can help inspire them to overcome the challenges we face today.<br><br>Editor's note: Vincent York moved to Ann Arbor to study classical saxophone at the University of Michigan in 1974. After graduation he joined the Duke Ellington Orchestra and recorded or played with many artists including Ella Fitzgerald, Sarah Vaughn, the Temptations and Aretha Franklin. He moved back and forth between the music scenes in New Orleans, New York and Detroit until founding the local non-profit organization Vincent York's Jazzistry in 1994. | |

## Source B

### Trends in average math and science scores by country:

**Table 4.** Trends in average mathematics scores of fourth- and eighth-grade students, by country: 1995 to 2007

| Grade four | | | | Grade eight | | | |
|---|---|---|---|---|---|---|---|
| | Average score | | Difference[1] | | Average score | | Difference[1] |
| Country | 1995 | 2007 | 2007–1995 | Country | 1995 | 2007 | 2007–1995 |
| England | 484 | 541 | 57* | Colombia | 332 | 380 | 47* |
| Hong Kong SAR[2] | 557 | 607 | 50* | Lithuania[3] | 472 | 506 | 34* |
| Slovenia | 462 | 502 | 40* | Korea, Rep. of | 581 | 597 | 17* |
| Latvia[3] | 499 | 537 | 38* | **United States[4,5]** | **492** | **508** | **16*** |
| New Zealand | 469 | 492 | 23* | England[4] | 498 | 513 | 16* |
| Australia | 495 | 516 | 22* | Slovenia | 494 | 501 | 7* |
| Iran, Islamic Rep. of | 387 | 402 | 15* | Hong Kong SAR[2,4] | 569 | 572 | 4 |
| **United States[4,5]** | **518** | **529** | **11*** | Cyprus | 468 | 465 | -2 |
| Singapore | 590 | 599 | 9 | Scotland[4] | 493 | 487 | -6 |
| Scotland[4] | 493 | 494 | 1 | Hungary | 527 | 517 | -10* |
| Japan | 567 | 568 | 1 | Japan | 581 | 570 | -11* |
| Norway | 476 | 473 | -3 | Russian Federation | 524 | 512 | -12 |
| Hungary | 521 | 510 | -12* | Romania | 474 | 461 | -12* |
| Netherlands[6] | 549 | 535 | -14* | Australia | 509 | 496 | -13* |
| Austria | 531 | 505 | -25* | Iran, Islamic Rep. of | 418 | 403 | -15* |
| Czech Republic | 541 | 486 | -54* | Singapore | 609 | 593 | -16* |
| | | | | Norway | 498 | 469 | -29* |
| | | | | Czech Republic | 546 | 504 | -42* |
| | | | | Sweden | 540 | 491 | -48* |
| | | | | Bulgaria | 527 | 464 | -63* |

■ Country difference in average scores between 1995 and 2007 is greater than analogous U.S. difference ($p < .05$)
□ Country difference in average scores between 1995 and 2007 is not measurably different from analogous U.S. difference ($p < .05$)
▨ Country difference in average scores between 1995 and 2007 is less than analogous U.S. difference ($p < .05$)
*$p < .05$. Within-country difference between 1995 and 2007 average scores is significant.
[1]Difference calculated by subtracting 1995 from 2007 estimate using unrounded numbers.
[2]Hong Kong is a Special Administrative Region (SAR) of the People's Republic of China.
[3]In 2007, National Target Population did not include all of the International Target Population defined by the Trends in International Mathematics and Science Study (TIMSS) (see appendix A).
[4]In 2007, met guidelines for sample participation rates only after substitute schools were included (see appendix A).
[5]In 2007, National Defined Population covered 90 percent to 95 percent of National Target Population (see appendix A).
[6]In 2007, nearly satisfied guidelines for sample participation rates only after substitute schools were included (see appendix A).
NOTE: Countries are ordered based on the difference in 1995 and 2007 average scores. All countries met international sampling and other guidelines in 2007, except as noted. Data are not shown for some countries, because comparable data from previous cycles are not available. The tests for significance take into account the standard error for the reported difference. Thus, a small difference between averages for one country may be significant while a large difference for another country may not be significant. Detail may not sum to totals because of rounding. The standard errors of the estimates are shown in tables E-1 and E-2 available at http://nces.ed.gov/pubsearch/pubsinfo.asp?pubid=2009001.
SOURCE: International Association for the Evaluation of Educational Achievement (IEA), Trends in International Mathematics and Science Study (TIMSS), 1995 and 2007.

## My Thought Processes

## Source B

### Trends in average math and science scores by country:

**Table 12.  Trends in average science scores of fourth- and eighth-grade students, by country: 1995 to 2007**

| Country | Grade four Average score 1995 | Grade four Average score 2007 | Grade four Difference[1] 2007–1995 | Country | Grade eight Average score 1995 | Grade eight Average score 2007 | Grade eight Difference[1] 2007–1995 |
|---|---|---|---|---|---|---|---|
| Singapore | 523 | 587 | 63* | Lithuania[2] | 464 | 519 | 55* |
| Latvia[2] | 486 | 542 | 56* | Colombia | 365 | 417 | 52* |
| Iran, Islamic Rep. of | 380 | 436 | 55* | Slovenia | 514 | 538 | 24* |
| Slovenia | 464 | 518 | 54* | Hong Kong SAR[3,4] | 510 | 530 | 20* |
| Hong Kong SAR[3] | 508 | 554 | 46* | England[4] | 533 | 542 | 8 |
| Hungary | 508 | 536 | 28* | **United States[4,5]** | **513** | **520** | **7** |
| England | 528 | 542 | 14* | Korea, Rep. of | 546 | 553 | 7* |
| Australia | 521 | 527 | 6 | Russian Federation | 523 | 530 | 7 |
| New Zealand | 505 | 504 | -1 | Hungary | 537 | 539 | 2 |
| **United States[4,5]** | **542** | **539** | -3 | Australia | 514 | 515 | 1 |
| Japan | 553 | 548 | -5* | Cyprus | 452 | 452 | # |
| Netherlands[6] | 530 | 523 | -7 | Japan | 554 | 554 | -1 |
| Austria | 538 | 526 | -12* | Iran, Islamic Rep. of | 463 | 459 | -4 |
| Scotland | 514 | 500 | -14* | Scotland[4] | 501 | 496 | -5 |
| Czech Republic | 532 | 515 | -17* | Romania | 471 | 462 | -9 |
| Norway | 504 | 477 | -27* | Singapore | 580 | 567 | -13 |
| | | | | Czech Republic | 555 | 539 | -16* |
| | | | | Norway | 514 | 487 | -28* |
| | | | | Sweden | 553 | 511 | -42* |

■ Country difference in average scores between 1995 and 2007 is greater than analogous U.S. difference ($p < .05$)
□ Country difference in average scores between 1995 and 2007 is not measurably different from analogous U.S. difference ($p < .05$)
▨ Country difference in average scores between 1995 and 2007 is less than analogous U.S. difference ($p < .05$)
# Rounds to zero.
*$p < .05$. Within-country difference between 1995 and 2007 average scores is significant.
[1]Difference calculated by subtracting 1995 from 2007 estimate using unrounded numbers.
[2]In 2007, National Target Population did not include all of the International Target Population defined by the Trends in International Mathematics and Science Study (TIMSS) (see appendix A).
[3]Hong Kong is a Special Administrative Region (SAR) of the People's Republic of China.
[4]In 2007, met guidelines for sample participation rates only after substitute schools were included (see appendix A).
[5]In 2007, National Defined Population covered 90 percent to 95 percent of National Target Population (see appendix A).
[6]In 2007, nearly satisfied guidelines for sample participation rates only after substitute schools were included (see appendix A).
NOTE: Bulgaria collected data in 1995 and 2007, but due to a structural change in its education system, comparable science data from 1995 are not available. Countries are ordered by the difference between 1995 and 2007 overall average scores. All countries met international sampling and other guidelines in 2007, except as noted. Data are not shown for some countries, because comparable data from previous cycles are not available. The tests for significance take into account the standard error for the reported difference. Thus, a small difference between the United States and one country may be significant while a large difference between the United States and another country may not be significant. Detail may not sum to totals because of rounding. The standard errors of the estimates are shown in tables E-20 and E-21 available at http://nces.ed.gov/pubsearch/pubsinfo.asp?pubid=2009001.
SOURCE: International Association for the Evaluation of Educational Achievement (IEA), Trends in International Mathematics and Science Study (TIMSS), 1995 and 2007.

## My Thought Processes

## Source C

| Excerpt from the Notebooks of Leonardo da Vinci | My Thought Processes |
|---|---|
| Definition of Perspective. | |
| | |
| [Drawing is based upon perspective, which is nothing else than a thorough knowledge of the function of the eye. And this function simply consists in receiving in a pyramid the forms and colours of all the objects placed before it. I say in a pyramid, because there is no object so small that it will not be larger than the spot where these pyramids are received into the eye. Therefore, if you extend the lines from the edges of each body as they converge you will bring them to a single point, and necessarily the said lines must form a pyramid with exact calculation.] | |
| [Perspective is nothing more than a rational demonstration applied to the consideration of how objects in front of the eye transmit their image to it, by means of a pyramid of lines. The Pyramid is the name I apply to the lines which, starting from the surface and edges of each object, converge from a distance and meet in a single point.] | |
| [Perspective is a rational demonstration, by which we may practically and clearly understand how objects transmit their own image, by lines forming a Pyramid (centred) in the eye.]<br><br>Perspective is a rational demonstration by which experience confirms that every object sends its image to the eye by a pyramid of lines; and bodies of equal size will result in a pyramid of larger or smaller size, according to the difference in their distance, one from the other. By a pyramid of lines I mean those which start from the surface and edges of bodies, and, converging from a distance meet in a single point. A point is said to be that which [having no dimensions] cannot be divided, and this point placed in the eye receives all the points of the cone. | |

## Source D

## Video, "Process of Animation"

*In this video-interview, Watch Mojo reporter talks to animation artist David Giraud about the process of creating characters for videogames. David describes the process of "Z-Brush," which is a 3-dimensional sculpting program. Z-Brush is like drawing and sculpting at the same time. David explains that working in Z-Brush is very close to the process an artist would use when working with clay. Further in the video, David discusses the differences between working with high-resolution vs. low-resolution graphics. High-resolution allows the artist to work on the fine details of a character's physical presence, and low-resolution is ultimately what the character becomes when people play the videogame. Moreover, the high-resolution characters are used for marketing purposes.*

| http://watchmojo.com/video/id/6131/ |
| :-- |
| **Video Notes:** |

**Your Outline:**

Write your essay on loose-leaf paper or in a notebook.

## Research Simulation Task – Life Skills

85 minutes

**Rationale:**

Imagine that your family is preparing on purchasing a vehicle that will be used for all five family members. Be conscious of the benefits and drawbacks when deciding to select between a Sports Utility Vehicle (SUV) and a four-door sedan.

**Task:**

You have reviewed four sources related to SUVs and four-door sedan vehicles. These four pieces provide information regarding some of the common benefits and disadvantages associated with each.

- **Source A:** "Latest Data Showing SUVs Safer Than Cars," *www. thecarconnection.com/news/1051239_latest-data-showing-suvs-safer-than-cars*

- **Source B:** Annual Gas Prices (1998-2011), Graph, *www.energy-trendsinsider.com/2012/03/14/charting-the-dramatic-gas-price-rise-of-the-last-decade/*

- **Source C:** "What You Should Know Before Buying a Sedan," *www.edmunds. com/sedan/before-buy.html*

- **Source D:** "Traffic" (Courtesy of Caroline Krueger)

Which would be most beneficial to a typical family of five? Write an informative piece that addresses the question and supports your position with evidence from **at least three of the four sources**. Be sure to acknowledge competing views. Give examples from past and current events or issues to illustrate and clarify your position. You may refer to the sources by their titles (Source A, Source B, Source C, Source D).

## Source A

| "Latest Data Showing SUVs Safer Than Cars" | My Thought Processes |
|---|---|
| SUVs are safer, right? You probably have a coworker, or someone in the family, who's always insisted that.<br><br>It wasn't always true, however. When really digging into the numbers in years past, it turned out that SUVs had a disproportionately high rate of rollover when they did crash, and that the fatality rate when they did roll—due to poor roof protection on many models—was disproportionately high.<br><br>Until the early 1990s, SUVs were undeniably more dangerous than cars, looking purely at fatality numbers and considering their poor emergency handling on the highway, but then the two numbers flipped and SUVs have been making more significant gains in recent years.<br><br>According to 2009-calendar-year statistics, as recently presented by the Insurance Institute for Highway Safety (IIHS), no matter which way you look at the numbers, they're now pointing to SUVs as a very safe choice—perhaps even a safer one.<br><br>Overall, just among drivers, 60 percent of passenger-car deaths in 2009 were in cars; 22 percent were in pickups; and 17 percent were in SUVs.<br><br>For all occupant fatalities in 2009, 52 percent involved a primary frontal impact, 27 percent a side impact, and just four percent a rear impact. Sixteen percent of all occupant deaths were attributed primarily to 'other' (representing rollovers, mostly).<br><br>**Rollovers still a key concern for SUVs**<br><br>But rollover remained the greatest concern for those considering an SUV. Still, nearly twice as many fatal accidents in SUVs (27 percent, versus 11 percent in cars) involved rollover in 2009. For single-vehicle crashes—such as running off the road avoiding an impact with a vehicle, or falling asleep—40 percent of SUV crashes, versus 21 percent in cars, involved rollover. Overall, 64 percent of total vehicle deaths for pickups and SUVs occur in those single-vehicle crashes, while for cars it's just 46 percent. | |

*(continued)*

| "Latest Data Showing SUVs Safer Than Cars" | My Thought Processes |
|---|---|
| A surprising 19 percent of 2009 vehicle fatalities involved rollover but no other significant impact, and 55 percent of all single-vehicle crash deaths involved rollover; furthermore, rollover deaths are more likely to occur in SUVs.<br><br>Here's where it gets interesting: Adjusted for number of registered vehicles, and only considering those vehicles 1–3 years old, SUVs are now far safer than passenger cars overall. For 2009, there were 39 occupant deaths per million registered SUVs—versus 82 for cars, and 94 for pickups.<br><br>**For SUVs, heavier isn't always better**<br><br>Larger cars (and pickups) tend to have the lowest fatality rates, the IIHS points out (see the chart we clipped below), but that's not true for SUVs—perhaps because of impaired accident-avoidance ability for the largest trucks. Very large trucks weren't as safe as the largest, heaviest cars, but midsize and large SUVs proved safer than mid-size or large cars.<br><br>"When you get to a particular (especially heavy weight class), weight doesn't help you but instead inflicts greater damage to other vehicles—and occupants. "Size and weight make a difference up to a point," summed IIHS senior vice president Anne Fleming.<br><br>But it appears that automakers are finally solving the rollover issue. Looking only at rollovers, driver deaths in SUVs actually dipped below those in cars for the first time in 2008, and they continued that trend for 2009—now at just 7 rollover deaths per million registered vehicles 1–3 years old, versus 13 deaths in cars.<br><br>The numbers might be good for SUVs, the IIHS still recommends large passenger cars over sport-utility vehicles as the safest vehicle type. | |

*(continued)*

| "Latest Data Showing SUVs Safer Than Cars" | My Thought Processes |
|---|---|
| "We acknowledge the improvement, but we're not ready to say they're better," said Fleming. While most of the dramatic improvement in rollover performance is due to improved roof protection, cars have some catching-up to do in the statistics as many models didn't get stability control until the past year or two, Fleming explained. The IIHS now tests vehicles on a regular basis for roof crush, but we're still also several years away from a stronger federal standard that will apply to all SUVs. | |
| "Purely in the interest of self-preservation, an SUV might very well be as good as a large car by now," said Fleming, but the potential damage you could do to other occupants should be considered, too. | |
| **Crossover vehicles the best compromise?** | |
| If you're dizzied by all these figures and percentages, you're not alone. What you need to take away from this is that SUVs have gotten a lot safer in recent years. And that it looks like mid-size or large cross-over vehicles—of the lowest, most carlike variety—might be the best compromise. | |
| The elephant in the room, of course, is that what we call SUVs today are in general very different than the SUVs of a decade ago. You're probably safer in one of the larger crossover vehicles that's also low enough to be maneuverable in an emergency and have a lower chance of rollover. Looking at the IIHS's list of Top Safety Picks, that would include vehicles like the Cadillac SRX and Chevrolet Equinox, Lexus RX, Subaru Tribeca, Subaru Forester, and Toyota Venza, among many others. | |
| Of course we're still open to arguments here. Cars handle better, so in the hands of a skilled driver, or one more at ease with the vehicle, the chances of an accident might be lower. | |
| Are there still other factors that aren't showing up in the numbers? What type of vehicle do you think is safest, and why? | |

*(continued)*

## SOURCE B

The following is a chart created from a United States consumer report regarding the average gas prices per year.

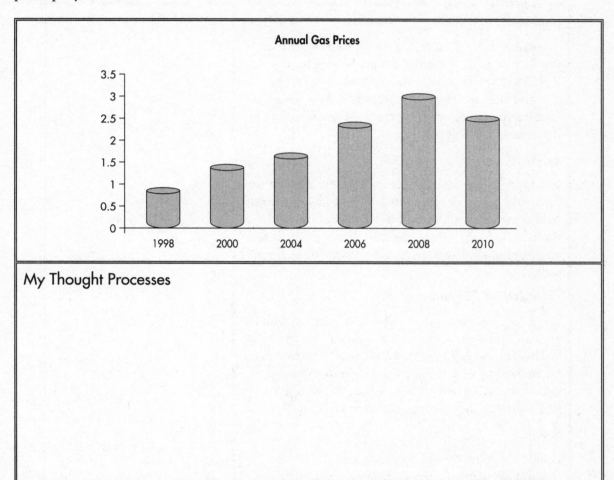

My Thought Processes

## Source C

| "What You Should Know Before Buying a Sedan" | My Thought Processes |
|---|---|
| **Size/Market Segment**<br><br>A sedan is defined as a vehicle with four doors that features a traditional trunk design, but we have included four-door hatchbacks among our recommended choices. There are three basic sizes: compact, midsize and large (or full-size). Some models don't fit neatly into any one group.<br><br>**Price**<br><br>Compact sedans can range from $10,000 for an economy sedan to more than $40,000 for a luxury model. Midsize sedans start around $18,000 and top off in the $80Ks. Large sedans run from the low $20Ks for your typical family sedan to more than $300K for an exotic.<br><br>**Engines/Fuel Economy**<br><br>You'll see four-, five-, six-, eight- and even 12-cylinder engines in this group, as well as hybrids and an all-electric car. An influx of new designs and technologies are improving fuel economy throughout the range of sedans, meaning that midsize sedans are getting the fuel economy that compacts used to achieve.<br><br>**Safety**<br><br>Family shoppers should check the availability of features like antilock brakes, front-seat side airbags, full-length side curtain airbags and stability control. Features like rearview cameras, parking sensors and knee airbags are becoming increasingly available on non-luxury sedans, while premium brands are utilizing high-tech electronics to warn inattentive drivers of blind-spot intrusion and impending collisions. Shoppers should be aware of crash test scores as well, but it should be noted that the National Highway Traffic Safety Administration adopted more strenuous testing procedures for last year, making the ratings of recently tested models incomparable with those tested in the past. | |

*(continued)*

| "What You Should Know Before Buying a Sedan" | My Thought Processes |
|---|---|
| **Luxury and Convenience Features**<br><br>Luxuries like automatic climate control, heated seats, iPod interfaces, navigation systems, keyless start systems and Bluetooth capability can often be found in *non*-luxury sedans. Look for them as you shop. Keep an eye open for multiple seat adjustments and plentiful cupholder and storage provisions.<br><br>**Passenger Capacity/Interior Space**<br><br>Most compact and midsize sedans can transport four adults in reasonable comfort. Taller families and those with five to carry should consider a large sedan.<br><br>**Luggage Capacity**<br><br>Generally, compacts offer 12–13 cubic feet of trunk space, midsize sedans offer 14–16 and large sedans offer 17–21. If you'll be hauling anything bulky, get a sedan with folding rear seats or a ski pass-through. Four-door vehicles with hatchbacks are the best choice for those who prioritize cargo space and versatility.<br><br>Do You Need All-Wheel Drive? Consumers should only pay extra for AWD if they regularly drive in snow or otherwise slippery conditions. Though the weight penalty of all-wheel drive is minimal in modern vehicle designs, there can be a compromise in fuel economy. Some sport sedans feature all-wheel drive to enhance control and stability during high-speed maneuvers. | |

*(continued)*

| "What You Should Know Before Buying a Sedan" | My Thought Processes |
|---|---|
| **Manual vs. Automatic Transmissions**<br><br>While traditional manuals with clutch pedals are still recommended for sport sedans and underpowered compacts, there are now several different kinds of automatics. The conventional automatic features a torque converter and sometimes can be shifted manually with either a lever on the center console or paddles on the steering wheel. Automated manual transmissions used to be the stuff of exotic sports cars, but now they've found their way into economy cars for their ability to maximize the power potential and fuel efficiency of low-powered engines. While such transmissions make manual shifting more responsive, they operate just like a normal automatic, although shift quality is generally less smooth. Finally, there's the continuously variable transmission (CVT), which automatically selects from an infinite ratio to keep the engine in a sweet spot of power and/or fuel economy. A typical downside of CVTs is the way they can drone during acceleration.<br><br>**Operating Costs**<br><br>Sedans are the standard by which all other vehicles are judged. Although sedan prices and sizes vary widely, buyers looking for low-cost transportation will inevitably end up with four doors and a trunk. Low-priced compact and midsize sedans are the cheapest to own; they don't use much gas, they don't cost a lot to insure and their lack of complexity keeps repair bills down. Luxury sedans may come with a limited free maintenance plan, but expect higher costs as they age. Higher-performance sedans often cost more to insure and maintain. | |

Source D

**My Thought Processes**

## Your Outline:

Write your essay on loose-leaf paper or in a notebook.
Be sure to see how you did by checking the charts at the end of the book.

## Research Simulation Task – World Languages

85 minutes

**Rationale:**

Your school district has decided to make the study of a foreign language a requirement for every school year, starting in first grade. Your Board of Education feels that requiring students to start learning a foreign language earlier, students will be able to utilize those skills in their future lives and careers.

**Task:**

You have reviewed four sources regarding the study of foreign language. These four pieces provide information on the role language has on an American citizen's prospective future.

- **Source A:** "Should Foreign Language Instruction Start Earlier in the U.S.?", *www.actfl.org/advocacy/discover-languages/for-parents/cognitive*

- **Source B:** "High School Education: Multiple Pathways and Student Choice," *www.huffingtonpost.com/659486*

- **Source C:** "Ease of Learning" Graph

- **Source D:** "The Importance of Teaching Your Child Two Languages" (Video), *http://watchmojo.com/video/id/9082/*

Do you agree or disagree with your school district's new foreign language requirement? Write an informative piece that addresses the question and supports your position with evidence from **at least three of the four sources**. Be sure to acknowledge competing views. Give examples from past and current events or issues to illustrate and clarify your position. You may refer to the sources by their titles (Source A, Source B, Source C, Source D).

## Source A

| "Should Foreign Language Instruction Start Earlier in the U.S.?" | My Thought Processes |
|---|---|
| *Foreign language programs are often one of the first items to be scrutinized and cut when elementary, middle, and high schools in the U.S. face poor performance evaluations or budget crunches. However, many studies have demonstrated the benefits of second language learning not only on student's linguistic abilities but on their cognitive and creative abilities as well. Duke TIP interviewed several experts in the field about the advantages of foreign language learning for children.* | |
| Martha G. Abbott, Director of Education for the American Council on the Teaching of Foreign Languages (ACTFL) | |
| Therese Sullivan Caccavale, president of the National Network for Early Language Learning (NNELL) | |
| Ken Stewart, 2006 ACTFL National Language Teacher of the Year; AP Spanish teacher at Chapel Hill High School in Chapel Hill, North Carolina | |
| Should Foreign Language Instruction Start Earlier in the U.S.? | |
| **Abbott:** It is critical that foreign language instruction be available to all students throughout their PK-12 academic experience. Knowing other languages and understanding other cultures is a 21st Century skill set for American students as they prepare to live and work in a global society. No matter what career students enter, they will be interacting with others around the world on a routine basis and doing business locally with those whose native language is not English. | |
| Beginning foreign language instruction early sets the stage for students' to develop advanced levels of proficiencies in one or more languages. In addition, younger learners still possess the capacity to develop near native-like pronunciation and intonation in a new language. Finally, young learners have a natural curiosity about learning which is evident when they engage in learning a new language. They also are open and accepting of people who speak other languages and come from other cultures. | |

*(continued)*

| "Should Foreign Language Instruction Start Earlier in the U.S.?" | My Thought Processes |
|---|---|
| **Caccavale:** Yes, because it has been shown to enhance children's cognitive development. Children who learn a foreign language beginning in early childhood demonstrate certain cognitive advantages over children who do not. Research conducted in Canada with young children shows that those who are bilingual develop the concept of "object permanence" at an earlier age. Bilingual students learn sooner that an object remains the same, even though the object has a different name in another language. For example, a foot remains a foot and performs the function of a foot, whether it is labeled *a foot* in English or *un pied* in French.<br><br>Additionally, foreign language learning is much more a cognitive problem solving activity than a linguistic activity, overall. Studies have shown repeatedly that foreign language learning increases critical thinking skills, creativity, and flexibility of mind in young children. Students who are learning a foreign language out-score their non-foreign language learning peers in the verbal and, surprisingly to some, the math sections of standardized tests. This relationship between foreign language study and increased mathematical skill development, particularly in the area of problem solving, points once again to the fact that second language learning is more of a cognitive than linguistic activity. A 2007 study in Harwich, Massachusetts, showed that students who studied a foreign language in an articulated sequence outperformed their non-foreign language learning peers on the Massachusetts Comprehensive Assessment System (MCAS) test after two to three years and significantly outperformed them after seven to eight years on all MCAS subtests. | |

*(continued)*

| "Should Foreign Language Instruction Start Earlier in the U.S.?" | My Thought Processes |
|---|---|
| Furthermore, there is research (Webb bibliography) that shows that children who study a foreign language, even when this second language study takes time away from the study of mathematics, outperform (on standardized tests of mathematics) students who do not study a foreign language and have more mathematical instruction during the school day. Again, this research upholds the notion that learning a second language is an exercise in cognitive problem solving and that the effects of second language instruction are directly transferable to the area of mathematical skill development.<br><br>The notion of "earlier is better" in language learning seems to be upheld by the fact that longer sequences of foreign language instruction seem to lead to better academic achievement, overall. Because second language instruction provides young children with better cognitive flexibility and creative thinking skills, it can offer gifted students the intellectual and developmental challenges they need and desire.<br><br>**Stewart:** Absolutely. Every piece of research in the field points to the benefits of starting a second language as early as three years of age. The other key to becoming proficient in another language is a long, continuous contact with the language. Until we have a well articulated PK-16 second language "buy-in" from legislators, school boards, administrators, and parents, the U.S. will continue to lag behind other nation, thus prolonging monolingualism. | |

## Source B

| "High School Education: Multiple Pathways and Student Choice" | My Thought Processes |
|---|---|
| The terms "vocational education" and more recently "career and technical education" have served historically as codes for programs or schools serving young people--often poor and minority youth--who are judged not capable of going on to post secondary education and, therefore, must be provided with a set of skills so that they can enter the workforce directly from high school. This judgment has created a two-tiered caste system of college-bound and work-bound education that is hardwired in our collective societal consciousness as the latest in a sorrowful lineage of caste systems that schools have created to funnel youth into pathways and bins based on such characteristics as disabilities, race, and class. | |
| Those caste systems are defunct. | |
| The world has changed. The economy has changed. The nature of work and the workplace have changed. Most everyone understands that there is, or certainly should be, a "career" and a "technical" aspect to all learning, just as there is, or should be, an applied, "hands-on" aspect to all learning. Can you imagine high school students aspiring to be architects, doctors, or lawyers who would not want to learn about the career and the technical aspects of their preparation for those professions? All high school education is, in large part, career education, just as all high school education is preparation for post secondary—make that lifelong—learning. | |
| Consider what many see as essential features of excellent career and technical education. | |
| • A personalized learning program focused on each student's career interests. | |
| • A thoughtful integration of academic and technical skills development. | |
| • Opportunities for each student to engage with adults working in the student's career interest area. | |

(continued)

| "High School Education: Multiple Pathways and Student Choice" | My Thought Processes |
|---|---|
| • Requirements that students exhibit skill and understanding through authentic performance demonstrations.<br><br>• Opportunities for students to obtain, in addition to a high school diploma, multiple forms of certifications and credentials in their career interests.<br><br>• All of the above provided in the workplace and community as well as the school.<br><br>You might conclude, as we have, that all high school students would be well served by programs with such features. Few high schools, however, offer them.<br><br>Consider also the by-now familiar list of skills employers want in their new hires, whether they arrive with a high school diploma or a two- or four-year college degree.<br><br>• The ability to construct and apply new knowledge across varying work activities.<br><br>• The ability to generate innovative solutions that require predicting, analyzing, forecasting, forming perspective, and recognizing patterns.<br><br>• The ability to communicate, using a variety of tools in multiple situations and cultures, particularly as a member of a team.<br><br>• The ability to integrate knowledge from multiple disciplines, including both the arts and sciences.<br><br>• The ability to transition across projects, firms, disciplines, and work/learning experiences.<br><br>• The ability to organize work and persist in its successful conclusion.<br><br>Again you might conclude, as we have, that all high school students need to demonstrate competence in these skills by graduation. Few high schools, however, teach or assess them. Even in our Big Picture Schools, focused as we are on learning in the workplace and the community, we are challenged to do so. | |

*(continued)*

| "High School Education: Multiple Pathways and Student Choice" | My Thought Processes |
|---|---|
| Observing the new world economy, we are reminded that it is not the career we choose that provides job security but our ability to use these essential skills, always prepared to make the inevitable shift to new work, perhaps in new industries, which the new economy will require.<br><br>All high school students need to have access to diverse program options that match their career interests and the ways they wish to pursue them. And within those programs, they need choices that allow them to customize their learning plans. Such programs will go a long way toward eliminating the caste system and turning America's promise of universal equity and access into programs and practices for all youth.<br><br>Might educators and policy makers, therefore, eliminate the increasingly useless separation between traditional college preparatory and career and technical education programs? Might it be more productive to envision one high school system with a continuum of multiple pathways and choices for students, all incorporating those features listed above, and leading to multiple destinations, not just traditional four year colleges, but community colleges, technical schools, even work or, in some cases, a year off for travel?<br><br>A small number of school districts throughout the country already provide multiple pathways through career-themed programs of study. Many more high schools need to follow their lead and go beyond that focusing on individual interests, essentially wrapping a career academy around each learner. Offering such choices will keep many more students from leaving school before graduation and ensure that many more graduates are prepared for success in their post secondary learning and careers.<br><br>The caste system is defunct. Let's get over it. | |

## Source C

The following chart depicts the rate of learning depending on a child's age, according to a series of scientific studies.

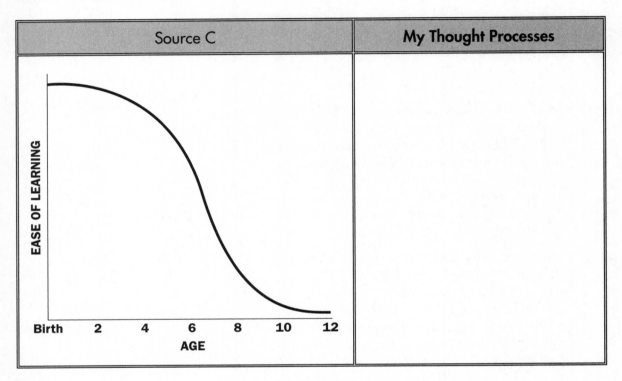

| Source C | My Thought Processes |
|---|---|

Source D

## The Importance of Teaching Your Child Two Languages

*In this interview video, Watch Mojo talks to Caroline Erdos, a speech language pathologist, about the importance of raising a child to speak two languages. First, bilingual children have been found to have better skills at problem solving. For adults, bilingual individuals tend to delay the onset of Alzeihmer's disease. In addition, Mrs. Erdos explains the importance of children—at home and at school—in receiving enough input of both languages in order to develop bilingual skills. That means, for instance, that a child would get equal time in hearing and speaking both Spanish and English. Mrs. Erdos goes on to exlain that children obtain a second language quite easily and rarely become confused when receiving instruction in both. Mrs. Erdos also continues to explain that children who are developing bilingual skills will "mix" languages together, even in the same sentence, which, she argues, is a healthy and normal phenomenon. Mrs. Erdos explains that it is never too late for a child to learn a second language. The only "negative effect" for a child to wait to learn a second language is that the accent in the second language tends to remain. The video ends by Mrs. Erdos explaining that parents should speak and operate 30% of the time in a second language if that child is to adequately learn the second language.*

| "The Importance of Teaching Your Child Two Languages" |
|---|
| http://watchmojo.com/video/id/9082/ |
| Video Notes: |

**Your Outline:**

Don't forget to use the charts at the end of the book after you write your essay.

## Research Simulation Task—Physical Education

85 minutes

**Rationale:**

In recent years, the structure of physical education programs has been heavily questioned. With obesity and healthy choices being a critical concern of our society, it is obvious that our schools' physical education programs require revisions.

**Task:**

You have reviewed four sources regarding the current state of our physical education programs. These four pieces provide information concerning the ways in which physical education can be altered to more readily influence students in a positive fashion.

- **Source A:** "New PE Trend Stresses Fitness and Fun," *www.educationworld.com/ a_curr/curr346.shtml*

- **Source B:** "Is PE a time waster?", *http://educationnext.org/dont-sweat-it/*

- **Source C:** "2012 Shape of the Nation Report: Quick Facts," *www.aahperd.org/ naspe/publications/upload/2012*

- **Source D:** Obesity Rates of American Youth, *http://educationnext.org/ dont-sweat-it/*

As you review the given sources, discuss possible ways in which our current physical education program can be modified to better impact our entire student bodies. Write an informative piece that addresses the question and supports your position with evidence from **at least three of the four sources**. Be sure to acknowledge competing views. Give examples from past and current events or issues to illustrate and clarify your position. You may refer to the sources by their titles (Source A, Source B, Source C, Source D).

## Source A

| "New PE Trend Stresses Fitness and Fun" | My Thought Processes |
|---|---|
| **Ingredients for Fitness Programs**<br><br>Inactivity in gym class is one of the problems with traditional programs, according to Paul Rosengard, executive director of SPARK. "We want programs that keep kids as active as possible," Rosengard tells Education World. "The programs should be fun, active, inclusive, and academically oriented."<br><br>SPARK staff members visit schools and evaluate their phys-ed curriculum for a fee, as well as provide curriculum and equipment. Many of the schools SPARK works with do not have the money for exercise equipment, so SPARK staff members suggest activities that don't require expensive equipment and curriculum modifications so more students can participate.<br><br>Fifth graders, for example, might prepare to play softball by working in pairs to field ground balls, so they can give each other feedback on their fielding technique. Then they can play a modified softball game, in which all the fielders have to relay the ball before it can be thrown home.<br><br>For a new spin on running laps, students can be assigned to see how many playing cards they can collect from a teacher while running for ten minutes. While they are cooling down, students can do a math problem using the numbers on the cards they collected, Rosengard explains.<br><br>**Starting a Lifelong Habit**<br><br>In the past few years, new activities have started to appear in gym classes, such as orienteering, mountain biking, and in-line skating, according to Kun. Some students and staff also have access to indoor exercise equipment, such as treadmills and stationary bicycles. | |

*(continued)*

| "New PE Trend Stresses Fitness and Fun" | My Thought Processes |
|---|---|
| An example of such a phys-ed program is at Madison Junior High School in Naperville, Illinois. Madison's gym now has a 40-station fitness center, with treadmills, stationary bicycles, heart-rate monitors, and a climbing wall. Students wear T-shirts that say "I'm Getting Fit for Life at Madison Health Club." The program emphasizes personal improvement instead of who can run the fastest mile; students run 12 minutes every week, and the teacher notes whether they increase their distances. | |
| "We are meeting the needs of every child who walks through the door," says Phil Lawler, a physical education teacher and the school's system phys-ed coordinator. "We don't want to make it so painful that we turn them off. The focus is on a healthy norm; what is good for their age, height, and weight." Students also play some games in phys-ed class and learn about eating healthfully and avoiding health risks. | |
| Lawler, at least, thinks the efforts in the gym are paying off in the classroom as well. Naperville's eighth graders made national news in April when they scored first in the world on the science portion of the Third International Mathematics and Science Study. | |
| "We [posted high scores] while offering quality, daily physical education," Lawler tells Education World. "I think they work hand in hand; [phys ed] was a contributing factor." Illinois is the only state that mandates daily physical education for students in sixth through 12th grades. | |
| Madison began its shift to a fitness-based phys-ed program about ten years ago, when staff began reading articles about the increase in the number of obese children. "We've been forgetting that kids are not living in the same world as we did growing up," says Lawler, noting the changes in lifestyle and increase in technology that keep kids inside. "They have multiple TVs, computers, and fast-food diets." | |

*(continued)*

| "New PE Trend Stresses Fitness and Fun" | My Thought Processes |
|---|---|
| **Changing Direction**<br><br>Another middle school that revised its phys-ed program is in Framingham, Massachusetts. Teachers at Fuller Middle School wanted a wellness theme throughout the building and noted that students were getting less physical activity, says James Carey, the Framingham district's director of health and physical education. Administrators applied for grants to help cover renovation costs and converted a standard multi-purpose gymnasium to a fitness center with between 60 and 70 machines, including equipment for disabled students.<br><br>Those students who take phys-ed twice in a six-day class cycle usually spend one day in the fitness center, Carey explains. At the middle schools without a fitness center, phys-ed teachers introduce students to lifetime activities, such as racquetball, badminton, and volleyball.<br><br>Equipment including treadmills and stationary bikes, much of it donated by local fitness centers and sports rehabilitation facilities, also was added to the weight room at the high school.<br><br>"We hoped to make it more user-friendly," by having more than just weights, Carey tells Education World. "Traditionally, fitness centers in high schools tend to be geared more toward male-dominated sports, such as football." During the day the center is open to phys-ed classes; after school, staff and students are able to use it.<br><br>Students at both the high school and the middle school play some sports in gym classes, but high school students learn to play tennis, golf, and croquet as well. And included in the plans for a high school renovation project is construction of a 5,000-square-foot wellness center. "We hope to have a state-of-the-art center," Carey says. | |

*(continued)*

| "New PE Trend Stresses Fitness and Fun" | My Thought Processes |
|---|---|
| **Following the Example**<br><br>Word of the programs is spreading and sparking interest among administrators in other districts. Recently, a group of phys-ed teachers, parents, and administrators from Davis County Schools in Owensboro, Kentucky, visited Madison Junior High School to see the fitness center and review the phys-ed curriculum.<br><br>Charles Green, director of middle and secondary schools for Davis County Schools, says that though the system currently has a traditional phys-ed program, staff members think it is time for a change. "We feel this is the way to go, with the emphasis on children's and young adolescents' health and increasing their cardiovascular knowledge," Green explains. School officials are talking with administrators at the local hospital, Owensboro Mercy Health Systems, to determine whether the hospital will help fund the change to a fitness program, he adds.<br><br>Federal funds now are available as well to pump up phys-ed programs. This month, the U.S. Department of Education released the guidelines for school systems applying for funds through the Physical Education for Progress Grant Program. The $5 million program provides grants so school systems can start, expand, or improve their phys-ed programs.<br><br>P.E.4Life's Flannery says her organization has mobilized support for the program and advocates that a review of physical education standards be part of overall national education reform efforts. "This is not just an education issue," adds Flannery of children's physical fitness. "This is a health, military readiness, and competitive workforce issue. We're on a mission." | |

## Source B

| *Yorktown High—"Is PE a time waster?"* | My Thought Processes |
|---|---|
| The countervailing pressures against increasing the physical education requirements are strong and widespread, and in plain view at Yorktown High, in Arlington, Virginia, a school that prides itself on producing high achievers. | |
| The student population at Yorktown is 69 percent white, 16 percent Hispanic, 9 percent Asian, and 7 percent African American, and only 17 percent of its students qualify for free or reduced-price lunches. Its diversity is evident as Rebecca Bonzano's 10 a.m. PE class of freshmen and sophomores begins to assemble one recent morning. Not only is there an ethnic mix, there are also goths and prepsters, nerds and jocks, fat kids and thin ones. By 10:07, they emerge from their locker rooms in blue-and-gray uniforms. Bonzano takes attendance. At 10:10, the class begins a few minutes of warm-up jogging, back and forth along a floor that has been set up with six volleyball nets. Some students walk, chatting with friends. | |
| At 10:15, the students sit down on the floor. Bonzano reads the standings after two weeks of volleyball competition. Students at Yorktown take a semester of PE and a semester of health in their first year. In the second year, they get three quarters of PE and a quarter of health. Each PE course consists of three-week units on different sports. Though physical exercise, known previously as gymnasium, has been a common part of American schooling since the 19th century, recreational games like basketball, flag or touch football, soccer, and softball were not introduced into the PE curriculum until the 1930s. The idea now is that if students learn sports, they will have a pleasant way to exercise after class and after graduation. | |

*(continued)*

| *Yorktown High—"Is PE a time waster?"* | My Thought Processes |
|---|---|
| Bonzano opens a bag of volleyballs, and at 10:16, the games begin. The teams are co-ed, each game lasts about five minutes, and the level of play is spotty. There are few rallies, few spikes, few sets, no digs. At any given moment, 1 student is attempting to play the ball and 11 stand and watch. | |
| At 10:44, a bell rings and the last volleyball game ends. In seconds, the students are in their locker rooms. They had been on the gym floor for 34 minutes. None had broken a sweat. By 10:50, the students are dressed and back on the floor, waiting for the bell at 10:53 that dismisses them. | |
| "That was one of my most challenging classes," Bonzano says after the students have gone, meaning that these students aren't enthusiastic about being in physical education. "In some of the other classes, you have kids cheering, getting into it. They play hard." | |
| Bonzano, in her 15th year of teaching, is unhappy with the role of PE at Yorktown. "In many respects it's a waste of time," she says. "I would have four years of PE and I'd have harder standards. You'd have to run a mile under a certain time, you'd have to do a certain number of curl-ups, and so on. As it is, we've watered down the fitness standards, and they're too easy. And the kids don't even have to meet them! We just pass them and promote them." She says that the old national fitness standards are not used anymore because they were too hard. | |
| But Bonzano does not expect this situation to change, because it satisfies the desires of too many constituencies. | |
| "We have parents who would like to cut PE further," she says. "They'd like more time for Advanced Placement academic classes. They're focused on their kids getting into the Ivy League, and they know those colleges don't care about PE grades." | |
| Like their parents, she says, Yorktown students are focused on building a résumé that will look good to selective colleges. PE has no role in that. | |

*(continued)*

## Source C

| "2012 Shape of the Nation Report: Quick Facts" | My Thought Processes |
|---|---|
| 1. 43 states (84%) mandate that schools must provide their students with elementary physical education. | |
| 2. 41 states (80%) mandate that schools must provide their students with middle school physical education. | |
| 3. 44 states (86%) mandate that schools must provide their students with high school physical education. | |
| 4. 38 states (75%) mandate that schools must provide their students with physical education in elementary, middle/junior high, and high school. | |
| 5. 6 states (12%: Illinois, Hawaii, Massachusetts, Mississippi, New York, and Vermont) require physical education in every grade, K–12. | |
| 6. 16 states (31%) have established mandated minutes/week for elementary physical education participation. | |
| 7. 18 states (35%) have established mandated minutes/week for middle school physical education participation. | |
| 8. 10 states (20%) have established mandated minutes/week for high school physical education participation. | |
| 9. 6 states (12%) have established mandated minutes/week for all grade levels for school physical education participation. | |
| 10. 50 states (98%) have adopted state standards for physical education. Only Iowa does not have physical education standards. | |
| 11. 28 states (55%) allow exemptions or waivers for schools regarding physical education time or credit requirements. | |
| 12. 33 states (65%) permit schools to allow students to substitute other activities for physical education class and/or credits for graduation. | |
| 13. 9 states (18%) require elementary schools to provide students with recess. | |

*(continued)*

| "2012 Shape of the Nation Report: Quick Facts" | My Thought Processes |
| --- | --- |
| 14. 11 states (22%) prohibit the practice of withholding physical activity, including recess, as punishment or for disciplinary reasons. | |
| 15. 11 states (22%) prohibit the use of physical activity as punishment for inappropriate behavior or for disciplinary reasons. | |
| 16. 13 states (25%) require a minimum weekly amount of physical activity time for elementary school students. | |
| 17. 7 states (14%) require a minimum weekly amount of physical activity time for middle school students. | |
| 18. 3 states (6%) require a minimum weekly amount of physical activity time for high school students. | |
| 19. 34 states (67%) require school districts to provide their local school wellness policies to the state education agency. | |
| 20. 27 states (53%) monitor the implementation of local school wellness policies. | |
| 21. 12 states (24%) distributed written physical education curriculum to schools/school districts in the past year. | |
| 22. 20 states (40%) distributed written goals and objectives for physical education programs to schools/school districts in the past year. | |
| 23. 17 states (33%) distributed student learning benchmarks for physical education to schools/school districts in the past year. | |
| 24. 15 states (29%) distributed a chart describing scope and sequence for physical education to schools/school districts in the past year. | |
| 25. 18 states (35%) distributed lesson plans or learning activities for physical education to schools/school districts in the past year. | |
| 26. 30 states (59%) allow required physical education credits to be earned through online physical education courses. | |

*(continued)*

| "2012 Shape of the Nation Report: Quick Facts" | My Thought Processes |
|---|---|
| 27. 17 states (33%) require online physical education courses to be taught by a certified physical education teacher. | |
| 28. 26 states (51%) require some form of student assessment in physical education. | |
| 29. 14 states (27%) require fitness assessments. 9 states (18%) require the use of a particular fitness assessment. | |
| 30. 12 states (24%) require collection of height and weight data by schools/school districts. | |
| 31. 9 states (18%) require collection of BMI data by schools/school districts. | |
| 32. 28 states (55%) require physical education grades to be included in a student's grade point average. | |
| 33. 21 states (41%) have a teacher evaluation system in place for physical education teachers. | |
| 34. 40 states (78%) require all who teach elementary school physical education to be certified/licensed. | |
| 35. 42 states (82%) require all who teach middle school/junior high school physical education to be certified/licensed. | |
| 36. 46 states (88%) require all who teach high school physical education to be certified/licensed. | |
| 37. 37 states (73%) require professional development/ continuing education to maintain/renew physical education teacher certification/licensure. | |
| 38. 10 states (20%) provide funding for professional development for physical education teachers. | |
| 39. 31 states (61%) actively support the National Board Certification process. | |
| 40. 1 state (2%: New York) requires each school district to have a licensed physical educator serve as a physical education coordinator for the district. | |
| 41. 42 states (82%) currently employ someone to oversee or coordinate physical education for the state. | |

(continued)

## Source D

### Obesity Rates of American Youth

The following chart is based on information that has been collected by a federal institution that actively regulates obesity rates of our American youngsters, ages 5–12.

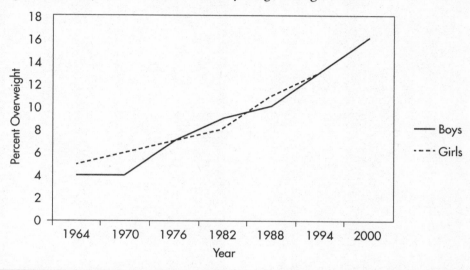

**My Thought Processes**

## Your Outline:

Don't forget to use the charts at the end of the book after you write your essay.

## CHAPTER 10

# Final Thoughts

To the students and educators who have used this book: We wish to impress upon you a thought as you further your adventures both in and out of education. Aristotle, the great Greek thinker, once mused, ""We are what we repeatedly do. Excellence, then, is not an act, but a habit."

Through the habit of completing the exercises and repeated practices of this book, we are confident that you will achieve excellence on the PARCC. There are some people in education who see testing as a negative—that testing interferes with the "real" education process. We, however, have a different viewpoint: The importance of the PARCC exam is not the test itself; it is not the research simulation task; it is not the literary analysis or the narrative essay. The importance of the exam is twofold: the authentic content that is used on the exam and the literacy skills that the exam requires of its takers. As for the content, we encourage you to continue reading literary works of great importance, especially those that give a broader and deeper perspective on the American experience and those that provide a wider landscape of the increasing global world in which we live. An excellent place to start would be to consult the reading list of the Common Core State Standards Initiative (CCSS). The Common Core is the multi-state curriculum upon which the PARCC is based. Reading the literature suggested by the Common Core will give you a definite advantage when taking the exam. The reading list is reproduced for you in the appendix.

Next, let's talk briefly about the skills you have gain in preparing for the PARCC. When this book asked you to "get your sources talking" on the research simulation task, we were actually asking you to synthesize information. Being able to condense data and to formulate a working thesis based upon these sources is a skill that will make you stand out among your peers. When this book asked you to write the literary analysis, we were testing your ability to read texts critically. Critical reading means the ability to ask the question "Why?" and to explore and talk about divergent ways of thinking about both fiction and nonfiction. Thinking critically is a must in the 21$^{st}$ century world in which we live. Finally, this book asked you to use your creativity and imagination when composing the narrative essay. Imagine how different our world would be if Steve Jobs, founder of Apple Inc., lacked imagination? We know that your imagination is one of the keys to success in your future.

If you followed this book well, we are confident that these three important skills—synthesizing, critical thinking, creativity—are ingrained within you. Good luck on the exam, and more importantly, best wishes to you in your future, regardless of what you decide to do. Remember Aristotle's words: You are what you repeatedly do.

# ACKNOWLEDGMENTS

## Chapter 2

Excerpt on pages 28–29 from THE GREAT FIRE by Jim Murphy. COPYRIGHT ©1995 by Jim Murphy. Used by permission of Scholastic, Inc.

Excerpt on page 36 from *Dragonwings* by Laurence Yep. COPYRIGHT ©1975 BY LAURENCE YEP. Used by permission of HarperCollins Publishers.

Poem on pages 41–43, "A Poem for My Librarian, Mrs. Long" from ACOLYTES by NIKKI GIOVANNI. COPYRIGHT © 2007 BY NIKKI GIOVANNI. Reprinted by permission of HarperCollins Publishers.

Excerpt on pages 58–59 from "The Golden Apple" from BLACK SHIPS BEFORE TROY by Rosemary Sutcliff, text copyright © 1993 by Rosemary Sutcliff. Used by permission of Delacorte Press, an imprint of Random House Children's Books, a division of Random House LLC. All rights reserved.

Excerpt on page 80–83 from "Abraham Lincoln's Great Laws of Truth, Integrity," *The Washington Times*. Reprinted by permission.

## Chapter 3

Excerpt on pages 112–113 from A WRINKLE IN TIME ©1962 by Madeleine L'Engle. Reprinted by permission of Farrar, Straus, and Giroux, LLC. All Rights Reserved.

## Chapter 4

Poem on pages 145–146 from "Caged Bird" from SHAKER, WHY DON'T YOU SING? by Maya Angelou, copyright ©1983 by Maya Angelou. Used by permission of Random House, an imprint of The Random House Publishing Group, a division of Random House LLC. All rights reserved.

Poem on page 167, "The Railway Train," by Emily Dickinson. Reprinted by permission of the publishers and the Trustees of Amherst College from THE POEMS OF EMILY DICKINSON: READING EDITION, edited by Ralph W. Franklin, ed., Cambridge, Mass.: The Belknap Press of Harvard University Press, COPYRIGHT © 1998, 1999 by the President and Fellows of Harvard College. COPYRIGHT © 1951, 1955, 1979, 1983 by the President and Fellows of Harvard College.

## Chapter 5

Pages 176–178, "One Third of Teens Use Cellphones to Cheat in School," by Zach Miners. Reprinted by permission.

## Chapter 6

Pages 194–198, *Poverty in America: Why Can't We End It?* by Peter Edelman from *The New York Times*, July 29, 2012 © 2012, The New York Times. All rights reserved. Used by permission and protected by the Copyright Laws of the United States. The printing, copying, redistribution, or retransmission of this Content without express written permission is prohibited.

Pages 199–203, *The Cost Of Space Exploration*, by Michio Kaku from Forbes.com, July 16, 2009 © 2009 Forbes. All rights reserved. Used by permission and protected by the Copyright Laws of the United States. The printing, copying, redistribution, or retransmission of this Content without express written permission is prohibited.

## Chapter 7

Image on page 252, *The Problem We All Live With*, by Norman Rockwell. Printed by permission of the Norman Rockwell Family Agency. COPYRIGHT © 1963 the Norman Rockwell Family Entities.

Pages 253–254, Jim Crow Laws, by Ronald Lewis. All rights reserved. Reprinted by permission of Scholastic Library Publishing, Inc.

Page 265, "Blood, Toil, Tears and Sweat: Address to Parliament." Reprinted with permission of Curtis Brown, London on behalf of the Estate of Sir Winston Churchill. COPYRIGHT © Winston S. Churchill.

## Chapter 8

Pages 286–290, "In Praise of Antibiotics," by Julian Davies. American Society for Microbiology. Reprinted by permission.

Pages 303–305, "5 Reasons Why Mars May Have Never Seen Life," by Bruce Dorminey, from Forbes.com, Nov. 15, 2012 ©2012 Forbes. All rights reserved. Used by permission and protected by the Copyright Laws of the United States. The printing, copying, redistribution, or retransmission of this Content without express written permission is prohibited.

## Chapter 9

Page 322–323, "Cutting Funding for Arts Education Makes No Sense as We Struggle to Create Jobs." Reprinted by permission.

Pages 330–332, "Latest Data Showing SUVs Safer Than Cars," by B. Halvorsob. Reprinted by permission.

Photograph page 337, "Traffic." Courtesy of Caroline Krueger.

Pages 340–342, "Should Foreign Language Instruction Start Earlier in the U.S.?" American Council on the Teaching of Foreign Languages. Reprinted by permission.

Pages 343–345, "High School Education: Multiple Pathways and Student Choice," by Elliot Washor. Reprinted by permission.

Page 347, "The Importance of Teaching Your Child Two Languages" (Video). *watchmojo.com*. Referenced by permission.

Page 354–355, "Is PE a Waste of Time?" by Bob Cullun. Reprinted by permission.

Pages 356–358, "2012 Shape of the Nation Report Quick Facts." Reprinted with permission from the American Alliance for Health, Physical Education, Recreation and Dance (AAHPERD), 1900 Association Drive, Reston, VA 20191, *www.aahperd.org*.

# Commonly Used Action Verbs

**Accept** To receive; to regard as true, proper, normal, inevitable

**Accomplish** To execute fully; to attain

**Adjust** To make slight changes in something to make it fit or function better

**Administer** Manage or direct the performance of duties or actions

**Adopt** To take up and practice as one's own; to accept or carry out a plan

**Advise** Recommend a course of action; offer an informed opinion based on specialized knowledge

**Analyze** Separate into elements and critically examine, to study or determine relationship or accuracy

**Answer** To speak or write in reply to a request

**Anticipate** Foresee and deal with in advance, give advanced thought or consideration, remedy in advance

**Apply** To put to use for a purpose; to employ diligently or with close attention

**Appraise** Evaluate the worth or merit of

**Approve** Accept as satisfactory; exercise final authority with regard to commitment of resources

**Arrange** Make preparation for an event; put in proper order

**Assemble** Collect or gather together in a predetermined order from various sources

**Assess** Determine the value or accuracy of; evaluate

**Assign** Specify or designate tasks or duties to be performed by others

**Assist** To give support or aid

**Assure** Give confidence, to make certain, guarantee

**Attain** To gain or achieve

**Attend** To be present for the purpose of making a contribution

**Articulate** To give clear and effective communication

**Audit** To make a formal examination or review

**Authorize** Approve; empower through vested authority

**Budget** To plan the allocation, expenditure, or use of resources, especially money or time

**Calculate** Make a mathematical computation; judge to be sure or probable

**Clarify** Make something clearer by explaining in greater detail

**Classify** To arrange or assign to a category

**Collaborate** Work jointly with; cooperate with others, acts as liaison providing a close relationship, connection, or link

**Communicate** To impart a verbal or written message; to transmit information

**Compare** Determine if two or more items, entries are the same and if they are not, identify the differences

**Compile** Put together information; collect from other documents

**Comply** To conform to something for example, a rule, law, policy, or regulation

**Compose** To create or arrange in proper or orderly form

**Conduct** Guide; carry out from a position of command or control; to direct or take part in the operation or management of

**Confirm** Give approval to, verify

**Consolidate** To join together as one whole

**Construct** To form by combining or arranging parts

**Consult** Seek the advice of others; to give professional advice or services; to confer

**Contribute** To play a significant part in bringing about an end or result

**Coordinate** Combine the actions of others to bring to a common result

**Correspond** Communicate with in writing

**Counsel** To give advice or guidance, to consult with

**Create** To bring into existence; to produce through imaginative skill

**Delegate** Commission another to perform tasks or duties that may carry specific degrees of accountability

**Design** Conceive, create and execute according to plan

**Determine** Resolve; fix conclusively or authoritatively

**Develop** Disclose, discover, perfect, or unfold a plan or idea

**Devise** Come up with something new — perhaps by combining or applying known or new ideas or principles

**Direct** Guide work operations though the establishment of objectives, policies, practices and standards

**Disseminate** Spread or disperse information

**Distribute** Deliver to proper destinations

**Document** To support with written information and records

**Draft** Prepare papers or documents in preliminary form

**Edit** To revise and prepare material (written, film, tape, soundtrack) for publication or display

**Endorse** Support or recommend; express approval

**Enhance** Improve; make better

**Ensure** Guarantee or make certain

**Establish** Bring into existence; enact an agreement

**Estimate** Forecast requirements; appraise, judge approximate value

**Evaluate** Determine or fix the value of; assess, careful appraisal

**Examine** Scrutinize closely (as to determine compliance)

**Execute** Put into effect or carry out

**Expedite** Accelerate the process or progress of

**Facilitate** To make a process easier to perform

**File** To arrange in a methodical manner

**Finalize** To bring something to a point at which everything has been agreed upon and arranged

**Forecast** To predict; to estimate in advance

**Formulate** Develop or devise

**Foster** To promote the growth or development of

**Generate** To bring into existence; to cause to be; to produce

**Greet** To welcome in a cordial, professional manner

**Guide** To show or lead the way to; to manage the affairs of; to influence the conduct or opinions of

**Gather** To collect; to accumulate and place in order

**Hire** To employ

**Identify** To ascertain the origin, nature, or definitive characteristics of

**Implement** Carry out; execute a plan or program

**Improve** Make something better; enhance the value or quality of

**Initiate** Start or introduce

**Inspect** Critically examine for suitability; carries with it the authority to accept or reject

**Instruct** To teach; to coach; to impart or communicate knowledge

**Insure** To make certain by taking necessary measures and precautions

**Interpret** To conceive the significance of something; to explain something to others

**Interview** To obtain facts or opinions through inquiry or examination of various sources

**Investigate** Study through close examination and systematic inquiry

**Issue** Put forth or distribute officially

**Lead** To guide or direct on a course or in the direction of; to channel; to direct the operations of

**Maintain** Keep in an existing state; uphold

**Manage** Exercise administrative, executive and supervisory direction

**Mediate** To oversee an attempt to resolve a dispute by working with both sides to help them reach an agreement

**Mentor** To provide advice and support to, and watch over and foster the progress of a less experienced person

**Modify** To make changes to

**Monitor** Watch, observe, or check for a specific purpose; keep track of

**Negotiate** Confer with others for the purpose of reaching agreement

**Notify** To make known

**Operate** Perform an activity or function

**Organize** To set up an administrative structure; to arrange or form

**Outline** To make a summary of significant features

**Oversee** To supervise, to watch or survey

**Participate** To take part in

**Perform** Fulfill or carry out an action or function

**Plan** Devise or project the realization of a course of action

**Prepare** To make ready for some purpose, use or activity

**Present** To introduce; to bestow; to offer to view

**Prioritize** To order or rank things according to their importance or urgency

**Proceed** Begin to carry out an action

**Process** Handle in accordance with prescribed procedures

**Promote** Encourage growth and development; further something by arranging or introducing it

**Proofread** To read a text in order to identify errors and make corrections

**Produce** To give shape or form to, to make or yield something

**Project** To estimate something by extrapolating data

**Propose** Declare a plan or intention

**Provide** Supply what is needed; furnish

**Purchase** To buy something using money or its equivalent

**Pursue** Employ measures to obtain or accomplish

**Recognize** To perceive clearly; to acknowledge with a show of appreciation

**Recommend** Advise or counsel a course of action; offer or suggest for adoption

**Recruit** To seek out others to become new members, students or personnel

**Refer** To send or direct for aid, treatment, information, or decision

**Register** To enter in a record; to enroll formally or officially

**Regulate** To bring to order or method of

**Report** Give an account of; furnish information or data

**Represent** Act in the place of or for

**Research** Inquire into a specific matter from several sources

**Resolve** To find a solution

**Respond** To reply or to react to

**Review** Go over or examine critically; examine or re-examine

**Revise** Rework in order to correct or improve

**Schedule** Plan a timetable

**Screen** To examine and separate nature of importance; to filter

**Secure** Keep free from risk of loss

**Select** Choose the best suited

**Serve** To be of assistance to or promote the interests of; to act in a particular capacity

**Sign** Formally approve a document by affixing a signature

**Solve** To find a solution for

**Specify** State precisely in detail or name explicitly

**Standardize** To bring into conformity to something established by authority, custom, or general consent as a model or criterion

**Submit** Yield or present for the discretion or judgment of others

**Summarize** Succinctly present an abstract of the main points either orally or in writing

**Supervise** Personally oversee, direct or guide the work of others with responsibility for meeting standards

**Support** To promote the interests or cause of

**Survey** To examine as to condition, situation, or value

**Track** To observe and monitor the course

**Train** Teach or guide others in order to raise to a predetermined standard

**Transcribe** Transfer data from one form of record to another without changing the nature of the data

**Update** To bring current

**Utilize** To make use of

**Verify** Confirm or establish authenticity; substantiate

**Write** To author; to draft

# APPENDIX B

## Transitional Words

| Types of Transitions | Transitional Words/Phrases |
| --- | --- |
| Similarity | also, in the same way, just as . . . so too, likewise, similarly |
| Exception/Contrast | but, however, in spite of, on the one hand . . . on the other hand, nevertheless, nonetheless, notwithstanding, in contrast, on the contrary, still, yet |
| Sequence/Order | first, second, third, . . . next, then, finally |
| Time | after, afterward, at last, before, currently, during, earlier, immediately, later, meanwhile, now, recently, simultaneously, subsequently, then |
| Example | for example, for instance, namely, specifically, to illustrate |
| Emphasis | even, indeed, in fact, of course, truly |
| Place/Position | above, adjacent, below, beyond, here, in front, in back, nearby, there |
| Cause and Effect | accordingly, consequently, hence, so, therefore, thus |
| Additional Support or Evidence | additionally, again, also, and, as well, besides, equally important, further, furthermore, in addition, moreover, then |
| Conclusion/Summary | finally, in a word, in brief, briefly, in conclusion, in the end, in the final analysis, on the whole, thus, to conclude, to summarize, in sum, to sum up, in summary |

# Key Charts

So, let's review some of the key charts that have remained integral throughout your reading of this test prep guide.

According to PARCC requirements, the following word counts apply to all reading selections:

| Grade level | Word count |
|---|---|
| Grades 6–8 | 400–1,000 words |

The PARCC requirements also deem a complexity rating for each text, which follows this protocol:

| Grade level | PARCC "Complexity" Determination |
|---|---|
| Grades 6–8 | 905–1185 |

The balance of texts on the Performance-Based Assessments and End-of-Year Assessments will shift by grade band.

| Grade level | Types of texts |
|---|---|
| Grades 6–8 | • Approximately forty (40) percent literary texts<br>• Approximately sixty (60) percent informational text |

In order to be deemed "college and career ready" for their grade level, students' progress on the PARCC ELA/literacy assessment will be determined by their performance level descriptor. PLDs are further explained below:

| Level | Policy-Level Performance Level Descriptor |
|---|---|
| 5 | Students performing at this level demonstrate a **distinguished command** of the knowledge, skills, and practices embodied by the Common Core State Standards assessed at their grade level. |

*(continued)*

| Level | Policy-Level Performance Level Descriptor |
|-------|--------------------------------------------|
| 4 | Students performing at this level demonstrate a **strong command** of the knowledge, skills, and practices embodied by the Common Core State Standards assessed at their grade level. |
| 3 | Students performing at this level demonstrate a **moderate command** of the knowledge, skills, and practices embodied by the Common Core State Standards assessed at their grade level. |
| 2 | Students performing at this level demonstrate a **partial command** of the knowledge, skills, and practices embodied by the Common Core State Standards assessed at their grade level. |
| 1 | Students performing at this level demonstrate a **minimal command** of the knowledge, skills, and practices embodied by the Common Core State Standards assessed at their grade level. |

Lastly, it seems as if the shift to PARCC and the Common Core require us to master a new language. We hope you find the acronym chart helpful as you move from one task to the next.

| Acronym | Actual Title | Explanation |
|---------|--------------|-------------|
| PARCC | Partnership for Assessment of Readiness for College and Career | The name of this particular assessment's consortium. |
| ELA | English Language Arts | This refers to the literacy skills used throughout these PARCC assessments. |
| CCR | College and Career Readiness | In order for students to be deemed as "college and career ready," they will have demonstrated the academic knowledge, skills and practices necessary to enter directly into and succeed in entry-level, credit-bearing courses in<br><br>College English Composition, Literature, and technical courses requiring college-level reading and writing. |
| CCSS | Common Core State Standards | These standards are aligned with the PARCC assessment. |

*(continued)*

| Acronym | Actual Title | Explanation |
|---|---|---|
| OWG | Operational Working Group | The groups of professionals formed to work forward and to revise assessments. |
| PLD | Performance Level Descriptor | A student's level determined by their performance on each assessment. |
| PBA | Performance-Based Assessment | This label is attributed to the three assessments you will take throughout the school year before the End-of-Year assessment. These include the narrative PBA, the literary analysis PBA, and the research simulation PBA. |
| MYA | Mid-Year Assessment | This assessment is taken in the middle of the school year. |
| EOY | End-of-Year Assessment | This assessment is taken at the end of the school year. |
| PCR | Prose-Constructed Response | The larger writing task that you will complete with each performance-based assessment. |
| EBSR | Evidence-Based Selected Response | When a second question on the PARCC is dependent on a student's answer to a first question. |
| TECR | Technology-Enhanced Constructed Response | A task that requires the student to use technology to capture student comprehension, including the following tasks: drag and drop, cut and paste, shade text, move items to show relationships. |
| WHST | Writing History, Science, and Technical Subjects | The interdisciplinary writing standard. |
| RST | Reading Science and Technical Subjects | The interdisciplinary reading standard. |
| RST | Research Simulation Task | The synthesis performance-based assessment that asks students to use information from a variety of sources to support their opinion. |

# APPENDIX D

## Suggested Reading

### Stories

Alcott, Louisa May. Little Women

Cisneros, Sandra. "Eleven."

Cooper, Susan. The Dark Is Rising

Hamilton, Virginia. "The People Could Fly."

L'Engle, Madeleine. A Wrinkle in Time

Paterson, Katherine. The Tale of the Mandarin Ducks

Sutcliff, Rosemary. Black Ships Before Troy: The Story of the Iliad

Taylor, Mildred D. Roll of Thunder, Hear My Cry

Twain, Mark. The Adventures of Tom Sawyer

Yep, Laurence. Dragonwings

### Drama

Fletcher, Louise. Sorry, Wrong Number

Goodrich, Frances and Albert Hackett. The Diary of Anne Frank: A Play

### Poetry

Carroll, Lewis. "Jabberwocky."

Dickinson, Emily. "The Railway Train."

Frost, Robert. "The Road Not Taken."

Giovanni, Nikki. "A Poem for My Librarian, Mrs. Long."

Hughes, Langston. "I, Too, Sing America."

Longfellow, Henry Wadsworth. "Paul Revere's Ride."

Navajo tradition. "Twelfth Song of Thunder."

Neruda, Pablo. "The Book of Questions."

Sandburg, Carl. "Chicago."

Soto, Gary. "Oranges."

Whitman, Walt. "O Captain! My Captain!"

Yeats, William Butler. "The Song of Wandering Aengus."

### Informational Texts: English/Language Arts

Adams, John. "Letter on Thomas Jefferson."

Churchill, Winston. "Blood, Toil, Tears and Sweat: Address to Parliament on May 13th, 1940."

Douglass, Frederick. Narrative of the Life of Frederick Douglass an American Slave, Written by Himself

Petry, Ann. Harriet Tubman: Conductor on the Underground Railroad

Steinbeck, John. Travels with Charley: In Search of America

## Informational Texts: History/Social Studies

Freedman, Russell. Freedom Walkers: The Story of the Montgomery Bus Boycott

Greenberg, Jan, and Sandra Jordan. Vincent Van Gogh: Portrait of an Artist

Isaacson, Phillip. A Short Walk through the Pyramids and through the World of Art

Lord, Walter. A Night to Remember

Monk, Linda R. Words We Live By: Your Annotated Guide to the Constitution

Murphy, Jim. The Great Fire

Partridge, Elizabeth. This Land Was Made for You and Me: The Life and Songs of Woody Guthrie

United States. Preamble and First Amendment to the United States Constitution. (1787, 1791)

## Informational Texts: Science, Mathematics, and Technical Subjects

"Geology." U*X*L Encyclopedia of Science

"Space Probe." Astronomy & Space: From the Big Bang to the Big Crunch "Elementary Particles." New Book of Popular Science

California Invasive Plant Council. Invasive Plant Inventory

Enzensberger, Hans Magnus. The Number Devil: A Mathematical Adventure

Katz, John. Geeks: How Two Lost Boys Rode the Internet out of Idaho

Macaulay, David. Cathedral: The Story of Its Construction

Mackay, Donald. The Building of Manhattan

Peterson, Ivars and Nancy Henderson. Math Trek: Adventures in the Math Zone

Petroski, Henry. "The Evolution of the Grocery Bag."

## Charts Used in this Book

## Narrative Graphic Organizer

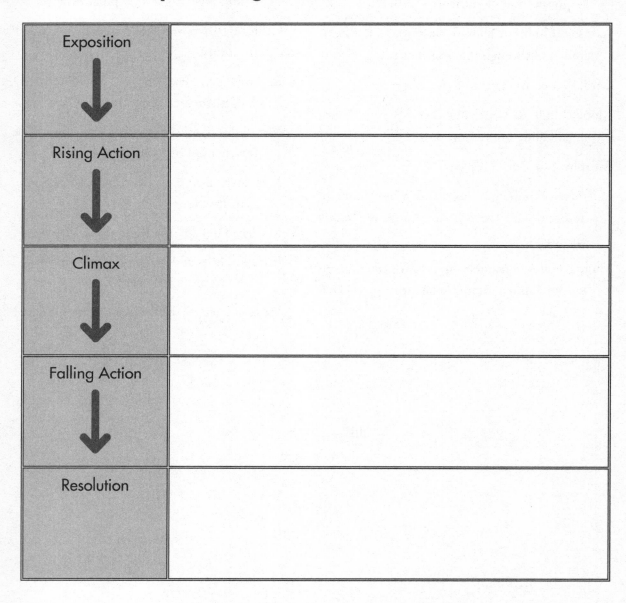

# Historical Account/Scientific Process Graphic Organizer

| Introduction of Historical Account/Scientific Process |
| --- |
| |

| Sequence of Main Events | | |
| --- | --- | --- |
| Event 1 | Event 2 | Event 3 |
| | | |

| Completion of Historical Account/Scientific Process |
| --- |
| |

# Literary Analysis Top-Hat Graphic Organizer

| Text 1 | Text 2 |
|---|---|
| Key Phrases: | |
| Analysis: | Analysis: |

| Common theme(s) in both works? |
|---|

# Literary Analysis Flowchart

| Step 1: Read the directions. Then, read the passage. |
| --- |

| Step 2: Note *some* literary and/or rhetorical devices as you read. And, write down the theme. |
| --- |

| Step 3: Ask yourself—Is the author conveying information to the reader or making an argument? |
| --- |

| CONVEYING INFORMATION? | PRESENTING ARGUMENT? |
| --- | --- |
| 1. Address theme in introduction. | 1. Discuss, generally, the writer's purpose for making the argument. |
| 2. Discuss the passage as a whole, involving a few devices, keeping in mind the overall theme of the passage throughout. | 2. Address logical fallacies and the appeals when needed. |
| 3. Close your essay with your final thought on the theme of the passage. | 3. Do not forget to use common sense—How is the author trying to persuade his/her audience? |
| | 4. Close your essay with your final thought on the theme of the passage. |

# RST Steps

| | |
|---|---|
| Step 1 | Read through the question carefully. Make sure to decipher if the question is asking you to convey an opinion, or to convey information/research objectively. |
| Step 2 | In the upper right-hand corner of your paper, simplify what the question is asking you to do. Put the question/task into your own words. |
| Step 3 | Circle the minimum amount of sources that need to be addressed. |
| Step 4 | Take notes with each of the sources. Address the source's main points. Underline actively. |
| Step 5 | After you've addressed and highlighted the main point of the source, make separate notes on the reliability of these sources. Is the source reliable in general? Is it slanted in any way? Do logical fallacies or "holes in argument" exist? |
| Step 6 | You've read through your sources. Choose the sources that you are most comfortable with, and put a star (*) in the upper right-hand corner of each source that you will be using in your research simulation task. |
| Step 7 | In source chart, copy your notes from your sources into each. |
| Step 8 | Now, look at the relationships of your sources. Do they agree with each other? Do they disagree? Use your source-relationship chart to begin thinking about how you will have your sources begin conversing with one another. |
| Step 9 | Complete the outline for your essay. |
| Step 10 | Complete your essay, using the outline/framework as a guide. |
| Step 11 | After you have completed your essay, go back to check that your sources have a conversation, and replace the verbs you've used to integrate these sources with the action verbs from the sheet provided. |

# Video Clip Note-Taking Organizer

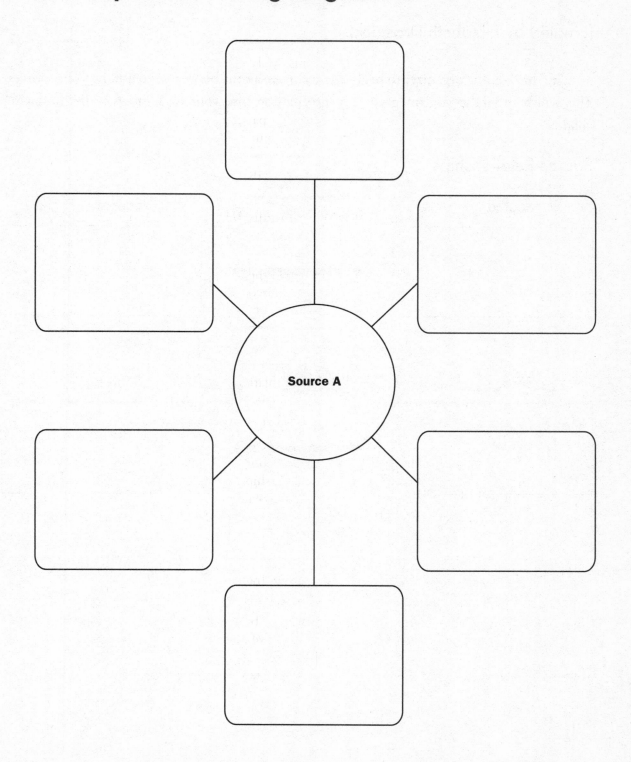

# RST Source Relationship Chart

## (created by Elizabeth Drosdick)

Use this graphic organizer to begin these conversations between and among your sources. This will help you as you integrate this information into your RST essays in the following chapters.

## Source Relationships

Source _____          (how does _____ interact with _____?)          Source _____

Source _____          (how does _____ interact with _____?)          Source _____

# Source Relationships

| Topic: | | |
|---|---|---|
| My Thesis Statement: | | |
| Source A | Source B | Source C |
| Exactly how do the sources talk with each other? | | |

# APPENDIX 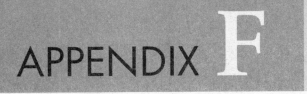 F

## Scoring Checklist

### Development of Ideas

❏ Did the author use evidence from the text?

❏ Did this evidence come from more than one source?"

❏ Did the author successfully have the two sources interact with each other?

### Organization

❏ Is there a clearly expressed introduction, body, and conclusion?

❏ Does the introduction have an attention-grabber and a clearly stated thesis?

❏ Do each of the body paragraphs support the thesis?

❏ Does the conclusion successfully answer the So What? question?

### Written Expression

❏ Does the author effectively use vocabulary, including content-specific words?

❏ Does the author utilize vivid and proper description?

❏ Does the author appropriately use transitional words throughout the piece?

❏ Is the style clear, concise, and to the point?

❏ Are any points in the essay ambiguous and unclear?

### Knowledge of Language Conventions

❏ Were there any mistakes in grammar, mechanics, and usage?

❏ Did the author go back and edit the work?

❏ Does the work read effortlessly?

❏ Does poor grammar become a distraction or a nuisance?

# Scoring Rubric for Analytic Writing

| Construct Measured | Score Point 4 | Score Point 3 | Score Point 2 | Score Point 1 | Score Point 0 |
|---|---|---|---|---|---|
| (Reading) Comprehension of Key Ideas and Details | Student cites convincing textual evidence to show a full understanding of his/her reading. | Student cites convincing textual evidence to show an extensive understanding of his/her reading. | Student cites textual evidence to show a basic comprehension of his/her reading. | Student cites textual evidence to show a limit comprehension of his/her reading. | Student cites little or no textual evidence; student does not exhibit close comprehension of his/her reading. |
| (Writing) Development of Ideas | Student response provides convincing reasoning and development that is appropriate to the task. | Student response provides clear reasoning and development that is largely appropriate to the task. | Student response provides some reasoning and development that is somewhat appropriate to the task. | Student response provides limited reasoning and development that is limited in appropriateness to the task. | Student response provides underdeveloped reasoning and development that is inappropriate to the task. |
| (Writing) Organization | Demonstrates purposeful cohesion, with well-executed progression of ideas. | Demonstrates a great deal of cohesion, and a logical progression of ideas. | Demonstrates some cohesion, and logically grouped ideas. | Demonstrates limited cohesion, making the writer's progression of ideas somewhat unclear. | Demonstrates a lack of cohesion. |
| (Writing) Clarity of Language | Establishes and maintains an effective style, including precise details and transitions. | Establishes and maintains an effective style, including mostly precise details and transitions. | Establishes and maintains a mostly effective style, including some precise details and transitions. | Establishes a limited effective style, including limited details and transitions. | Inappropriate style, with little to no precise language. |
| (Writing) Knowledge of Language and Conventions | While command of the language exists, few grammatical issues may exist. | While command of the language exists, distracting grammatical issues may exist. | While inconsistent command of the language exists, few patterns of grammatical issues may exist. | While limited command of the language exists, a series of grammatical issues may exist. | Demonstrates little to no command of language. Frequent and varied grammar and usage errors. |